TEACHING GLOBAL HISTORY

Teaching Global History challenges prospective and beginning social studies teachers to formulate their own views about what is important to know in global history and why. It explains how to organize the curriculum around broad social studies concepts and themes and student questions about humanity, history, and the contemporary world. Chapters include lesson ideas, sample lesson plans with activity sheets, primary source documents, and helpful charts, graphs, photographs, and maps. High school students' responses are woven in throughout. Additional material corresponding to each chapter is posted online at **http://people.hofstra.edu/alan_j_singer**

The traditional curriculum tends to highlight the Western heritage, and to race through epochs and regions, leaving little time for an in-depth exploration of concepts and historical themes, for the evaluation of primary and secondary sources, or for students to draw their own historical conclusions. Offering an alternative to such pre-packaged textbook outlines and materials, this text is a powerful resource for promoting thoughtful reflection and debate about what the global history curriculum should be and how to teach it.

Alan J. Singer is professor of secondary education and director of social studies education in the Department of Teaching, Literacy and Leadership at Hofstra University in Long Island, New York and the editor of *Social Science Docket* (a joint publication of the New York and New Jersey Councils for Social Studies).

TEACHING GLOBAL HISTORY

A Social Studies Approach

Alan J. Singer

Routledge
Taylor & Francis Group

NEW YORK AND LONDON

First published 2011
by Routledge
711 Third Avenue New York, NY 10017

Simultaneously published in the UK
by Routledge
2 Park Square, Milton Park, Abingdon, Oxon OX14 4RN

Routledge is an imprint of the Taylor & Francis Group, an informa business

Library of Congress Cataloging in Publication Data
Singer, Alan J.
Teaching global history : a social studies approach / Alan J. Singer.
p. cm.
1. Social sciences–Study and teaching. 2. Social sciences–Research. 3. Social science
teachers–Training of. I. Title.
H62.S4774 2011
907.1'2–dc22
2010041697

ISBN 13: 978–0–415–87548–6 (hbk)
ISBN 13: 978–0–415–87549–3 (pbk)
ISBN 13: 978–0–203–83236–3 (ebk)

Typeset in Bembo and Stone Sans by
Keystroke, Station Road, Wolverhampton

Printed and bound in the United States of America on acid-free paper.

I am 60 years old and sometimes it is hard to remember what I am struggling for.

Then I remember that I am struggling for the future of my grandchildren, Gideon and Sadia. Then I remember I am struggling for the future of other people's grandchildren as well. This book, which is about teaching about the past, is dedicated to the future – to all of our grandchildren.

CONTENTS

PREFACE

In 1968, my friend Ken Silver and I hitched along the U.S. Pacific coast from San Francisco to British Columbia. Along the way we hiked, camped, searched for the fabled "Big Foot," and argued. We had just completed our freshman year in college and we were both very committed to somewhat rigidly held philosophical beliefs. As a crude Marxist, in the way only an 18-year-old can be, I argued that all human action was dictated – dictated – by individual and collective economic need in a socially stratified conflict-riddled society. Ken, a bit of an anarchist enamored with Friedrich Nietzsche, refused to accept any narrow restrictions on his free choice and individualism, and claimed he was much more motivated by the desire for power. The arguing went on for three months until we finally came to blows and agreed to halt the discussions before someone was injured.

In 40 years as a social studies teacher I have continued to argue about human nature and the nature of society and history with anyone who is willing to team up with me. In some ways, this book is a continuation of those arguments.

Teaching Global History was originally intended as a companion book for the methods text *Social Studies for Secondary Schools: Teaching to Learn, Learning to Teach, 3rd edition* (Routledge, 2008). Over time it developed its own logic and it is now designed to stand on its own. I hope secondary education social studies methods teachers and their students find it useful.

In the Hofstra University social studies education program for pre-service teachers, all students take a course "Global History in the Curriculum" that is supposed to help them integrate their knowledge of world history into a more or less coherent narrative. Feedback from social studies department chairs and coordinators who are members of the local and state councils for social studies have raised that this is a major area of weakness for beginning teachers. This book was specifically designed to address that problem.

I confess that I have been teaching for almost 40 years and I am still working on my own "coherent narrative." But that is the way it is supposed to be. As a secondary education methods teacher I think the best I can hope to achieve is to influence the way teachers and their students think about the past and the world and stimulate them so they keep thinking about these things their entire lives. Maybe they will have more success than I have at putting things together in a meaningful way, but I am not sure.

Recently, I opened a staff development workshop on U.S. foreign policy at the end of the 20th century by having participants discuss historian Eric Hobsbawm's belief that the United States is the greatest threat to world peace at the start of the 21st century (http://www.stwr.org/united-states-of-america/the-us-imperial-triangle-and-military-spending.html, accessed June 27, 2010) and Senator Robert Byrd's statement that the lack of debate in the United States, especially in the United States Senate, over the proposed invasion of Iraq in 2003, suggested the country was dangerously "'sleepwalking' through history" (http://www.commondreams.org/views03/0212-07.htm, accessed June 27, 2010). I argued that while as teachers they might not agree with either position, it was their responsibility to introduce their students to these positions.

If secondary school students learn anything in a global history class, they should recognize that the world is a complicated place and it is not so easy to understand. As United States President Barack Obama noted in his speech upon receipt of the Nobel Peace Prize, "the instruments of war do have a role to play in preserving the peace. And yet this truth must coexist with another – that no matter how justified, war promises human tragedy" (http://www.msnbc.msn.com/id/34360 743/ns/politics-white_house/page/2/, accessed December 27, 2009). I know it sounds a bit like an Orwellian formulation, but Obama is probably right that peace requires the willingness to go to war. It is just that in the summer of 2010, I do not agree with him about when this willingness needs to be translated into action, especially when it comes to continued U.S. military involvement in Iraq and Afghanistan. These are things readers of this book will hopefully think about as they jump back and forth between past and present, exploring what I call a social studies approach to global history.

My second goal is to promote questioning by both students and teachers. Questions lead to the formulation of hypotheses, which leads to research, which leads to possible answers, broader theories, and new questions. Questions are what transform disconnected students into thinkers, historians, and active participants in a democratic society. When I read a book on a new topic I start by jotting down notes, but soon I am writing questions in the margins and before long I am having arguments with the author. I hope readers write questions in the margins of this book and launch into arguments with me. I can be contacted via email at catajs@hofstra.edu. You are also invited to use my website, http://people.hofstra.edu/alan_j_singer (accessed June 1, 2010) and to respond to my blog on Huffington Post.

A third goal I have is for secondary school students to start discovering connections between people, places, events, and inventions. Knowledge is so often compartmentalized, especially in a topic as broad as global history, that discovering connections, and I mean discovering them not being told about them, is part of the excitement of the game. I try to share my connections throughout this book.

I find that connections and discovery are the things that people remember. My wife and I were driving in southwestern France trying to find the site of famous Paleolithic cave paintings. After a few hours my wife asked, "How much further?" I pointed to limestone cliffs on the side of the road that had been undercut by water in the past. "Do you remember, we saw very similar cliffs in Mesa Verde when we visited Anasazi ruins and they were laced with caves? We are here!" And we were.

In recent years, environmental historians, brought into the forefront by concerns over global warming, have helped to draw connections between events and civilizations on opposite sides of the world. It is kind of amazing but after about 100,000 years of relative cultural stagnation, the Earth got a little warmer, agriculture was discovered in different places, and civilizations took off.

This book is organized into four broad sections. In Part I, Chapters 1–6, I discuss topics and questions I believe you need to consider as you think about global history and develop a global history curriculum, units, and lessons. They include "What is a social studies approach to global history?"; "What is important to know and why?"; "How should global history teachers address controversial or sensitive issues?"; "Why is global history usually European chronology with tangents?"; and "What does a theme-based global history curriculum look like?" At the end of each chapter in every section are teaching ideas. Sample classroom material corresponding to each chapter is available online at http://people.hofstra.edu/alan_j_singer (accessed October 17, 2010).

Part II, Chapters 7–12, grew out of a series of articles I wrote for *Social Science Docket*, a joint publication of the New York and New Jersey Councils for Social Studies. Each chapter focuses on a specific debate in the global history curriculum. While they are narrowly focused they have broader implications. I know this is hubris, but I modeled my approach on a series of columns Stephen Jay Gould wrote for *Natural History* magazine. Topics discussed in this section include: "Why does the grand narrative of Western civilization play such a central role in most global history curricula?"; "What would global history look like if it were written from a Chinese perspective?"; "Who and what should be included in history?"; "How should we teach about religion?"; "Why revolution?"; and "Are there multiple perspectives on the European Holocaust and genocide?"

Part III, Chapters 13–16, focuses on waves of globalization since the start of the Columbian Exchange. Topics discussed in this section include: "How did the Columbian Exchange transform the world?"; "How did capitalism, industrialization, and imperialism lead to global transformation?" and "What does the future hold?"

Part IV, Chapters 17, 18, and 19, suggest resources for teaching global history. Included in these chapters are recommended websites, autobiographies, fictional works, movies, historical works, and a lesson plan format.

THREE VERY IMPORTANT NOTES

1. I am not "anti-Wiki." Many of the problems of unreliability with Wikipedia (http://www.wikipedia.org/, accessed March 30, 2010), the online encyclopedia, have been addressed. The rule I follow in my own work, and my recommendation to teachers and secondary school students is that Wikipedia should be a first source but not the last.
2. I have edited and/or excerpted dozens of primary source documents for the teaching activities included in this book. I have tried to peg them to different academic performance levels. Some versions are going to be too difficult for some students and classes. These are recommended sources and questions. Teachers need to reedit them to make them accessible to their specific students and classes.
3. Please visit my website, http://people.hofstra.edu/alan_j_singer (accessed October 17, 2010), and download material specifically designed for this book as courses packs, lesson plans, articles, and curriculum packages. Lesson materials for use by teachers that I helped develop are also available in *Social Science Docket*. Back issues are available online at the website of the New York State Council for Social Studies (http://www.nyscss.org, accessed October 17, 2010).

ACKNOWLEDGMENTS

I am the Graduate Director of the secondary school social studies program in the Department of Teaching, Literacy and Leadership of the Hofstra University School of Education, Health and Human Services (SOEHHS). The Hofstra New Teachers Network (NTN) is a network of students and student teachers currently in the program, alumni, secondary school social studies teachers and administrators, cooperating teachers, field supervisors, and Hofstra faculty. NTN maintains an email newsletter, sponsors conferences, organizes support teams for new teachers, and promotes participation in teacher development activities.

Although I no longer teach in secondary school classrooms on a full-time basis, I have been fortunate that members of the NTN have welcomed me into their classrooms to experiment with new lessons, activities, and approaches to teaching. Most of the classroom material used in this book was developed with the help of former students from the Hofstra University teacher education program who remain involved as members of the New Teachers Network, participants in conferences, contributors to online discussions, as cooperating teachers, and as adjuncts. Throughout the text I try to give credit where it is due, but teaching ideas constantly change as they get kicked around in discussion and it is hard to say who first came up with a particular suggestion. If I left someone out, or if I changed an idea as it incubated in my own mind, I apologize.

Some of the teachers who have assisted me deserve special recognition. Michael Pezone, Law, Government, and Community Service Magnet High School, Queens, NY and Adeola Tella, Uniondale (NY) High School have been involved in this project from the start. Michael Mullervy, Uniondale (NY) High School, and Jessica Cartusciello, Island Trees High School (Levittown, NY) worked through the standard global history curriculum with me even though they knew I would be criticizing it. Claire Lamothe, Christopher Verga, and Christa Kadletz checked out websites and edited copy. Jessica Sutherland typed documents. Patricia Halpin assisted with the design of the cover and other illustrations. The New York and New Jersey State Councils for Social Studies have been very supportive and have allowed me to use their journal, *Social Science Docket*, as a sounding-board for my ideas about teaching global history.

This book could not have been completed without support from the staff of the Curriculum Materials Center in Hofstra University's Axinn Library, the secretarial and administrative staff of the Hofstra University SOEHHS, and the invaluable assistance of Naomi Silverman and her staff who gave me a chance to put 40 years of arguing into print.

My most important collaborators continue to be Maureen Murphy, the Graduate Director of English Education at Hofstra and Judith Y. Singer, former director of the MLE Learning Center in Brooklyn and former Associate Professor of Elementary Education at Long Island University–Brooklyn Campus. Judi was a full partner in the development of the educational philosophy and teaching approaches that undergird this book. Our grown children, Heidi, Rachel and Solomon, deserve special credit for years of ingenuity and patience as I experimented with them on approaches to teaching, as do my grandchildren, Gideon and Sadia, who are my latest victims. Their willingness to continually argue with me has helped keep many a flight-of-fancy grounded in the reality of schools "as they are," while recognizing the potential of education "as it can be."

ACTIVITIES

PART I

Designing a Global History Curriculum

1

WHAT IS A SOCIAL STUDIES
APPROACH TO GLOBAL HISTORY?

This chapter defines a social studies approach to global history, discusses the key role of questioning in historical research and teaching, questions traditional approaches to teaching about global history, and introduces recommended historians.

The poem, "A Worker Views History" by Bertolt Brecht is really a series of rhetorical questions (http://www.cs.rice.edu/~ssiyer/minstrels/poems/1406.html, accessed April 24, 2009). The poet asks readers to consider who built the fabled wonders of the ancient world and died in wars of conquest and voyages of exploration. His point is that historians generally describe the triumphs and tragedies of the rich and powerful, but ignore the lives of masons, cooks, workers, and the enslaved, ordinary people who did the work and fought the battles that made the events and developments of the past possible and created the world we live in today.

teaching for social justice

In the last line of the poem, Brecht seems to sigh because there are "so many questions" that need to be asked and considered. Asking questions, loads of questions, simple questions and hard questions, is what historians do. They then try to find answers to their questions through research, but the best ones know that each discovery about the past inevitably leads to a new round of questions.

Unfortunately, few secondary students ever see history as a process of questioning and discovery of which they can become part. Too often their textbooks and teachers present the past as a collection of facts to be learned because someone smarter than them decided it was important to know them and because they will be quizzed about their ability to memorize information on a unit test or standardized assessment.

history as an active process

One of the global history textbooks I used in the 1990s was *History of the world* (Perry et al., 1990) published by Houghton Mifflin. The first reading passage in the book is titled "Why Study World History?" Although the passage begins with a question and asks questions throughout, they are just devices for providing students with a simplified "fairy tale" view of the past. There is no evaluation of what is presented. It requires no student thinking. In fact, the book does the thinking for students.

According to the Houghton Mifflin textbook:

> In the 1760's in America, people also studied world history. In those days, world history meant the history of the Middle East, Greece, Rome, and England. Some Americans studied world history then because they had military responsibilities. They needed to learn about the battles and wars of the past, in order to fight those of the present. Others studied world history because they were in business, buying and selling on four continents. Other Americans studied world history because they cared about the great poets and thinkers and artists of the past. How else could you learn to make poems or art of your own American kind?
>
> (Perry et al., 1990: xx)

The statement suggests a level of literacy and education far beyond what actually existed in colonial British America at the time. Perhaps the elite studied world history, but certainly not the mass of people or the 25% of the adult population that was enslaved. Even those who studied history did not pretend to be interested in world history. They were attracted by the fabled empires of the ancient Mediterranean world and England from the Roman era onward.

Parts of the statement are simply wrong. The colonists certainly did not plan to emulate Hannibal and use elephants to cross the Appalachian Mountains. In fact, their experience during the French and Indian War made them suspicious of traditional European warfare. During the colonial and early national period artists in the Americas studied and reproduced European art forms. It was not until after the War of 1812 that they stopped looking towards Europe for inspiration and started to become American artists.

Later in the same section, the publisher tells students:

> You are one of the relatively few human beings in the world today who is a citizen of a politically free nation. You therefore have a special birthright and a special obligation. You have been given a right to rule that once only kings and nobles had. You must learn from world history at least one lesson: the right to rule can be gained, and it can be lost.
>
> (Perry et al., 1990: xxi)

My primary problem with this section is its ethno-centrism. In 1990 the population of the United States was 248,709,873. The population of the twelve nations in the European Union, which was also made up of "politically free" countries, was approximately 350 million people. India, with a population of 850 million people at that time, also claimed to be a democracy. To me, the argument for America's unique mission reads dangerously like a justification for world domination, and while concern with the loss of self-government is a significant concern, it is not the only or even the most important lesson to be learned from the study of history. What about the demands of the French Revolution for liberty, equality, and brotherhood? What about justice, democracy, and freedom?

If I were assigned to use the Houghton Mifflin textbook in a global history class today, I would have the students read and discuss the passages. Then I would challenge them to uncover possible biases and to draw up a series of questions for the authors and publishers expressing our concerns. One of my colleagues at Hofstra University, who was also a high school social studies teacher before becoming a teacher educator, used to have her students write questions and comments on post-it notes and insert them into the textbook as they read. This project encourages students to think critically and debate with the authors as they study history. Bill Bigelow and Bob Peterson advocate a similar approach in *Rethinking our classrooms: Teaching for equity and justice* (2007).

In linear notes in the teacher's edition, social studies teachers are directed to ask students "How can an examination of the world's past benefit a free nation"? That the United States is a free nation

analyzing the textbook

and uniquely so is not to be questioned. In fact, that is the key "lesson" to be learned from this textbook's presentation of history.

Curiously, some of the world's most renowned thinkers, "dead white European men" celebrated in many of the textbooks, have been skeptical about this approach to history and the study of history in general. In 1759, Voltaire declared, "The history of the great events of this world are scarcely more than the history of crimes" (Seldes, 1966: 714). Lord Acton of Great Britain, best known for the statement "Power tends to corrupt, and absolute power corrupts absolutely" (36), also warned, "History is not a web woven with innocent hands" (38). Otto von Bismarck, chancellor of Prussia, disdainfully dismissed history as "simply a piece of paper covered with print; the main thing is still to make history, not to write it" (97), while Napoleon is believed to have asked, "What is history but a fable agreed upon?"(519). I wonder if as youths they were forced to sit in classes where teachers committed to the idea of immutable truth babbled on in great detail about the important facts of the past and textbooks presented history as allegory in order to proselytize about the key lessons students needed to absorb?

A major theme of this book is that as teachers, we go about understanding history and its importance in the wrong way. We put the cart in front of the horse when we start with "facts" instead of questions. This is why I advocate a social studies approach to the study of history, an approach that starts with questions about the present and future, uses these questions to interrogate the past, and utilizes the past to help students answer their questions and formulate new ones.

Of course history unfolds chronologically; it moves in only one direction, but it does not have only one starting point or take just one path. Prior to 1492 the histories of the eastern and western hemispheres were quite distinct and the histories of different regions within the hemispheres (e.g., North and Sub-Saharan Africa, East and South Asia, and Western Europe in the eastern hemisphere) were following largely independent paths where change occurred at different rates of development. History is like a river with multiple sources that are flowing into the mainstream at different speeds. And sometimes, unexpectedly, it leaps its banks and cuts new channels.

The Flow of History

While it is helpful to look at sequence, connection, and change over time, it is also useful to make leaps and comparisons between regions and time periods, to explore tangents and dead-ends, and to examine societies that developed alternative ways of governing, producing, thinking about the world, and living. While I respect chronology and the chapters of this book roughly follow the chronology of human history, I am not imprisoned by it. There is no reason why teachers cannot jump around as we make comparisons across time and place as long as we bring our students with us. While this may make the study of history more complicated, a major theme I want students to explore is complexity. The world in all of its diversity, both past and present, is not a simple place to understand.

"Why is the World the Way it is Today?"

A social studies approach to global history starts with student questions, questions about why the world is the way it is today. It organizes the curriculum, units, and individual lessons in order to go back and forth across time, to examine case studies from the past, to help us gain insights into the human condition, and to stimulate questions about the present. Everyone in our classes is not going to become a historian; in fact, very few will. But educated citizens in a democratic society need to think about the past and raise questions about the present so that they can be informed and active participants in shaping the future.

FIGURE 1.1 Global history as a river.

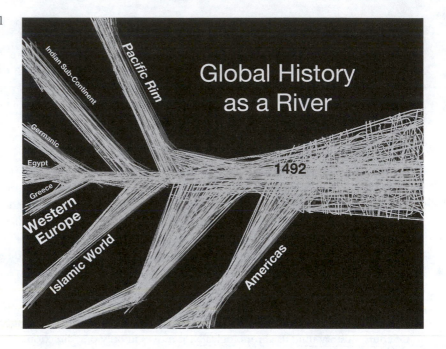

I opened a lesson in Adeola Tella's ninth-grade global history inclusion class by tossing out a soccer ball, an idea I adapted from a classroom activity developed by Bill Bigelow (1997), an editor of the magazine *Rethinking Schools*. Any student who caught the ball would tell us something about it and then toss it to someone else.

Adeola had told her class they would spend three days discussing the question "Why is the world the way it is today?" They would also try to figure out what their own questions are about things happening in the news.

Many of the twenty-four students in Adeola's class, overwhelmingly male and all either African American or Latino, had serious reading and writing problems and were hesitant to participate in class discussions. Two learning specialists usually worked with Adeola, assisting with group projects and helping students who were having difficulty completing their assignments.

The first student who caught the ball described it as a "sphere" and threw it to a friend. Other answers, roughly in sequence, were "round," "multi-colored," "the world plays soccer," "octagon," "covered with symbols," "mostly white," "used to play a sport," "patterns," "filled with air," "made by Adidas," "barcode," "used," "made in Pakistan," and "round like the Earth."

Eventually, as finding something new to say became harder, I asked a student to pass me the ball. Adeola, who was writing down student responses, read them back to the class. Then I asked, "Which of these answers has anything to do with social studies or the world today?" Someone said, "well it looks like a globe," but no one else spoke. So I asked, "What about where it was made?"

Some students knew where Pakistan was and located it on a map. Many were surprised that it wasn't just a "small" country. Students knew a few other things as well. "It was poor." "They had wars there." One young man asked if the soccer ball was made with child labor. He had heard that children worked in factories in many poor countries. Another young man, whose family immigrated to the United States from El Salvador, said children there work, especially on the farms. I asked why that was important and discussion started anew. This time, students began to question me.

They wanted to know, "Is child labor really happening today?"; "Is this like slavery?"; "How did I know this soccer ball was made by children?"; "Why are some people so poor and others so rich?"; "Does global trade make the world better or worse?"; "Why is this our problem? Shouldn't we just be concerned about what happens in the United States?"; "Won't the soccer balls cost more if they are made by adults?"; and "Don't we need more jobs in this country?"

I confessed I did not know the history of this particular soccer ball, but there was evidence that children stitched soccer balls together by hand in Pakistan and in other poor countries. I projected a series of pictures onscreen that I downloaded from websites sponsored by anti-child labor advocacy groups, as well as the United Nations, UNICEF, National Geographic, the International Labor Organization, and the United States Department of Labor. They showed children working in factories and fields, fishing, breaking rock into gravel, and making and hauling bricks.

Approximately 120 million of the world's children work full time. According to a report by the British affiliate of UNICEF, one child in twelve around the world today is forced into the "worst forms" of labor, including slavery, the sex trade, and hazardous and illicit activities (http://www.unicef.org.uk/publications/pdf/ECECHILD2_A4.pdf, accessed June 27, 2010).

Discussion of the slides led to three additional questions. "Are rich countries like the United States helping or hurting the world?" "Does our great wealth cause them to be poor?" "If our wealth causes their poverty, what should we do about it?"

On the second day, students worked in teams of six with help from Adeola and her co-teachers. Teams received newspapers, poster paper, and markers. They had to identify and write on the poster paper three newspaper headlines for international news articles that help explain why the world is the way it is today. Next they had to write down on a separate piece of paper why they chose each of these headlines, what the articles were about, what the articles tell us about the world, and any new questions they have. They also had to locate countries mentioned in the articles on a world map.

On the third day, each team selected one news article to present to the class. There were articles on the drug trade across the U.S./Mexican border; an attack on a hospital in Sri Lanka by a local militia; poverty, disease, and war in Zimbabwe; and economic problems in China. In follow-up discussion, students identified a range of additional questions. Why do people keep having wars? Who is a terrorist? Why would someone become one? Are national borders still important in today's world? Can national governments stop international crime? Does global trade (globalization) make countries weak? How come the things that people need to live are too expensive for them to buy?

Again, I couldn't answer their questions. I could not even start to answer them in the few minutes we had left. Instead, we decided to write their questions on poster board and hang them on the wall. Adeola agreed that they would talk about their questions and try to answer them as they learned about world history during the course of the school year. I agreed to visit their class periodically to see how they were progressing, especially because I wanted to know their answers to the question, "How come the things that people need to live are too expensive for them to buy?"

Over the years I have done similar activities in global history classes and in workshops for teachers. In one workshop, I gave global history teachers headlines and brief excerpts from three articles published in the March 31, 2009 edition of *The New York Times* ("Haiti's Woes Are Top Test for Aid Effort"; "Rampage in Pakistan Shows Reach of Militants"; and "Janet Jagan, Chicago Native Who Led Guyana, Dies at 88"). After a short discussion on the significance of the articles and a lot of questioning, I broke workshop participants into five small groups and asked them to make lists of their own questions about global history. Their lists of questions were amazing, gave a real sense of what teachers are thinking about, and would take years to explore.

Questions included "Why does religion impact on history?"; "What makes a civilization civilized?"; "Why are women usually treated as inferior?"; "Why do the West and White people dominate the world?"; "What would have happened if everyone was the same race?"; "Who decides what type of government is superior?"; "Is world peace a reasonable goal?"; "Are there moral absolutes?"; "What obligations do we have to others?"; "Is technology making the world better or worse?"; "How can we know what's true when governments and media are all biased?"; "When is it exploration and when is it exploitation?"; "What is the difference between a terrorist and a freedom fighter?"; "Is it all about oil (battles for scarce resources)?"; "Who benefits and who suffers from globalization?"; "What happens when global warming undermines our ability to survive?"

Researching answers to these questions would involve a high school class in exploring the full scope of global history. For example, discussions about the role of religion in society take place in units on early human cultures, ancient civilizations, empires that emerge in China, India, the Mediterranean world, and Meso-America, the development of feudalism in Europe and Japan, cross-cultural conflicts between Christian and Islamic societies, the spread of trade across Asia and Africa, the European Renaissance and Reformation, the creation of modern states, and genocide and war in the modern world.

Historians Question History

Many prominent historians, while reflecting on the historical process, have emphasized the importance of questioning. Marc Bloch was a French historian during the first half of the 20th century whose area of expertise was European feudal society. He is of interest here because of his life as well as because of his work as an historian. Bloch was a veteran of World War I where he served as an officer in the infantry and was awarded the Légion d'honneur, France's highest military decoration. Bloch was also a Jew and colleagues recommended that he leave Europe as war between France and Germany seemed imminent at the end of the 1930s. Instead, Bloch, at the age of 52, returned to active duty in the French army to defend his country.

After France's defeat, Bloch was a leader of the anti-Nazi resistance until he was captured in June 1944, just after the allied invasion at Normandy. Bloch was imprisoned, tortured, and executed. While awaiting execution, he wrote *The historian's craft* (1953), which was published after his death. It is the final testament of an activist and historian in which he discusses the value of one of the things he holds most dear, the study of history. In a quote that gives a sense of the seriousness of the man as a professional historian, he apologizes to readers, readers he knows may never see his text, for not using footnotes and standard citations. "The circumstances of my present life," he writes, "the impossibility of reaching any large library, and the loss of my own books have made me dependent upon my notes and memory" (6).

Bloch opened the book by sharing some personal anecdotes, including an exchange he had had years earlier with his young son. "Tell me, Daddy," the boy says to him, "What is the use of history?" (3). It is this question and challenge from his son that Bloch thinks about while a German prisoner and it serves as the "point of departure" for his book.

A few pages later, Bloch describes difficult questions being asked of him again, but in a different form and a very different setting. A member of the French military general staff confronted Bloch as German troops were entering Paris in June 1940. The officer wanted to know, "Are we to believe that history has betrayed us?" (6).

As a social studies teacher and as a teacher educator, I discovered the most important follow-up question during the course of discussion is to simply ask "Why?" over and over again as we seek to explain events. Bloch, as an historian, arrived at the same conclusion in the last chapter of his book where he explores historical causation. "The scholar," Bloch argues "is content to ask: 'Why?' and he [*sic*] accepts the fact that the answer may not be simple."

As anybody who has tried to explain something to a four-year-old knows, any attempt to answer the question "why" only leads to more questions, usually just "why," "why," "why," "why." Because of this, Bloch's answer to his son (and the French general staff) ends up being more an explanation of how historians seek to answer questions than a discussion of answers that must always remain tentative. But the questions remain paramount because they give us direction. For Bloch, "There is no waste more criminal than that of erudition running, as it were, in neutral gear, nor any pride more vainly misplaced than that in a tool valued as an end in itself" (86).

E. H. Carr, author of *What is history?* (1961) is another historian who revels in asking questions and places them at the forefront of his craft. Carr argues that the "historian is necessarily selective" and must consciously question the underlying assumptions that are shaping choices and conclusions. He calls "the belief in a hard core of historical facts existing objectively and independently of the interpretation of the historian a preposterous fallacy, but one which is very hard to eradicate" (10). As examples, Carr challenges historical knowledge about ancient Greece and the European medieval world, his own areas of specialization. According to Carr, in a passage that echoes Brecht's poem, our knowledge about ancient Greece is defective because we draw conclusions about the entire Mediterranean world based on "what fifth-century Greece looked like to an Athenian citizen" but ignore "what it looked like to a Spartan, a Corinthian, or a Theban – not to mention a Persian, or a slave or other non-citizen resident in Athens" (12). Similarly, historians conclude that people in Europe during the Middle Ages were "deeply concerned with religion," but this is based on reports written by people who themselves were deeply concerned with religion.

Throughout the book, Carr challenges historians who are concerned with collecting facts while they deny that they make interpretations or have underlying assumptions. He accuses them of writing "propaganda or historical fiction." They "merely use facts of the past to embroider a kind of writing which has nothing to do with history" (33).

One statement by Carr could well be considered his reply today to teachers, State Education Departments, and textbook companies that argue for a fact-based curriculum. In a defense of historical questioning, Carr explains: "As any working historian knows, if he stops to reflect what he is doing as he thinks and writes, the historian is engaged on a continuous process of moulding [shaping] his facts to his interpretation and his interpretation to his facts. It is impossible to assign primacy to one over the other" (34–35). History, according to Carr, "is a continuous process of interaction between the historian and his facts, an unending dialogue between the present and the past" (35). History is about asking and trying to answer questions.

Social Studies Approach

Historian Sean Wilentz (1997) of Princeton University has argued that secondary school teachers must present the "pastness of the past" and not turn the study of history into a "mere prologue of the present" with topics selected based on their current "relevance to our own world." While I disagree with Wilentz, I think he clearly identifies the fundamental difference between how some historians view the understanding and teaching of history and what I call a social studies approach.

There are a number of problems with the traditional global history curriculum. The challenging problem is probably related to the wealth of possible detail to include in a crowded curriculum. How do teachers decide what is important for students to know? What bears mentioning? What requires a lesson? What topics demand an entire unit? The abundance of information influences the way we teach history. There is tremendous pressure to race through epochs and regions, dictating names and dates, with little time available for an in-depth exploration of concepts and historical themes, for the evaluation of primary and secondary sources, and for students to draw their own historical conclusions.

A second problem is that most social studies teachers in the United States have significantly more extensive background in European and United States history than in the history of the non-Western world. The tendency to highlight the Western heritage in global history curricula is supported by the idea that what is really important to know about the history of the world happened in Europe, an idea that has been championed by many leading scholars, including Arthur Schlesinger Jr. (1992) and Orlando Patterson (1991).

According to this Western triumphalism position, civilization started in ancient Greece, traveled through Rome to medieval and modern Europe, landed in the Americas along with Columbus, and reshaped the world through Enlightenment ideas (including democracy) and the power of industrial capitalism and imperialism. It finally culminated in U.S. global expansion after World War II. At best, the examination of the history of the rest of the world is tangential to this process.

In this version of "history," everything else is at best a curiosity or at worst irrelevant. It is almost as if the future was predetermined and contingency and human efficacy eliminated. One way I challenge this conception is to ask students to examine the world in 1435, just before Portuguese sailors exploring the West African coast precipitate the Columbian Exchange. If you were a gambler, which region would you bet would emerge as dominant in world affairs during the next 300 to 500 hundred years: the Americas, Australia, Sub-Saharan Africa, the Islamic World, China and Japan, South Asia, or Western Europe? Western Europe was war torn and technologically backward. The United States would not even exist for hundreds of years. Meanwhile the Islamic World dominated trade in the eastern hemisphere and China was the most populous region in the world and probably its best governed.

Present and Past

A social studies approach to teaching global history is directly concerned with ideas and issues being discussed today, rather than just a compilation of events from the past. For example, teachers often ask me for interesting lesson ideas on relatively obscure topics such as absolute monarchy in 17th- and 18th-century Europe. The first question I always ask them is why they believe it is important for students to know about the topic. Most cannot think of reasons other than that it is in the textbook or might appear on a standardized test.

But if you think about the current world scene, significant reasons to examine absolute monarchy in Europe do emerge. We are looking here at a case study in the process of nation-state building. As the United States and the West try to develop democratic governments in Iraq and Afghanistan, it is legitimate to explore the process by which other countries developed democratic institutions in the past. Are there necessary stages that nations have passed through during this process? Have alternative strategies been attempted or successful? Can some stages be "skipped" and nation-building collapsed in time? Have national unity and cohesion and the development of a viable political and economic infrastructure sometimes been enhanced by authoritarian regimes? In other words, was absolute monarchy in 17th- and 18th-century Europe an essential step in the development of modern Western democratic societies? As I have written over and over in this chapter, the keys to understanding are the questions that we ask.

In addition, if our focus is on the process of nation-building rather than just European absolute monarchies in the 17th and 18th centuries, there are important comparisons that can be made with developments in other parts of the world and in other time periods, including India and China as they succumbed to European imperialism in the 18th and 19th centuries, Japan's decision to industrialize and become an imperialist power itself, and the problems faced by African and Asian independence movements in the post-World War II period.

Balancing Breadth and Depth

A social studies approach to global history is based on the idea that teachers need to balance the breadth of historical coverage with occasional in-depth case studies. Everything cannot be covered extensively, but for students to appreciate the historical process and the work of the historian, some things must be. Because it is a case study approach, examples can be drawn from outside what the teacher normally perceives as the main historical narrative, creating space for more extensive examination of the non-Western world throughout the curriculum. For example, most teachers (and hopefully some of our students) are familiar with the travels of Marco Polo along the silk route and how they helped cement economic and cultural ties between Western Europe and Eastern Asia on the Eurasian continent. But thousands of merchants and travelers were making the trip along this route and others were helping develop the infrastructure and networks binding different regions of the earth together, not just Marco Polo and his family. Teachers can just as easily focus on non-Western global travelers such as Rabban Sauma, an ethnic Turk and Eastern Orthodox monk who was born in northern China in the first half of the 13th century, Abu Abdullah Ibn Battuta, a North African merchant whose memoirs include reports on his visits to eastern and western Africa and the Indian subcontinent, and Zheng He, the 15th-century Chinese admiral whose ships plied the Indian Ocean.

Of course students might want to know which of these explorers were historically more significant and why they had never heard about the non-Western travelers before. They also might want to know what roles women played on the trips, at the way stations, and at the home base. These are excellent questions that will lead to research, analysis, debate, conclusions, and more questions, which according to Bloch and Carr is the process of historical study, and which is the primary goal of a social studies approach to history.

Empowering students to ask questions and seek their own answers does pose a pedagogical problem, especially for teachers who are trying to prepare them for tests. Students might not focus on the questions you would choose, value what textbook authors selected to include, or come up with the same answers that state and district administrators prefer them to "discover." Social studies teachers have to remember that disagreements about interpretation, the search for information to support conclusions, and the presentation of ideas in lively debate, are at the core of what learning, the study of history, and active involvement as citizens in a democratic society are supposed to be all about. In one memorable lesson that I observed, a fifth-grade class discussed trans-Atlantic European exploration of the western hemisphere and wanted to know how people went to the bathroom. The lack of privacy led to a discussion about whether women could be explorers. This in turn led to a discussion of the role of women in history and a research project on the role women played in the European conquest and settlement of the Americas. Somewhere down the line, students discovered how long skirts acted as portable bathrooms and provided a measure of privacy as women crossed the Great American Plains on wagon trains.

Sources and Historians

Nobody is an expert on everything. This book is not intended as a comprehensive history of all human endeavors. It largely focuses on the questions and debates that I have found interesting over the years and tries to suggest ways of thinking and teaching about the past.

I was nervous about writing this book, partly because of enormous gaps in my knowledge about large swathes of the world. The older I get and the more I study, the more I realize how much I do not know about so many things. Readers will certainly discover things I left out that should have been included, especially in discussions of Sub-Saharan African and Asian societies. Hopefully the things I chose to include will turn out to be accurate and my conclusions will not be too far-fetched. I promise to respond if you email me at catajs@hofstra.edu about things that should be added, dropped, or changed in future editions.

Almost this entire book is based on my reading of secondary sources. To help me organize my ideas as I started to write, I reread *A brief history of the human race* (2003) by Michael Cook. Cook, whose area of historical expertise is the Islamic world, is also a big proponent of asking big questions about the past to better understand the present. For Cook, these include, "Why has human history been crowded into the last ten thousand years?"; "Why has it happened at all?"; "Could it have happened in a radically different way?"; and "What should we make of the disproportionate role of the West in shaping the world we live in?" I also found Cook's comparisons of development in different parts of the world and what happens when regional civilizations butt up against each other very useful.

For discussions of human beginnings and what makes us human, I drew heavily on Marvin Harris, a cultural anthropologist whose many works explore the origins of human society and the relationship between environment and culture. Among his books, I recommend *Our kind* (1989) and *Cows, pigs, wars and witches* (1974). I found V. Gordon Childe's work on pre-historic societies and the transition from Paleolithic to Neolithic society – *What happened in history* (1942) and *Man makes himself* (1951) – interesting and useful. Jared Diamond's *Guns, germs, and steel: The fates of human societies* (1997) was especially helpful for exploring the development of river valley civilizations and the collision of regional "worlds" following the Columbian Exchange. A number of books about the impact of human societies on their environments and environments on human societies use traditional and early agricultural societies as examples. Three of the better sources are Eugene Linden's *The winds of change* (2006), Jared Diamond's *Collapse* (2005), and Cormac Ó Gráda's *Famine: A short history* (2009).

For sections in which I discuss the ancient world I generally relied on traditional sources including M. I. Finley (1963) and Martin Bernal (1987). Basil Davidson (1995) is the best-known chronicler of the history of Africa. Eric Williams (1970) plays a similar role for the Caribbean. I confess that for many areas and time periods, especially for Asia, I turned to upper-level high school and college introductory textbooks to fill in blanks. I have spent a lot of time considering the role of religion in different places and epochs. I find Karen Armstrong's series of books about religion in history accessible and comprehensive, although I often did not agree with her focus or interpretation (Armstrong, 1993).

Norman Cohn, author of *The pursuit of the millennium: Revolutionary millenarians and mystical anarchists of the Middle Ages* (1970), presents an interpretation on the role of religion in history that I found especially helpful as I formulated my own ideas. Cohn examined Christian society in Europe from the Middle Ages through the Protestant Reformation including the Crusades. His primary thesis was that during periods of "mass disorientation and anxiety" the poor and displaced expressed dissatisfaction with their conditions and even formulated revolutionary goals through millenarian and messianic beliefs and religious-inspired mass movements that challenged temporal authority. Significantly, once these forces were unleashed, they took on a life of their own and assumed power that traditional religious authorities could not control.

In his work, Cohn did not hesitate to draw connections between his historical scholarship and analysis of the contemporary world. He believed that part of the appeal of 20th-century autocratic leaders like Hitler and Stalin was their "messianic" ability to connect their vision with the aspirations of the disoriented and anxious poor of the modern epoch.

Among the historians who discuss the impact of the Columbian Exchange on the modern world I recommend two very highly. Fernand Braudel's work, including *Capitalism and material life, 1400–1800* (1973), examines economic development and everyday life in European society and the developing relationship between Europe and the rest of the world during the period of exploration, conquest, and colonization. Robin Blackburn (1988, 1997) specializes in the history of new world slavery, both its institutionalization and its eventual abolition.

The historian I find most helpful in defining recent historical epochs is Eric Hobsbawm. Hobsbawm's research and writing spans the last quarter of the second Christian millennium (roughly 1750–2000). I learned much from Hobsbawm about capitalism, industrialization, imperialism, and revolution. *The age of extremes: A history of the world, 1914–1991* (1994) is a comprehensive survey of the 20th century in which Hobsbawm attempts to explain the development of the modern world.

Concluding Note about Language

Questions of language often reflect broader historical disagreements, and certainly expose sensitivity and insensitivity. I try to be politically sensitive rather than politically correct (e.g., people are enslaved rather than slaves), although as political and cultural currents shift and groups or movements assert control over their own destinies, this is not an easy task. In the study of history and in historical writing an effort to respond to changing usage is complicated because primary source documents often use dated and even offensive language about racial, ethnic, and national groups and women. To ignore this language, and the attitudes they reflect, distorts the past.

As a historian and teacher I try to avoid using the term "human progress" because one of the questions I discuss with students is whether history should be seen as a generally positive progression, with some road bumps, from a "primitive" past to "modern" present, or as a much more complex path with many twists and turns and often no clear direction. I also refer to hunting and gathering and agrarian societies as "traditional" rather than as "primitive," because primitive connotes that their members are culturally backward.

Because terms have historical and political implications and the world is constantly changing, I sometimes cannot make up my mind what language to use and I shift back and forth when teaching or writing. For example, is it more useful to describe collectively the United States, Western Europe, Australia, and Japan as the First or Capitalist World, which is what it was called during the Cold War (1945–1990), or as the industrialized, post-industrial, capitalist, modern, developed, affluent, or economically advanced world? Part of the problem is that with globalization, while it continues to dominate the world economy, much industrial production takes place elsewhere.

In the same way it is hard to find a term to describe what used to be called the Third World or unaligned bloc before the collapse of the Soviet Union eliminated the Second World or socialist bloc. "Developing" or "underdeveloped" are relatively neutral descriptive terms, but they mask that these regions were massively exploited by imperialist powers for hundreds of years and were misdeveloped to support their industrial economies.

It is also hard to categorize countries such as China and India, which have emerged as industrial powers but where most of their populations remain impoverished; Russia which seems to be in a constant state of flux; micro-states that flourish as financial centers and niche economies, such as Singapore, Brunei, Bahrain, and Djibouti, and at least temporarily Ireland and Iceland, and some of the oil-rich countries that have great wealth, economic influence, and small indigenous populations such as Saudi Arabia and Kuwait. My tendency is to call the United States, Western Europe, Australia, Japan, and the countries tied into their industrial and financial networks (including the banking and wealthy OPEC states) the "Western Bloc," describe China, India, and perhaps Russia as emerging or "Second Tier" powers, and to continue to call the undeveloped or misdeveloped third world the "Third World." However, I remain open to better ideas.

TEACHING IDEAS

The teaching ideas and activities at the end of each chapter and posted on my website http://people.hofstra.edu/alan_j_singer can be used in different ways depending on your goals, the grade-level and academic performance of your students, and the way your curriculum is organized. These are recommended activities, and teachers will need to adapt them and reedit documents to fit different situations.

 With a higher performing class you might want to begin the year with a debate on the value of studying history (Activity 1) and use current events articles to define student questions (Activity 2). In New York State, where global history is taught in high school in ninth grade (Human Origins through European Enlightenment) and tenth grade (French Revolution through today) I usually start ninth grade with the soccer ball lesson discussed earlier in the chapter that is used to identify student questions about the world we live in. With different students, you can use this activity again in tenth-grade classes. However, I generally begin with a discussion of the events and people who changed the world (Activity 3). Teachers can also return to this activity at the end of the year so students can reconsider their decisions based on what they learned during the course of study. Activities 4–8, which are available online, can be used at the start of the school year to introduce themes, interspaced into the curriculum to reinforce them, or as part of culminating and review activities as students prepare for assessments. Activity 9, available online, introduces students to the continuing problem of famine in the modern world.

Activity 1. Of What Value is History?

Instructions: Some of the world's most renowned thinkers have been skeptical about the value of studying history. According to the French philosopher Voltaire, "The history of the great events of this world are scarcely more than the history of crimes." Lord Acton of Great Britain warned, "History is not a web woven with innocent hands." Otto von Bismarck, chancellor of Prussia, dismissed history as "simply a piece of paper covered with print; the main thing is still to make history, not to write it." Napoleon is rumored to have asked, "What is history but a fable agreed upon?" Do you agree or disagree with history's critics? Explain.

Activity 2. Headlines from *The New York Times*, March 31, 2009

Instructions: The headlines and the excerpts from articles below appeared in a recent edition of *The New York Times*. Working in teams, examine and discuss the headlines and excerpts, locate places mentioned on your world map, and answer questions 1–3.

Questions

1. What is the main point of each headline and excerpt?
2. Based on your knowledge of current events and the information presented here, what questions do you have about these reports?
3. Using these reports and questions as a starting point, what broader questions do you have about what is taking place in the world today?

Haiti's Woes Are Top Test for Aid Effort

by Neil MacFarquhar, A5

"About 46 million more people are expected to tumble into poverty this year amid the largest decline in global trade in 80 years, according to the World Bank. The results ripple through every index. An additional 200,000 to 400,000 infants, for example, may die every year for the next six years because of the crisis, the bank said."

Rampage in Pakistan Shows Reach of Militants

by Sabrina Tavernise, Waqar Gillani and Salman Masood, A1

"The attackers hopped over a crumbling brick wall, wearing backpacks and belts with dangling grenades. They were young and wore beards, and by 7:30 a.m. on Monday, they were firing automatic weapons into an unarmed crowd of young police recruits."

Janet Jagan, Chicago Native Who Led Guyana, Dies at 88

by Simon Romero, A24

"Again, their politics, along with their admiration for Fidel Castro's revolution in Cuba, caused alarm in a foreign capital—this time, Washington. According to long-classified documents, President John F. Kennedy ordered the Central Intelligence Agency in 1961 to destabilize the Jagan government. The C.I.A. covertly financed a campaign of labor unrest, false information and sabotage that led to race riots and, eventually, the ascension of Forbes Burnham, a black, London-educated lawyer and a leader of the People's Progressive Party who had become a rival of the Jagans. He became president and prime minister in 1966."

Activity 3. Events (or People) That Changed the World

Instructions: At the end of the 1990s, in preparation for celebration of the start of a new millennium, many groups and individuals created lists of the most important or significant people and events in human history. *Life* magazine published a list of the "Top 100 Events of the Last Millennium" (http://www.tostepharmd.net/hissoc/top100events.html, accessed June 6, 2010). The top ten events from the list are included here. Students can research these events and evaluate their impact on human history. During the course of studying global history they can create their own "top" 100 lists of people and events. As part of the project they need to explain the criteria they used for making these choices and ordering people and events and write a paragraph about each event or person. They should be prepared to defend their choices and explain why certain groups of people (e.g., women) and regions of the world are over- or under-represented.

Life Magazine List

1. Gutenberg prints the Christian Bible, Germany, 1455
2. Columbian Encounter, Spain and the Americas, 1492
3. Luther launches Protestant Reformation, Germany, 1517
4. James Watt patents the steam engine, England, 1769

5. Galileo establishes sun-centered solar system, Italy, 1610
6. Robert Koch develops germ theory of disease, Germany, 1882
7. Gunpowder first used in weapons, China, 1100
8. Declaration of Independence, United States, 1776
9. Hitler and Nazis come to power, Germany, 1933
10. Compass used to navigate, China, 1117

2

DEBATING CURRICULUM: WHAT IS IMPORTANT TO KNOW AND WHY?

> This chapter looks at curriculum debates and the role of national and state history standards, assessments, and textbooks in defining the global history curriculum. It encourages teachers to become historians themselves and to constantly explore what is important to know.

While working on this chapter during the summer of 2009, I received an email from an alumnus of the Hofstra program who had just completed his first year as a social studies teacher at a small urban high school. He had used many of the activities and projects he learned about in methods classes and was pleased with the response of students. However, he was worried because the principal spoke with him at the end of the school year and insisted that if he wanted to work at that school he had to apply the state standards rigorously and be much more focused on preparing students for the standardized Global History assessment test that they had to take at the end of tenth grade. This young teacher wanted to be true to his principles, but he also needed to hold on to his job.

When we spoke, he was much relieved that I had some of the same conflicts with my supervisors as a beginning teacher and that I did not think he was "selling-out" by addressing the principal's concerns. I shared with him some of the things I learned as I figured out how to maintain my integrity as a teacher and an historian while negotiating life in a bureaucratic school system.

Standards and Assessments

The first thing I learned was that standardized state social studies assessments overwhelmingly test student subject area literacy. Students who read and write on grade-level perform well on these tests whatever the particular content focus of a teacher. In one high school I had a colleague who made students copy and memorize what I considered to be essentially meaningless lists of European monarchs. Students learned little about history from these lists and to her chagrin there never were any questions about her favorite monarchs on the assessment test. Despite this approach, her top performing classes did as well on the tests as similar groups in the school and her lower performing classes did just as poorly.

In my experience, students who are interested in what you are discussing and the projects you are doing in class are more likely to pay attention and remember key ideas. They do more and better work and almost always perform better on the state assessments. Working in difficult schools where cutting and truancy were major problems, one of my biggest achievements was getting students to attend class until the end of the year and to show up for standardized tests. My passing percentages were not significantly different from other teachers in our school, but they were based on a much higher percentage of students from my classes who actually took the tests.

Experienced teachers I work with as a student teaching field supervisor generally find state and national content standards less than useful as guides to lesson planning, the creation of activity sheets, and daily teaching. When they are required to refer to "The Standards" in their lesson plans they do little more than write "Addresses Standard 2" or maybe "Addresses Standard 2a."

Too often the phrase aligning a curriculum, unit, or lesson with the appropriate national, state, or local standard is just a synonym for turning to the next chapter in the textbook. The textbook is where the meat is added to the skeletal standards. Unfortunately, textbooks are produced by publishing conglomerates whose primary goal is to maximize profits, even when it means accommodating conservative state legislatures and cautious educational agencies. The result is that textbooks and curricula are heavy on lists of "facts" while underlying assumptions go unstated and unquestioned and controversies go unexamined.

Satisfying the Standard

Most of what are called state or national content standards are so broadly framed and so generic in language that anything you choose to teach, as long as it is related to the topic, satisfies the standard. For example, the National World History Standards for Era 6 (http://nchs.ucla.edu/standards/worldera6.html, accessed June 6, 2010) describes the period between 1450 and 1770 as the first "global age" and standard six for this era recommends that students examine "major global trends" between those years including demographic and political boundary shifts, economic and technological changes, and "patterns of social and cultural continuity . . . in the context of a rapidly changing world." A teacher can focus on any topic from the period or region, as long as students end up understanding the impact of different factors (multiple causation) on historical continuity and change. We should be presenting students with case studies that illustrate specific ideas, not an all-encompassing list of everything that happened.

As a high school teacher, and in classes for pre-service teachers examining the global history curriculum, I focus on the impact of the Columbian Exchange, especially the trans-Atlantic slave trade, on human history. The Columbian Exchange precipitates enormous demographic shifts, promotes the development of capitalism, and centers world power in the North Atlantic. However, other teachers whom I respect are more interested in the history of ideas and focus on the Renaissance, Reformation, Scientific Revolution, and Enlightenment in Europe, which they argue sets the stage for Europe's transcendence in the 19th century.

I suspect, although I have not seen it done, a teacher could do a very effective job teaching about this period of global interaction while addressing the standards and preparing students for assessments, by focusing on the history of west, south, or east Asia (See Chapter 8). Michael Cook, in *A brief history of the human race* (2003), tells much of the story of humanity from the perspective of the Islamic world and the regions it dominated. He even uses the Islamic scholar, Tabari (c. 900), to discuss the nature of history itself. Tabari argued, "no knowledge of the history of men of the past . . . is attainable . . . except through information and transmission provided by informants and transmitters . . . this knowledge cannot be elicited by reason or inferred by internal thought processes" (9).

What is Important to Know?

State and national content standards are generally effective at showing teachers how topics they might cover in an individual lesson are connected to broader social studies and historical themes. Standard 2A for Era 6 of the National World History Standards recommends that students be able to "describe characteristics of the family and peasant society in early modern Europe and explain changes in institutions of serfdom in eastern and western Europe." This is to be used to teach students how to "analyze cause-and-effect relationships."

Between 1450 and 1750 AD, the period covered by this standard, global events, especially the impact of the Columbian Exchange, unleashed forces that transformed life for the European peasant and can be used to show the connections between the macro and the micro worlds. Rather than just looking at family structure or reviewing the feudal hierarchy, I see this topic as an opportunity to explore the impact of global events on the everyday life of ordinary people and the problem of exploitation when people have little or no control over the institutions that govern their society.

One change was the closing of the commons, at first in England, and then in other parts of Europe. Traditionally open village land available for common use as a source of pasture and wood had helped sustain peasant life. But the commercial revolution that followed the Columbian Exchange with the introduction of new products and economic practices stimulated the desire of landholders to enhance their income. They stripped away the rights of peasants, driving them off of land that could be used more profitably to grow grains for new markets. Some peasants rebelled and their rebellions were brutally suppressed. Others migrated to cities where they became a new class of urban poor. Many migrated to the Americas, either by choice or under duress, some as free men and women, but most as bonded labor. The end of feudalism in most of Europe in the early modern period, rather than being motivated by a push for democracy and equality, was precipitated by new economic conditions and marked by intense exploitation and little regard for the impact of changes on the people being affected.

Ultimately, my advice to the young friend I mentioned at the beginning of this chapter was to continue to teach in ways that engaged his students. But to also be prepared to explain to his principal where the topics fit into the standards and how his lessons and the projects prepared students for the assessment. For example, every time they examined pictures, songs, or artifacts in class, students had to use what they uncovered to answer an umbrella question about the topic, making the lesson, in effect, practice for a document-based essay.

Curriculum Debates

In the poem "To a Mouse" (1793) (http://www.robertburns.org/works/75.shtml, accessed June 6, 2010), Scottish poet Robert Burns observes a hard-working field mouse as it builds a nest, only to have it destroyed by the farmer who is plowing the field. Burns draws the lesson that despite preparation and effort there are no guarantees of success in life for either mice or men. The best-planned activities can go astray because of uncontrollable outside forces.

This is a statement against historical determinism and in favor of contingency, the intervention of unanticipated factors. It is also a warning to the rich and powerful that economic downturns can weaken the strongest businesses and that the thousand-year "Reich" and empires where the sun never sets are really ephemeral.

You would think historians would apply this lesson on the impact of unanticipated forces to curriculum debates, but many do not. They are too often trapped by the belief that the best ideas and arguments will be incorporated into textbooks and curriculum guides, and forget to factor in political and economic considerations in the debate over what gets taught and why.

Voluntary national history standards, developed by the National Center for History in Schools at UCLA (NCHS) with funding from the federal government through the National Endowment for the Humanities, were released to the public in 1994. The initial draft included suggested approaches to the study of history, statements outlining broad historical themes, lists of topics to analyze, and suggestions for how some of the themes and topics could be taught in social studies classes. The general statements included in the document were largely ignored in the ensuing debate, but the standards and the people who developed them were excoriated because of conservative political opposition to proposals about what could be taught to illustrate the broader historical ideas. Eventually the NCHS issued a revised set of standards without the recommended classroom activities. This document, because it avoided the controversy over specifics, was widely accepted (Singer, 2008: 108–110).

Concern about the details of the standards was not just restricted to rightwing groups. The Council on Islamic Education, which viewed the overall approach to history in the standards favorably, prepared a systematic critique of the way they addressed, or failed to address, Islam's role in global history (http://www.cie.org/categories.aspx?id=N&CategoryId=62&m_id=30, accessed June 6, 2010). While most of their comments focus on bias in language, a major concern was that, "although the *Standards* expressly acknowledge Muslim civilization's dominance over a wide area and a long chronological period, only isolated reference is made to the influence of Islam and Muslims upon cultures of the East or the West, unless they are specifically Muslim cultures."

National Standards for World History

I have some significant problems with the National Standards for World History in their current version (http://nchs.ucla.edu/standards/world-standards5-12.html, accessed June 6, 2010). It is a cautious document that arose out of controversy and the sense that somehow you could develop a document that satisfied everyone. My biggest problem is that because of its surrender to political pressure, it is just not as useful as it should be.

The National Standards for World History present history as a finished product. It is as if historians and teachers know all they need to know about the past and its impact on the present and that their primary task is to find more or less interesting ways to convey this information to students. They present no controversy over interpretations of history or suggest that there are significant gaps in knowledge. While they talk about developing historical skills, there is no sense that students will participate as historians. In fact, they add very little to traditional textbook accounts. In addition, after reading through the standards, teachers have no sense of how they should progress to engage students as historians.

Although it acknowledges, "Not all of the events in world history that students should address can be bracketed within one of the nine eras presented in this chapter," they follow the nine standard eras, ranging from human origins to the contemporary world. So bent on avoiding controversy, they introduce the section on human beginnings by stating, "So far as we know, humanity's story began in Africa." This is presented as if some other explanation is being seriously considered. The summary does not use the term "evolution." It speaks of biological change, and does not make clear that "our early ancestors" were not biologically modern human beings.

In what I find misleading, the curriculum claims "human history became global at a very early date" as populations migrated around the world and as "humans learned how to grow crops, domesticate plants, and raise animals." A major point of contention among historians who are specialists in different regions is how much of the similarity between cultures is a result of diffusion and how much is parallel development caused by human responses to similar environments. For example, how much were early civilizations in Egypt (Nile River valley) and India (Indus River

Valley) influenced by Mesopotamia (Tigris–Euphrates River Valley), where developments seems to have occurred a few hundred years earlier than in the other two places. Strict chronological presentation leaves out that often developments are unconnected and take place at different rates and follow different paths, definitely up to 1500 AD and in many parts of the world into the 20th century. There is a general overemphasis in the National Standards for World History on global development in a world where people lived in localities and at most there was regional interaction. Rather than providing students with predigested answers, I prefer a curriculum where students debate diffusion versus parallel development and the reasons for cultural similarity and requires them to provide specific examples to support their conclusions.

Why Study This Era?

The best part of the National Standards for World History is the question at the end of each era: "Why Study This Era?" For example, study of this era helps students understand what it means to be human including our "common past," that early "cultural forms, social institutions, and practical techniques . . . laid the foundations for the emergence of all early civilizations . . . the possibilities and limitations of human control over their environment . . . the variety of social and cultural paths that different societies may take; and the acceleration of social change through time" (http://nchs.ucla.edu/standards/worldera1.html, accessed June 27, 2010). What is striking is that these main ideas really permeate the curriculum, not just one era. As students study each historical period they reexamine many of the same historical factors, adding depth to their understanding of the forces that promote historical continuity and change.

Typically, Era 3 is identified as the era of Classical Traditions, Major Religions, and Giant Empires, 1000 BCE–300 CE. Among major topics is the emergence of religious systems including Judaism, Christianity, Buddhism, Hinduism, Confucianism, and Daoism. All appeared in this period as systems of belief capable of stabilizing and enriching human relations across large areas of the world and providing avenues of cultural interchange between one region and another. Each of these religions united peoples of diverse political and ethnic identities. Religions also, often enough, divided groups into hostile camps and gave legitimacy to war or social repression. But why religion developed in this period is never asked, nor how differences reflected specific historical circumstances.

In Era 4, the National Standards for World History argue that one of the most dramatic developments of this 700-year period (300 AD to 1000 AD) was the rise of Islam as both a new world religion and a civilized tradition encompassing an immense part of the eastern hemisphere. Commanding the central region of Afro-Eurasia, the Islamic empire of the Abbasid dynasty became in the 8th to 10th-century period the principal intermediary for the exchange of goods, ideas, literacy, and technologies across the hemisphere.

Concluding Thoughts

In the most recent edition of *Social Studies for Secondary Schools* (2008), I explain that over the course of my career as a high school social studies teacher and as a teacher educator I developed "a deeper awareness of the importance of teacher conceptual knowledge of history and the social sciences" (xiv). My concerns there, and here, are related to teaching practice, but also to my broader goals. Unless teachers are "committed to the continuous growth of their own knowledge and understanding," I worry "they will fall into the habit of using easily available print and online material that is attractive, even seductive, but is superficial and largely misleading." In addition, if we do not know enough about the past and contemporary society to distinguish between analysis and propaganda, how will our students "develop the knowledge and skills needed to become active and critical citizens of a democratic society" (xiv)?

If the National World History Standards, or individual state standards, stimulate teachers to think more broadly about what is important to know and why in global history, they serve a vital pedagogical function. However, if they are only a relatively incomplete pacing calendar or test-prep guidelines, they are less than useful and probably have a negative impact on teaching and learning global history.

TEACHING IDEAS

In the previous chapter, we discussed having students participate in framing essential questions, based on their own interests and contemporary concerns, that can provide a focus for examining global history. As they interrogate the past to figure out what happened in history and why, they can also question local, state, and national global history standards and decide where they agree or disagree with what government agencies have decided should be included in the curriculum. As a class project, they can write a critique of the standards from their individual and collective perspectives and submit it to the appropriate officials for review (Activities 1 and 2).

Examining and questioning curriculum standards is not just an exercise. Internationally there has been sharp debate over sex education guidelines developed by UNESCO in 2009 as part of its campaign to reduce the rate of H.I.V. infections among young people. Much of the opposition has centered in the United States where conservative religious groups have opposed references to masturbation and discussions of condom use, sexually transmitted diseases, and the assertion that "legal abortion performed under sterile conditions by medically trained personnel is safe." Activity 3 involves global history students studying contemporary problems in this debate.

Examining the nature of knowledge and truth (Activity 4) has deep roots in different classical traditions. It is a major topic in both Greek philosophy and the writings of the imperial Chinese philosopher Confucius. In his *Analects*, Confucius argued, "The object of the superior man is truth. Food is not his object . . . The superior man is anxious lest he should not get truth; he is not anxious lest poverty should come upon him." He also defined knowledge: "When you know a thing, to realize that you know it; and when you do not know a thing, to allow that you do not know it: this is knowledge."

Questioning received truth is at the core of the Socratic Method as presented in the writings of Plato and led to a death sentence for Socrates on charges that he corrupted the youth of Athens. Interestingly, in *Crito* Socrates accepts his fate. He refuses to escape because he believes such defiance would undermine the authority of the state. Activity 5 compares the attitudes toward authority of Socrates and Confucius.

Questioning authority and received truth was an essential feature of the European Renaissance, Reformation, and Enlightenment; however in these periods it also existed in dynamic tension with the idea that social order required supporting the institutions of society (Activity 6). Students should also examine ideas about knowledge, attitudes toward questioning, and challenges to authority in other classical traditions (Activity 7).

Activity 6 is a play written and performed by a team of students in Michael Pezone's tenth-grade class in response to reading about and discussing the scientific revolution and the trial of Galileo. The assignment is designed to promote oral and written literacy, as well as academic seriousness and historical understanding. Many of the students in Michael's school, Law, Government and Community Service Magnet High School, have significant academic difficulty. In a follow-up discussion, students examined the way in which the play differed from established historical facts and argued over whether Galileo's legacy would have been different if he had refused to confess and instead continued to challenge the authority of the Roman Catholic Church. It is reproduced from an article Michael wrote for the New York/New Jersey State Councils of Social Studies (Pezone, 2008).

Activity 1. Democracy Chronology

Instructions: Diane Ravitch and Abigal Thernstrom were two of the leading conservative opponents of multiculturalism during the 1980s and 1990s and were influential in shaping social studies and history curricula. From 1991 to 1993 Ravitch was an Assistant Secretary of Education during the first Bush presidency. Thernstrom served as vice-chair of the U.S. Commission on Civil Rights during the second Bush presidency. In 1992 Ravitch and Thernstrom published *The democracy reader: Classic and modern speeches, essays, poems, declarations, and documents on freedom and human rights worldwide* (New York: HarperCollins). In Section 1, Classical and European Thought, they present what they see as the pathway of democracy from Thucydides (*The Peloponnesian War*) through Plato (*The Republic*), Aristotle (*The Politics*) to Thomas Aquinas (*Summa Theologia*) and Niccolò Machiavelli (*The Discourses*).

Questions

1. Can the ideas discussed by Thucydides, Plato, Aristotle, Thomas Aquinas, and Machiavelli reasonably be considered democratic in the modern sense of the word? When do institutions we would recognize as democratic emerge? Explain.
2. How did "democratic" ideas leap across time from ancient Greece to early modern Europe?
3. Could democracy and democratic institutions develop independently unrelated to other historical events that are taking place? Explain.

Activity 2. Debating the World History Standards

Instructions: You have been appointed to be the student representative on a committee rewriting your state's global history standards. In preparation for the committee's next meeting you have been asked to prepare a 250–word statement on one of the following issues that will be discussed:

1. Should the Roman Republic and Empire receive special attention and be covered in a separate two-week unit or should it be treated the same way as other ancient societies?
2. While Egypt is physically located on the continent of Africa, should the ancient kingdom of the Pharaohs be considered an African, a Middle Eastern, or a Mediterranean civilization, or something else?
3. Should Islamic societies in the Middle Ages (roughly 600 AD–1200 AD) receive as much attention in the curriculum as Christian societies in Europe?
4. European imperialism brought capitalism, industrial development, Christianity, modern medicine, and democratic institutions to colonized countries in Sub-Saharan Africa. Should it be portrayed as exploitative or beneficial?

5.   Chinese civilization, while initially more advanced than civilization in Europe, remained essentially stagnant for thousands of years. How much attention does it merit in the global history curriculum?

Activity 3. UNESCO Sex Education Guidelines

Background: In 2009, international sex education guidelines designed to reduce the rate of HIV infections among young people around the world were proposed by UNESCO, an agency of the United Nations. The proposed guidelines provoked a wave of criticism from conservative and religious groups, many based in the United States. They argued that the guidelines exposed children to sexual information while they were too young to fully understand, promoted pre-marital sex and abortions, and violated parental rights.

Proponents of the guidelines argued that in the absence of a vaccine to prevent AIDS, education was the most potent weapon against the spread of the disease. UNESCO officials estimated that only 40% of young people aged 15 to 24 have accurate knowledge of how HIV/AIDS is transmitted and that people in this age group account for 45% of all new cases of the disease.

Instructions: Examine the international sex education guidelines developed by UNESCO (http://unesdoc.unesco.org/images/0018/001832/183281e.pdf, accessed June 6, 2010). Write a 1,000-word essay commenting on the guidelines and the problems they are intended to address and your view of the issues in the debate, including your response to both critics and advocates of the guidelines.

Activity 4. How Do We Know What We Know? – A Greek Perspective

Instructions: The philosophers of ancient Greece, especially Socrates, Plato, and Aristotle, were very concerned with the nature of truth and the process by which people acquire and can be certain about knowledge. In these statements, adapted from the original quotes, they discuss some of their beliefs and questions about the nature of knowledge and how we know what we know. After you have read the passages, clarify your understanding of what they are saying, and be prepared to explain your views on the nature of truth and knowledge.

FIGURE 2.1
The Parthenon, on top of the Acropolis in Athens, Greece, is where Socrates and his students met.

A. Socrates questions the existence of absolute truth in a dialogue with Cratylus

I suspect the study of what truly really exists is beyond the ability of you and me to determine. Knowledge of things does not just come from naming them. To acquire true knowledge, things must be carefully studied and investigated. One problem in acquiring true knowledge is that everything seems to be in a state of flux. If things are constantly changing, how can we claim to have true knowledge about them. Is it possible to determine whether there is some eternal unchanging nature in things?

(http://classics.mit.edu/Plato/cratylus.html, accessed June 6, 2010)

B. Plato compares knowledge with opinion in *The Republic*

When a person looks at objects after the light of day is no longer shining, we see dimly, and are nearly blind. But when we examine objects on which the sun shines, we see them clearly. The soul is like the eye. When the soul looks at something that is true, it understands this truth and shines with intelligence. But when the truth is obscured by twilight the soul only sees opinion. It goes blinking about, and is first of one opinion and then of another, and seems to have no intelligence.

(http://classics.mit.edu/Plato/republic.7.vi.html, accessed June 6, 2010)

C. Aristotle discusses whether objects or truth exist independently of human knowledge

It is true that if an object does not exist, there can be no knowledge about it. There will no longer be anything to know. However, it is equally true that, an object may exist even if people do not have knowledge about it.

(http://aristotle.thefreelibrary.com/Categories/2-1, accessed June 6, 2010)

Activity 5. Socrates and Confucius Discuss Responsibility and Authority

Instructions: Both Socrates and Confucius discussed the relationship between the individual and the state and the obligation of the individual to respect and obey state authority. Examine passages A and B and answer questions 1–4.

Questions

1. What are the key arguments made by each of the philosophers?
2. Do you agree or disagree with their ideas about the responsibility of individuals to obey those in authority? Explain.
3. In your opinion, are these ideas valid today? Explain.
4. Write a paragraph where you present a response to either Socrates or Confucius.

Passage A

We know very little about the ideas of the Greek philosopher Socrates other than what is reported in the writings of his disciple Plato. According to Plato, Socrates (470–399 BC) spent his adult life questioning received truth. He believed that people hide their ignorance to protect their positions of power and influence. His constant questioning made him enemies among the Athenian elite. In 399 BC he was put on trial, accused of subverting the morals of the youth of Athens. He may have been accused because he questioned the ability of fragile democratic institutions to reach just decisions. Socrates was found guilty and sentenced to death. When he refused to flee Athens, he was executed. In the *Crito*, Plato has Socrates explain to one of his followers why he will obey the law even if it means his death:

> Imagine that I am about to play truant, and the laws and the government come and interrogate me: "Tell us, Socrates . . . do you imagine that a State can subsist and not be overthrown, in which the decisions of law have no power, but are set aside and overthrown by individuals?" . . . He who disobeys us is, as we maintain, thrice wrong: first, because in disobeying us he is disobeying his parents; secondly, because we are the authors of his education; thirdly, because he has made an agreement with us that he will duly obey our commands; and he neither obeys them nor convinces us that our commands are wrong; and we do not rudely impose them, but give him the alternative of obeying or convincing us; that is what we offer and he does neither.
>
> (http://classics.mit.edu/Plato/crito.html, accessed June 6, 2010)

Passage B

The teachings of Confucius (Kong-tzu or Master Kong, 551–479 BC) were not written down until long after his death. In the *Analects*, a collection of sayings, he did not discuss the responsibility of individuals to obey the dictates of rulers in depth. However, a major part of his philosophy was the responsibility of youth to obey and respect their parents. Confucius called this filial piety. Most historians believe that in Confucius' system of beliefs, filial piety also describes the relationship that should exist between the individual and rulers:

> I asked what filial piety is. The Master said, "It is being obedient . . . That parents, when alive, should be served according to ritual; that, when dead, they should be buried according to ritual; and that they should be sacrificed to according to ritual.
>
> The duties of universal obligation are five . . . The duties are those between ruler and subject, between father and son, between husband and wife, between elder brother and younger, and those in the intercourse [interaction] of friends.
>
> It is rare for a man whose character is such that he is good as a son and obedient as a young man to have the inclination to transgress against his superiors; it is unheard of for one who has no such inclination to be inclined to start a rebellion . . . Being good as a son and obedient as a young man is, perhaps, the root of a man's character.
>
> (http://www.wsu.edu/~wldciv/world_civ_reader/
> world_civ_reader_1/confucius.html, accessed June 6, 2010)

Activity 6. Trial of Galileo – An Alternative Possibility

Background: Galileo Galilei (1564–1642 AD) was an Italian scientist whose use of a telescope to study the solar system played an important part in the 17th-century scientific revolution in Europe. Based on his observations, Galileo challenged the idea that the Earth was the center of the solar system. Instead he proposed a heliocentric model with the planets orbiting the sun. His research and conclusions brought him into conflict with leaders of the Roman Catholic Church who embraced the geocentric (Earth-centered) model of the solar system. In 1632, he was tried by the Inquisition and found "vehemently suspect of heresy." When he was threatened with execution, he agreed to recant his beliefs. He spent the rest of his life under house arrest.

Instructions: This play was written by high school students who were unhappy that Galileo disavowed his findings about the solar system in order to save his life. If you were Galileo, would you have recanted or resisted? Why? Read and discuss this alternative contemporary version of the trial of Galileo in your groups. In groups, you will write and be prepared to perform your own skit about the trial of Galileo. In your skit, you must mention and explain specific ideas and information (scientific method, geocentric and heliocentric views, etc.) If you wish, you can change the outcome of the trial. Use your imaginations! Your written script must fill at least three pages, front and back (double-space and write neatly).

Galileo's Story: An Alternative Version

NARRATOR: Galileo walks around talking to himself about his brand-new discovery. He had used the newly invented telescope and observed that Jupiter's moon revolved around Jupiter, which brought him to strongly agree with the heliocentric (sun-centered) theory. When he discovered this he immediately dialed the number of his closest friend.

GALILEO: Hello.

FRIEND: Hello Galileo, what have you been up to?

GALILEO: I was looking through this hot new telescope I just made and I noticed the coolest thing. From my observations I also have a little problem. The universe is sun-centered. It can't be earth-centered. There is just no possible way. The church and all in authority are wrong. But what am I going to do about this?

FRIEND: Well I am here for you. You are one of my best friends. I promise that if the church ends up catching you and threatens to put you to death, I am here as your friend and lawyer.

GALILEO: Well thank you, I got to go. If anything comes up I will contact you.

NARRATOR: Little did Galileo know that his best friend was not the only one listening. There was someone spying on him. The anonymous person called up church officials and reported what they heard. The church immediately called for the trial of Galileo. The trial went as follows.

PROSECUTOR: Are you aware Galileo that you have gone against church teachings, gone against the beliefs of your family, but more importantly you have gone against God?

GALILEO: I did what I did and said what I said. This is my discovery. I am proud to say I have proved you wrong. All my life I have been taught to follow what was told to me and now I have proof that you are wrong and what has been told to me is wrong. I am the one to prove you all wrong!

PROSECUTOR: So you admit all of these accusations. You have made these discoveries and stated them for all to hear. Please do us a favor and state them again so there will be proof to put you to death.

GALILEO: I have stated it once and I will not state it again. I will not apologize either. If you have something wrong with your ears, well then so be it. But you know what I have stated. Whether or not I state it again, you will be putting me to death, will you not?

PROSECUTOR: Oh, yes. We will put you to death no matter what. But you do not ask me any questions. I ask the questions around here. I am a representative of the church. I am the lawyer. It is not my decision to put you to death. Your future, if you will have any, lies in the hands of the judge.

NARRATOR: Just then the lawyer for Galileo comes into the room. All changes as she walks in.

FRIEND: Sorry I'm late, it's a long story. May I have a moment with my client?

PROSECUTOR: Yes go ahead.

FRIEND (TO GALILEO): So what is going on? Will they be trying to put you to death? I am so sorry that I am late but it wasn't my fault. I cannot, I mean I will not let them put you to death.

GALILEO: It's okay you were late, it is only my life we are talking about. I have a plan. You see the windows right there? I am going to escape. You are my dear friend and you can come with me if you would like.

FRIEND: I would love to go with you but they will kill us both and I am not willing to lose my life. I will miss you though. I wish you the best of luck. I hope they will not capture you. You do know that if you get caught after this, things will be even worse. You will probably have a more painful death.

GALILEO: Yes, I know, but the thing you don't get is that in order to kill me, they have to catch me first.

Activity 7. What it is Important to Know: A Buddhist Perspective

Source: http://www.thenagain.info/Classes/Sources/Buddhist.html#First, accessed June 6, 2010.

Instructions: This is an edited version of a conversation between the Buddhist monk Malunkyaputta and his spiritual advisor, The Blessed One, about what is important to know. Read the passages and answer questions 1–4.

Questions

1. What does Malunkyaputta want to know from The Blessed One?
2. What does Malunkyaputta promise in exchange for this knowledge?
3. How does The Blessed One respond?
4. In your opinion, what is the "message" of this conversation?

MALUNKYAPUTTA: If the Blessed One will explain to me, either that the world is eternal, or that the world is not eternal . . . or that the worthy person neither exists nor does not exist after death, in that case I will lead the religious life under the Blessed One.

THE BLESSED ONE: Pray Malunkyaputta, did I ever say to you, 'Come, Malunkyaputta, lead the religious life under me, and I will explain to you either that the world is eternal, or that the world is not eternal . . . or that the worthy person neither exists nor does not exist after death?

MALUNKYAPUTTA: No, indeed, Reverend Sir.

THE BLESSED ONE: That being the case, vain man, whom are you so angrily denouncing? The religious life does not depend on the dogma that the world is eternal; nor does the religious life depend on the dogma that the world is not eternal. Whether the dogma obtain that the world is eternal, or that the world is not eternal, there still remain birth, old age, death, sorrow, lamentation, misery, grief, and despair.

3

HOW SHOULD GLOBAL HISTORY TEACHERS ADDRESS CONTROVERSIAL OR SENSITIVE ISSUES?

In this chapter I argue that teachers should encourage students to discuss controversial and sensitive issues as they explore global history. However, the study of them must be done in responsible ways. Sensitive topics are often the same topics students think about in their own everyday lives or are exposed to in the media. Controversies about the past capture student interest and as they explore them students get a fuller sense of people and events.

Evolution. Human origins. Race. Gender. Religion. Sex. Sexuality. Just the thought of addressing these topics in a social studies class unnerves most new teachers and even many experienced teachers. What is safe to say? How will students, parents, administrators, and local officials respond? On the other hand, these are exactly the topics that generate student interest and excitement about studying history. I was interested in them when I was in high school, certainly more interested in them than in anything taught in school, and I bet you were also. Today, with the availability of the Internet, the real question is whether students will discuss these topics in class with teachers in thoughtful ways, or find questionable information on their own that they will circulate surreptitiously among themselves.

My advice about any controversial topic is to teach about it, albeit in a responsible way. That means being clear what is important to know and why. While something may be true, it might not be the most important thing to focus on, or even introduce, in a lesson or unit. We might have examined a topic with considerable scrutiny in an upper-level college elective, but that does not mean you should cover it in a high school global history class. We cannot include everything. For example, Martin Luther definitely wrote anti-Semitic tracts. But in a unit on the 16th-century religious Reformation in Europe, Luther's challenge to the authority of the Roman Catholic Church and the reasons why it was successful tell us much more about events and ideas during that era than do his opinions about Jews. On the other hand, in the introduction to a unit on the 20th-century European Holocaust, a high school global history teacher could legitimately decide to include material on European anti-Semitism in earlier periods to provide students with background to the events that will be taking place.

Responsible Teaching

Being a responsible social studies teacher means preparing materials and lessons rather than responding to student statements or questions off the top of your head. There is nothing wrong with saying to a class that we will answer a question or talk about a topic on another day. And being responsible means alerting your supervisor in advance when you are trying something out of the ordinary, seeking advice from colleagues and sharing materials with them, and promoting discussion of controversial material in department meetings.

Being responsible also means allowing students to express their views and explore options instead of just giving them your answers. However, we have an obligation to make it clear to students that whatever our personal beliefs are, we are expected to teach a curriculum with intellectual roots in the European Enlightenment. It offers a scientific view of global history emphasizing cause and effect, change over time, and material explanations (geographic, economic, technological) for events. We are not studying what people thought their God or Gods told them to do, but what they did because of their beliefs, or justified by their beliefs, in these Gods.

I might agree with the 18th-century English theologian Bishop Usher that a Supreme Being created the Earth in six days about 7,000 years ago, much as it is described in the Book of Genesis, the first book of the Old Testament, or I might believe the Huron creation story that honors "First Woman" for starting the world we live in on the back of a great turtle. But the global history curriculum, drawing on the scientific research of Charles Lyell (1797–1875), an English geologist, and Charles Darwin, the founder of biological evolution who initially trained to be a theologian, presents the Earth as billions of years old, the human family as millions of years old, and the start of the earliest river valley civilizations approximately 7,000–8,000 years old.

Confronting Racism and Imperialism

The Brooklyn (New York) Public Library removed the children's picture book *Tintin au Congo* (Hergé, 1991) from its shelves and categorized it for restricted viewing in 2007 because the content, which promoted Belgium colonialism in Africa, was racially offensive (Cowan, 2009). In a typical scene Tintin, who is a White youth, lectures Black African children on the merits of Western civilization, a "civilization" that brought brutal economic exploitation, torture, and war to the Congo region. In addition, the Congolese are depicted in the book as less than human. They speak pidgin, or broken, French and their features are exaggerated to make them appear monkey-like.

The problem with removing the book from the shelves, however, is that an invaluable primary source for examining the meaning of imperialism and the pervasiveness of the racist ideology that supported it has been hidden away from public view. Should other similar literary sources supporting European imperialism in Africa and Asia, such as the works of Joseph Conrad and Rudyard Kipling, especially Kipling's poem "The White Man's Burden" (http://www.wsu.edu/~wldciv/world_civ_reader/world_civ_reader_2/kipling.html, accessed June 7, 2010), be expunged from library shelves? Can they "safely" be read in English or global history classes as representative of the policies they championed? I believe they can and should be part of the curriculum and I suggest some lesson ideas at the end of this chapter.

Human Origins

One of the most awkward lessons I participated in involved evolution, human origins, race, and religion all woven together. I was observing a student teacher presenting his first high school demonstration lesson with a ninth-grade class just starting the global history curriculum. The students were discussing a textbook passage about the origin of different hominid species, including biologically modern humans, in the East African Rift Valley. The discussion was meant to be a very brief introduction to a lesson that would focus primarily on Stone Age culture and set the stage for the Neolithic Revolution, the discovery of agriculture, and the beginning of human civilization.

The student teacher was Black. The cooperating teacher was Black. All 22 of the students were Black. I was the only non–Black person there. A few minutes into the lesson, one of the students glanced at the back of the room where I was sitting. "I don't know about that guy," he said while pointing at me, "but my ancestors weren't monkeys."

His comments were followed by a profound silence laced with expectation. None of the other students reacted outwardly, and neither the cooperating, nor student teacher, seemed to know where to go next. I raised my hand and the student teacher, thankful, called on me.

I said that I was not upset and wanted to thank the student for raising fundamentally important questions that social studies students need to consider. He was not only demanding evidence that humans and other modern primates had evolved from the same ancestors, but was also questioning whether the different human groups that we call races have the same origin and are part of the same human family. People have been asking these questions forever and still debate the answers today. I suggested that the student teacher go on with his lesson as planned, but that he, the cooperating teacher, and I meet to plan another lesson that would allow the class to explore these issues directly.

The class was satisfied, the student teacher and cooperating teacher were relieved, and now we had a chance to teach about the topic in a thoughtful and organized way that involved students in sifting through and evaluating evidence. Activity sheets provided students with a chronology of human evolution generally accepted in the scientific community, a map of the East African Rift Valley with major fossil finds marked, a map of human migration, and some quotes including Darwin's speculation that humans had evolved in Africa. The teachers also assured students that definitions of race and the problem of racism would be explored in depth in future units when the class discussed the Columbian Exchange and the trans–Atlantic slave trade.

Everyone was not entirely convinced about human origins from the additional discussion, including, I suspect, the teachers. But that was not the goal of the lesson. The primary goal was to introduce students to a scientific approach to understanding history where evidence is carefully evaluated and criteria are established for making judgments about the past. An additional goal was to demonstrate to students that their views are valued and that they are part of the process of examining historical information, drawing conclusions, and connecting the past with issues under discussion in the present.

While in this case my approach worked well, sometimes I have botched it badly. I have misjudged what the students were actually interested in or I have gone too far off on a tangent. But the bottom line is that to ignore controversy and play it safe is to ignore the very topics that capture and hold on to student interest. It is also to write out of history some of the most profound forces impacting past, present, and future.

Unless we understand and accept biological evolution and the shared bonds connecting all members of the human species, it is difficult to challenge racism or uncover its underlying causes. It is also nearly impossible to explain the development of science and its profound impact on human history.

Grappling with Human Sexuality

To pretend that humans in the past were somehow asexual removes from consideration one of the primary causes of demographic pressure for expansion, environmental degradation, and the social combustibility that led to revolution. It also covers over the exploitation of women, eliminates explanations for the development of gender roles and for their transformation in the modern era, ignores the use of sex as a weapon in warfare, court intrigue, and diplomacy, leaves unexplained the focus on certain parts of the human body in the art of many cultures, and eliminates one of the powerful factors binding people together in families and in alliances.

I was thirty-five years old and a teacher for more than a decade when I visited Pompeii, the Roman port city buried by the eruption of Mount Vesuvius in 79 AD. I literally crawled through the dusty streets on my hands and knees so I could more closely examine the ruins and artifacts. According to a two-page well-illustrated spread in *World history: Patterns of interaction* (Beck et al., 2005: 166–167) published by McDougal Littell, "much of what we know about Roman homes comes from archeological excavations of the ancient cities of Pompeii and Herculaneum." There is a drawing depicting the villa owned by a wealthy Roman, a reproduction of a wall fresco showing a young couple, and a photograph of lava casts of two people, possibly a mother and child, buried by the eruption.

What is missing in this coverage of Pompeii, and was missing in high school and college classes when I was a student, is any discussion of the "economy" of the city. It was a port city visited by ships from the Roman fleet and commercial vessels depositing amphora of olive oil and other goods from around the empire. But what is the most striking to visitors because it is so unexpected are the rows of dwellings decorated by statues, signs, and walls illustrated with human body parts and sexual activities showing the particular specialty of the house. After time at sea or spent in battle, men visited these houses for physical relief and enslaved women catered to their needs. I am not suggesting that we show students pornographic images in class, but they should know that life in ancient Rome was not just technological achievement, flowery speeches in the Senate, and generals leading their troops in victorious combat.

Seeing people as sexual animals helps students understand that these were people biologically just like us who were grappling with many of the same problems that we confront, although under different circumstances. At times, conflicts involving sex and reproduction, especially when they involved the inheritance of feudal lands and privileges, directly influenced historical events. Eliminating sex also means eliminating human sexuality and sexual identity, which keeps gays invisible and supports biases against their normalcy. Students are often surprised to learn that cultural and sexual mores they assume are universal and eternal actually differ from place to place and time to time.

FIGURE 3.1 The author, somewhat younger, at Pompeii.

Why Religion?

Most global history teachers are committed to respecting human cultural diversity. One of the ways they engage students in the similarities and differences in cultures is by examining religious practices and beliefs. Nearly every global history textbook has an extended section comparing the world's "great" religions. For example, McDougal Littell's *World history: Patterns of interaction* (Beck et al., 2005) has a sixteen-page "pull-out" (pp. 282–297) describing what the publisher considers to be the major world religions and ethical systems, with illustrated two-page spreads on Buddhism, Christianity, Hinduism, Islam, Judaism, and Confucianism. The section concludes with a chart comparing numbers of adherents for each religion, the name of its God or primary Gods, its founder, holy book, leadership structure, and principal beliefs.

But what is missing in this section and throughout the book is a more systematic exploration of the role religion and different religious groups and beliefs have played in history. Part of the reason is that teachers and textbook companies are afraid to offend anybody. They forget that our job is to teach about the different roles religion has played in history, both positive and negative, and the reasons religions have played these roles. Students remain free to embrace whatever spiritual beliefs they want to.

Philosopher and historian Ernst Cassirer (1946) and many anthropologists argue that religious belief, which was initially inseparable from magic, provided early human groups with a way to explain what was to them a largely incomprehensible world. Just prior to my writing this chapter, my almost five-year-old grandson asked me what God was. He is a big fan of super-heroes (what almost five-year-old isn't?) and was very happy with my response that some people believe there is a magician who lives in the sky who has special powers. One way I help students understand the multiplicity of religious beliefs and some of their similarities and differences is to compare creation stories from different cultures. An excellent source is *In the beginning: Creation stories from around the world* by Virginia Hamilton (San Diego: Harcourt, 1988). Hamilton retells twenty-five creation stories including myths from ancient and traditional societies and two drawn from the Judeo-Christian Book of Genesis. I generally have students compare abbreviated versions of between three and five of the creation myths, including one of the stories of Genesis, and ask them "Which of the stories is true?" What usually comes out of our discussion is that none of the stories is supported by historical or scientific evidence; that each of these stories, which have some remarkable similarities, tries to explain things that are beyond people's ability to figure out using observation and reason; and that their own personal religious beliefs, as well as the beliefs of others, are usually based on what they were taught when they were children and as part of a family and a culture.

The other thing I try to do is to remove religion from its pedestal and treat is as just one among a number of social institutions including government, the military, the educational and legal systems, and the economic organization of society to produce goods and services. Believers might claim they were acting in the name of God or following her instructions, but our concern was with the way religion as an institution supported the growth of a community or civilization in general and the special interests of specific groups within the society. Both the Christian Crusaders and the Islamic defenders of Jerusalem claimed to be the agents of God, as did both George W. Bush and Osama bin Laden in recent years. The questions then, as they are now, are "Whose interests were being advanced by these wars?" and "Why did different groups coalesce in support of these campaigns?"

Students should understand that religion has often been an arm of state power and the institutions of state and religion were often indistinguishable. In Imperial China Confucianism served as both a religious and secular philosophy. Between approximately 700 AD and 1800 AD the Islamic religion was the unifying force that held together a vast empire that stretched from the

Atlantic coast of Spain to the Philippines and Indonesia and into Sub-Saharan Africa. In Spain in the 16th century the Inquisition was used to root out potential opposition to Catholicism and the crown and in 17th-century France the ministers who ran the government were often from the highest ranks of the clergy.

At the same time religion has been a force for revolutionary challenges to the status quo. In the eastern Mediterranean, Jewish dissidents rose up in the name of their God against Babylonian, Greek, and Roman domination, including one leader who might have been Jesus of Nazareth. In Europe during the Protestant Reformation of the 16th and 17th centuries and in the Islamic world of the 20th and 21st centuries, mass political movements that appealed to the lower classes presented their revolutionary message in religious terms.

Where are the Women?

As the number of students, especially women, who have taken feminist or women's studies courses in college has grown, so has the tension around teaching about the role of women in different societies. Usually every class of prospective social studies teachers has women who are committed to broadening coverage of women in the global history curriculum and men who remain skeptical about female contributions. I address this in two ways that can be easily adapted for a high school global history class. I have students examine lists of the major figures in world history that were prepared by different publishers during the frenzy leading up to the second millennium. One question that they quickly ask is where are all the women? On a list of a hundred people there are generally not more than three or four women.

I follow with a simple assignment that they are hard pressed to complete – working individually, list twenty women prominent before the 20th century who you feel should be considered for this list, and be prepared to explain your recommendation. Few students, even some of those who studied women's history, can come up with as many as five names.

The issue becomes: Are we just ignorant of the accomplishments of women, have the accomplishments of women been covered over or overlooked because of discrimination and because most history books have been written by men, or have women really done less significant things than men either because of ability, because they are wired differently as mothers and care-givers, or because of oppressive conditions in male-dominated patriarchal societies?

As a follow-up, students search through their textbook to examine its coverage of women and attach their own additions and commentaries where they feel it is necessary to provide adequate coverage of the role of women in global history.

Part of the problem in deciding why women do not regularly appear in the global history textbooks is because the historical record and its coverage of women is often so sketchy. One way to address this is to focus on women specifically while studying different historical epochs such as their role as factory workers during the Industrial Revolution. Another strategy is to look at women who led dissident movements in the past (such as Joan of Arc in 15th-century France, Anne Hutchinson in 17th-century New England, and Dorothy Hazzard and Mary Cary, prominent "levelers" during the religious upheaval in 17th-century England) trying to understand why women, who were denied traditional leadership positions in these societies, rose to prominence in these movements. This sets the stage for the study of social movements in the modern era, the 20th and 21st centuries. Women have been prominent in struggles for equality and human rights on a number of fronts. Four sisters, known collectively as Los Mariposas, were instrumental in the opposition to the Trujillo dictatorship in the Dominican Republic during the 1950s and early 1960s and became martyrs after three of them were assassinated. Rigoberta Menchú became well known during the campaign for the rights of indigenous people in Guatemala and won a Nobel Peace

Prize. Aung San Suu Kyi has become the international symbol of the movement to democratize Myanmar (Burma). Jian Qing was one of the "Gang of Four" that led the Cultural Revolution in China in the 1960s. Winnie Mandela ran the day-to-day struggle against apartheid in South Africa while many of the prominent male leaders were imprisoned. Both Jian Qing and Winnie Mandela were later heavily criticized and placed on trial for excesses committed under their leadership, which in itself challenges stereotypes that female leaders are not as strong-willed or as emotionally hardened as men. One reason for focusing on these particular struggles where women had leadership roles is because it exposes students to regions of the world that are rarely addressed in the global history curriculum.

If high school global history teachers cannot generate classroom battles over these topics they are not trying. The trick, which comes with preparation and teaching experience, is to use the controversy and the interest it generates in students, to get them to think about and learn the history.

Recommended Websites

There are a number of websites that provide teachers with material they can use to include more women in the global history curriculum. *Women in World History* (http://www.womeninworld history.com, accessed May 19, 2010) contains lessons, biographies, and documents. *Women in the Ancient World* (http://www.womenintheancientworld.com, accessed May 19, 2010) explores the status, role, and daily life of women in ancient Egypt, Rome, Athens, Israel, and Babylonia. Most of the information provided about women in the ancient world survives through accounts provided by men, since very few women were able to read and write. *Feminist Foremothers* (http://www.pinn. net/~sunshine/march99/whm_99.html, accessed May 19, 2010) is a collection of writings by European women from 1400 to 1800. *Western Philosophy* (http://oregonstate.edu/instruct/phl302/ philosophers, accessed May 19, 2010), a site maintained by Oregon State University, introduces students to European philosophers from the 16th to 18th centuries. It covers a fair number of women including Sor Juana Ines de la Cruz (Spain/Mexico), Émilie, Marquise du Châtelet-Laumont (France), Margaret Lucas Cavendish, Anne Finche, Viscountess Conway, Damaris Cudworth, Mary Astell, Catharine Trotter Cockburn, and Mary Wollstonecraft (England), Sophie Charlotte and Elisabeth of Bohemia (Germany), and Queen Kristina Wasa (Sweden).

TEACHING IDEAS

Activity 1 challenges students to compare their own religious beliefs about the creation of the universe and mankind with beliefs held by members of traditional societies in the past. Students tend to believe their own beliefs are true, but many discover that the other creation stories have as much validity. They realize they believe what they believe because they were raised within a particular system of beliefs. A website sponsored by the University of Georgia contains a number of creation stories from different indigenous cultures (http://www.gly.uga.edu/rails back/CS/CSIndex.html, accessed May 19, 2010). Activities 2–9 are available online at http://people.hofstra.edu/alan_j_singer.

Activity 2 uses a poem by Lucretius Roman (99–55 BC), a Roman poet and philosopher, to question the idea that God or Gods intervene in the daily affairs of people. Activities 3 and 4 challenge student assumptions about sexual behavior in the past and also in the present. Activity 3 asks them to debate whether positive attitudes toward same-sex relationships in certain ancient civilizations should be included as part of the curriculum. Daniel McNamara, a social studies teacher in New Rochelle, New York, developed a lesson where global history students are asked to be members of the editorial board of a textbook company (McNamara, 2002: 12). They must decide whether the company's global history textbooks should inform readers that Roman Emperor Hadrian (emperor from 117 to 138 AD) was gay and that the statues he commissioned of young men were depictions of his male lover Antinous. I like the concept of the activity, but think it is better applied to examining same-sex relationships in ancient Greece where it was more central to the culture. Among classical works that discuss same-sex relationships among men are *The Symposium* by Plato (http://classics.mit.edu/Plato/symposium.html, accessed June 7, 2010) and *Life of Pelopidas* by Plutarch (http://classics.mit.edu/Plutarch/pelopida.html, accessed June 7, 2010). Plato offers a treatise on the importance of love. Plutarch reported on the Sacred Band of Thebes, a renowned military fighting force consisting of pairs of male lovers. This is a particularly important historical document given the frequent hostility in the U.S. military toward same-sex relationships and student biases. The activity sheet comes with questions. Victor Jacarino (Herrick High School, Searington, NY) recommends that in addition students have a formal debate on the issue, write editorials or op-ed pieces for a newspaper, or write journals or blog entries on the topic.

Activity 4 uses archeological discoveries at Pompeii to introduce students to sexual practices in Rome. This activity, as presented here, is intended for teachers to help you determine what is important to know about life in ancient Rome. It can be adapted for classroom use (I think it should be) but first it should be discussed with supervisors. The problem with ignoring human sexuality is that students will discover much of the information here on their own, using the Internet. Be sure to preview any Internet sites before recommending them to students.

Activities 5–8 contain a series of documents and exercises exploring the treatment of women and ideas about gender equity in different historical periods.

In my experience, one of the more difficult topics to address in 20th-century global history is the continuing conflict between the state of Israel, which identifies itself as a Jewish homeland, and the occupied territory of Palestine, which is largely Arab and Islamic. Israel has strong support in the United States among both Christians and Jews who view it as the biblical homeland of the Jews, as a military ally in the eastern Mediterranean and Southwest Asia, and as a relatively democratic country with a similar European-based Western heritage. However, critics, including most Islamic nations, view the state of Israel as a Western usurper that is occupying what were Arab lands for over 1,000 years and which were illegally seized.

One year as a high school teacher I had students whose families had immigrated to the United States from both Israel and Palestine and our classroom was in a perpetual state of war, with other Jewish and Islamic students taking sides as well. Many teachers are afraid to teach about the history of the region and issues involved today, let alone offer an opinion, fearful of incurring community anger. Yet given student interest, and the United States' involvement in the region, it is a topic that needs to be addressed. It is also important because it shows just how difficult it is to use history to explain the causes of events and conflicts and to point to equitable solutions.

Over the years I have sought out and used Israeli sources written by participants in events who were uncomfortable with Israeli government policy, particularly the occupation of Palestine. Historian Benny Morris (1997) is a decorated Israeli veteran who has also refused to participate in military actions he considers illegal or immoral. Morris has frequently criticized the Israeli government and military for provoking Palestinian actions and covering over their own responsibility for events. He argues that the statement by General Moshe Dayan, the Israeli military Chief of Staff, presented in Activity 9, is indicative of the attitudes of Israelis during the 1950s towards the Arab–Israeli conflict. A well-documented Palestinian perspective on the Arab–Israeli conflict is presented by Rashid Khalidi in *The iron cage, the story of the Palestinian struggle for statehood* (Boston: Beacon, 2006).

Activity 1. Creation Stories from Around the World: Which Version is True?

Instructions: In the book, *In the beginning: Creation stories from around the world*, Virginia Hamilton retells stories from different cultures where people explain their beliefs about the origins of the world of humankind. Read the five excerpts below from Hamilton's book and answer questions 1–3.

Questions

1. In what ways are these stories similar? How do you explain these similarities?
2. Which story comes closest to your own religious beliefs? Explain.
3. In your opinion, why did people tell these stories about human origins and the formation of the world?

A. Raven the Creator, as Told by the Inuit People of Greenland

The first man still lay inside the pea pod. Four days passed, and on the fifth day, he pushed with his feet. He broke through the bottom of the pod and fell to the ground. Raven changed into a man. He walked around first man to get a good look at him. "I made that vine!" said Raven. "I never thought something like you would come from it." Raven made more animals, moved his wings, and brought them to life. He made a figure out of clay much like Man's, although different. When the figure had dried in the palm of his hand, he waved his wings several times. It came to life. It was a lovely woman. She got up, grew up, and stood beside Man (3–7).

B. Phan Ku the Creator, as Told in China about 600 BC

Phan Ku burst from the egg. He was the first being. He was the Great Creator. Phan Ku was the size of a giant. He grew ten feet a day and lived for 18,000 years. Phan Ku separated sky from earth. He chiseled out the earth's rivers. Phan Ku placed the stars and moon in the night sky and the sun into the day. Only when Phan Ku died was the earth at last complete. The dome of the sky was made from Phan Ku's skull. Soil was formed from his body. Rain was made from his sweat. And from the fleas that lived in the hair covering him came all of humankind (21–23).

C. Divine Woman the Creator, as Told by the Huron People of North America

A woman fell from a torn place in the sky. She was a divine woman, full of power. The animals decided the woman needed earth to live on. Turtle said, "Dive down in the water and bring up some earth." The woman took it and put it all around on Turtle's shell. That was the start of the earth. Dry land grew until it formed a country, then another country, and all of earth. To this day, Turtle holds up the earth (59–63).

D. Olorun the Creator, as Told by the Yoruba People of Nigeria

Olorun, Owner of the Sky, and the Highest Being, called the chief of the divine ones to him. This chief was Great God. Olorun told Great God, "I want you to make some firm ground down below." He gave Great God a shell. There was a small amount of earth in the shell. Great God did as he was told. He went down to the marshland, sliding down the spider silks. Then he threw the earth out of the shell and spread it about him. He put the pigeon and the hen on the bit of the earth from the shell. The pigeon and the hen began scratching and scratching the earth with their feet. That was how the firm, hard ground came to be. The first people came down from heaven. Olorun sent them down to earth to live (73–77).

E. Yahweh the Creator, as Described in the Judeo-Christian Book of Genesis

Yahweh, the Lord God, made the earth and heavens. Then the Lord God formed man out of dust from the ground, and he breathed into his nostrils the breath of life. Out of the ground the Lord God formed every beast of the field and every bird of the air. The Lord God took one of Adam's ribs and closed up its place with flesh. The rib which the Lord God had taken from Adam He formed into Eve (123–125).

4

WHY IS GLOBAL HISTORY USUALLY EUROPEAN CHRONOLOGY WITH TANGENTS?

This chapter examines how global history curricula calendars are traditionally organized around chronology and discusses why the focus tends to be on the history of European civilization. It offers an alternative social studies approach, based on attention to themes and essential questions with case studies and comparisons between regions and epochs, that broadens the scope of the curriculum.

In my experience, what generally passes for a global history curriculum or textbook is actually the chronology of European history with tangents. I do not think there is any deep-seated conspiracy or racism involved in this. There are four problems inherent in the design of traditional chronology-based global history curricula. (1) It is not meaningful to talk about an integrated global history before 1492 and probably not before European imperialism and industrialization remade the world in the 19th century. (2) The chronology of events in the different regions of the world do not line up easily and the European chronology is the best documented, certainly in English. (3) Historians, college courses, and hence social studies teachers have narrow areas of specialization, usually the United States and Europe. (4) The continued study of history in the traditional way by teachers leads to curriculum calendars overburdened by information overload.

The First 100,000 Years or So

Modern human beings emerged as a biological species over 100,000 years ago. Unlike the cavemen from the GEICO commercials who act like everyone else but look distinctly different, the skulls and skeletons of our most immediate human ancestors, the Cro-Magnon (originally discovered at a site in southwestern France) or Qafzeh-Skhul (from a site in modern-day Israel) were anatomically modern. They could have easily ridden on the New York City subway or walked the streets of any cosmopolitan city without attracting attention, assuming they were dressed in contemporary clothing. But they did not ride the subways or visit other cities, because cities and subways did not exist, and would not exist for tens of thousands of years.

These early modern humans lived in small bands dependent on hunting, fishing, and food gathering for survival and had virtually no contact with anyone outside their immediate range. Even after the Neolithic Revolution and the start of the gradual transition to agricultural production about 13,000 years ago, people continued to live in separate localized worlds. Because of this isolation, it took more than 5,000 years for agriculture to spread from the Mesopotamian–Egyptian region across Europe and Africa (Diamond, 1997: 35–41, 181).

THE POOP THEORY OF HISTORY

This may seem a bit irreverent for some teachers, but the students love the idea of the "Poop Theory of History" and try to find additional evidence to support it as they study global history. Basically the idea is that poop/buffalo chips/feces played a crucial role in human history at a number of key points. For example, human poop contributed to the agricultural revolution as hunter/gatherers swallowed seeds and then pooped at temporary settlements. When they returned to these sites they found plants enriched by fertilizer. Later, poor sanitation played a major role in the spread of diseases as populations grew more concentrated and spurred urban design. Meanwhile, in some traditional cultures, animal poop is used as a source of fuel. In this theory I also include cow burps. The world's one-and-a-half billion cows are ruminants. They eat enormous volumes of grasses and their burps, and to a lesser extent their farts, are a major cause of methane emissions into the atmosphere and of global warming (http://animals.how stuffworks.com/mammals/methane-cow.htm, accessed July 18, 2010).

Independent Chronologies

Prior to the Colombian Exchange at the start of the 16th century, there are separate local histories of peoples, cultures, and states and there are regional trans-national histories of empires, trade networks, and geographic zones such as the Incan Andean Empire, Sub-Saharan kingdoms, the Islamic world, the Mediterranean world, or China and its neighbors. Each of these has its own chronology and pace of development. Interregional interaction is at a minimum and events in one part of the globe rarely impact on the other areas. There is no meaningful global history.

The best examples of the way chronologies do not line up are the differences in the rate of development between civilizations in the Americas and Eurasia. Humans migrate from Eurasia to the Americas over the course of tens of thousands of years, the earliest documented human settlements in Alaska are only about 14,000 years old (Diamond, 1997: 46), and in the Americas most groups are forced by isolation and geographic conditions to develop the accoutrements of civilization independently. Agriculture appeared in the Americas about 5,000 years ago, roughly 3,500 years after it emerged in Mesopotamia (Southwest Asia) (Diamond, 1997: 100). American civilizations trailed Eurasian development and were very vulnerable when the first conquistadores arrived from Europe.

In a global history course organized chronologically, Mayan civilization would be discussed after the fall of Rome and as contemporaneous with the rise of Islam in southwest Asia and North Africa. However, it makes much more sense for students to compare the Mayan world with the Old World river valley civilizations. A question asked by students, or that you can ask them, is "How were the Mayans able to develop their civilization without a great river to depend on for water, irrigation, and transportation?"

Even after Columbus, it took roughly 300 years for the Americas, Africa, and Asia to be more or less integrated into a global system. Conquest, settlement, enslavement, trade, war, and ultimately economic and industrial development on new scales were needed before most of the world could truly be said to be on the same page chronologically, albeit not in the same place developmentally.

History or Social Studies?

Another problem is related to the debate over whether secondary school teachers should be teaching social studies, integrating history with significant aspects of anthropology, sociology, economics, political science, and geography, or a more or less straight historical chronology, whatever difficulties exist in piecing it together. In some sense this is a false debate. I am trained as a historian to focus on chronology, change over time, but I have always utilized insights gained from the social sciences to understand the past and its relationship to the present. Most contemporary historians do not hesitate to do the same.

Anthropology provides insight into the growth and development of human cultures, human inventions, materials, spiritual and artistic creations, institutions, relationships, beliefs, values, and practices. As anthropologists delved deeply and systematically into the way of life of different peoples and compared different cultures, they contributed to ongoing debates about human nature. Generally, anthropologists draw conclusions about the development of culture from studies of small, traditional societies where they can make in-depth observations of entire communities and account for outside influences. More recently they have applied anthropological approaches to study contemporary societies.

Economics examines how societies, both past and present, produce and distribute the goods and services that people, communities, and nations need to survive. Because economic recommendations impact sharply on government policies, they involve some of the most controversial issues in the social sciences. Major economic topics include the impact of technology, trade, and economic interdependence on societies; the environmental impact of economic decisions; the role of government in managing economies; relationships between privately owned corporations and workers (class conflict and cooperation); and the acquisition and use of scarce resources (including the displacement of indigenous people, colonialism, and imperialism). Economics helps us better understand corporate and government decisions that contributed to famine, precipitated depressions, and permitted man-made disasters such as the BP oil leak that polluted large parts of the Gulf of Mexico.

Geography helps focus attention on global interdependence, including increased attention to the non-Western world, its contributions to world history and culture, and its role in contemporary world affairs. The study of geography also elevates our concern for the impact of environmental issues, like pollution, resource depletion, and global warming, on the quality of human life and the importance of understanding global demographics and population diversity. The tools of geography are crucial for defining and comparing regions of the world, understanding the relationship between people and place; examining the migration of people, plants, and animals; explaining ways that the physical world influences human development; and exploring the ways that human development has changed the physical world. While all of these topics are contemporary in nature, geography also examines forces that played major roles throughout human history.

Political science examines who has the power to make decisions in societies (power and citizenship), how they are made (government), rules and procedures for enforcing decisions (laws), and the impact of decisions on societies (justice and equity). The study of political science often includes philosophical queries, and examines the values, dilemmas, choices, and broader belief systems (ideologies) that shape political decisions. It is a discipline that is rooted in the systematic comparison of societies.

Sociology examines human relationships and institutions in complex contemporary societies. Its goal is to establish theories that explain events, activities, and ideas about human interaction and group behavior. The study of social inequality and its impact on individuals, groups, and societies is an area where sociology, political science, economics, and history all overlap. In some approaches to the study of history, especially those identified with the work of Karl Marx, social inequality in the form of class conflict is the major engine generating historical change. In *The communist manifesto*, originally published in 1848, Marx and his collaborator Frederick Engels argued:

> The history of all hitherto existing society is the history of class struggles. Freeman and slave, patrician and plebeian, lord and serf, guild-master and journeyman, in a word, oppressor and oppressed, stood in constant opposition to one another, carried on an uninterrupted, now hidden, now open fight, a fight that each time ended, either in a revolutionary re-constitution of society at large, or in the common ruin of the contending classes.
>
> (Marx and Engels, 1964: 2)

A major advantage of a social studies approach that integrates history and the social sciences in the curriculum is that it focuses on comparisons both between regions and also across time periods, including comparisons between past and present. This makes student-generated essential questions about the world we live in today even more meaningful for understanding the past.

Thematic Strands

Thematic strands developed by the National Council for the Social Studies (http://www.social studies.org/standards/strands, accessed June 4, 2010) are designed to specifically draw attention to the interaction of history with the different social sciences. One strand emphasizes that human beings create, learn, and adapt culture to understand themselves as individuals and members of broader groups. The strand stresses that while human cultures exhibit both similarities and differences, all cultures are dynamic and constantly in the process of changing. Another focuses on the relationships between science, technology, and society from the development of the earliest stone tools through modern computerized societies that would not be able to function without the technology and science that supports them.

Other strands examine the interaction between people, places, and environments; the development of individual and group identity; institutions such as schools, churches, families, government agencies, and the courts that play an integral role in maintaining societies; how people create and change structures of power, authority, and governance; how people organize for the production, distribution, and consumption of goods and services; global interdependence and the increasingly important and diverse global connections among world societies; and the ideals, principles, and practices of citizenship.

The strand that focuses on history (Time, Continuity, and Change) encourages students to "draw upon historical knowledge during the examination of social issues" and "develop the habits of mind that historians and scholars in the humanities and social sciences employ to study the past and its relationship to the present in the United States and other societies." This strand supports the identification of student-generated essential questions about the world we live in today as a guide for exploring and to understanding the past.

AP World History

The Advanced Placement World History course of study takes a similar thematic approach to organizing the global history curriculum and is well worth exploring at some depth (http://www.collegeboard.com/student/testing/ap/history_world/topic.html?worldhist, accessed June 4, 2010). My main criticisms of AP curriculum suggestions are first that they limit what is essentially a social studies approach to understanding the past to students in advanced classes. I think a thematic approach should be applied to all classrooms on all academic levels. Second, although the curriculum description stresses that students should develop the habits of mind of historians, such as using documents and other primary source evidence to construct and evaluate arguments and identifying "global patterns and processes over time and space while connecting local developments to global ones," pressure for students to receive high scores on what is essentially a fact-intensive AP test produces a content-driven curriculum focusing on the memorization of detail rather than analysis and understanding.

The AP program recommends five overarching themes that provide "unifying threads" for making comparisons between regions and time periods. The AP themes are: (1) interaction between humans and the environment, which includes demography, disease, migration, patterns of settlement, and technology; (2) development and interaction of cultures, which includes religions, belief systems, philosophies, and ideologies, science and technology, and the arts and architecture; (3) state-building, expansion, and conflict, which includes political structures and forms of governance, empires, nations and nationalism, revolts and revolutions, and regional, trans-regional, and global structures and organizations; (4) creation, expansion, and interaction of economic systems, which includes agricultural and pastoral production, trade and commerce, labor systems, industrialization, and capitalism and socialism; and (5) development and transformation of social structures, which includes gender roles and relations, family and kinship, racial and ethnic constructions, and social and economic classes.

In recent years, the International Baccalaureate program based in Geneva, Switzerland has promoted more interdisciplinary and thematic learning, which I support. At this point, in the United States the program is primarily offered in elite private schools, some affluent suburban communities, and academically selective public schools. Schools must pay a $10,000 fee to participate and for access to online curriculum material. It remains unclear whether the level and amount of work it demands from high school students will allow it to be used on a wider basis or whether it is much more than an effort to provide special credentials for students applying to elite private universities (Lewin, 2010: 1). In 2010, the International Baccalaureate program claimed to involve over 800,000 students in 139 countries (http://www.ibo.org, accessed July 3, 2010).

Compartmentalization

The way in which knowledge and university courses are organized has contributed to the difficulty in developing a meaningful global history curriculum. Most history professors specialize in relatively narrow geographical regions and time periods and what is taught in classes is highly compartmentalized. History majors end up specializing in the history of one part of the world, usually the United States or Western Europe. When they become secondary school teachers they draw off what they know best. My doctoral dissertation is on the United Mine Workers Union during the era of handpicked coal-mining, a practice that was phased out in the United States during the 1920s. In the high school U.S. history curriculum, the era of handpicked coal-mining gets about ten minutes of coverage when I introduce students to labor union songs from the era.

When I was an undergraduate student at the City College of New York in the 1960s, I concentrated on studying European intellectual history (Renaissance through the present) and took the minimum number of courses in other areas. Because I was earning social studies teacher certification, I had to take two classes from non-traditional regions and I satisfied this requirement with a class on the history of Latin America from conquest to independence and another titled "American Negro History" – a class that should have been considered part of the history of the United States. In graduate school at Rutgers University, I switched to United States Social History with a heavy focus on the American working class between the Civil War and the end of the Great Depression. What I know about the history of the rest of the world I learned on my own, either as a companion to my teaching or through independent reading. I am not fluent in any language besides English so I am dependent on secondary sources, translated documents, and textbooks when studying the non-European, non-U.S. world. I became interested in developing a genuine global history curriculum, not because of my training as an historian, but because of a commitment to multiculturalism and a growing awareness that areas of the world beyond where I happen to live (United States) or am comfortable visiting (European world) have had a profound influence on the past and an even greater influence on the present. The 21st century may be the "Chinese century" in the way the 20th century was dominated economically and militarily by the United States and the 19th century by Great Britain (Fishman, 2004: 24).

The Full Scope of History

The span of knowledge covered in global history is impossibly broad. Who could possibly be an expert on every region of the world in every time period? Social studies teachers who are avid students of history find that the more they learn, the more they discover what they do not know. In addition, the new information they acquire is generally in much too much detail for a high school survey class. As a result, most teachers end up following the textbook; it is just easier. The more thoughtful ones create their own curriculum calendar, but recognize that coverage of many parts of the world is somewhat superficial.

There are some legitimate reasons for following the European-Western timeline. The European narrative stretching from ancient Greece through the contemporary North Atlantic world is the most coherent and best documented. For good or bad, with post-Columbian conquest, colonization, the Industrial Revolution, and imperialism, European societies shape the modern world.

The real problem is that places in the world that are not part of this grand narrative are usually treated as tangents to the main story. They are visited as distant curiosities or when their histories intersect with the European timeline, usually times of war and conquest. Approaching history this way masks diversity, eliminates alternative ways of organizing societies, and suggests pre-determinism – what happened had to happen. By focusing exclusively on the European timeline, the contingent nature of history as a result of the actions of individuals, the struggles by groups, surprise discoveries, and unanticipated disasters, is lost and all of these factors are removed from the equation as significant historical forces.

Developing a Curriculum Calendar

Michael Mullervy, a former student and current cooperating teacher with the Hofstra University program, made his global history calendar available for examination in this book. It is designed for first-year high school students who take global history as part of a two-year sequence. The first year, which Michael teaches, covers the time span from pre-history through the 18th-century European Enlightenment.

Michael is a very conscientious teacher and his lessons and activities are well planned and creative. He uses a relatively standard global history calendar; however, he lists aim questions for each lesson rather than topics, which is something I encouraged him to do during his pre-service teacher education classes. Each lesson is designed so that at the end of the lesson students have learned what they need to know to be able to answer the question.

Michael teaches in an overwhelmingly minority school (probably close to 100% of the students), and he has a strong commitment to introducing his students to the diversity of world civilizations; his curriculum calendar, however, still illustrates some of the problems I have been discussing. After seven initial lessons that introduce students to social studies concepts, important geographical skills, and essential questions (in the third lesson they question the accuracy of the textbooks), students begin the study of history with two eight-lesson units that cover early humans, the Neolithic Revolution, and the origin of river valley civilizations. This unit includes one lesson each on Sumer, Babylon, Egypt, the Indus Valley, and China. These are followed by seven lessons on ancient Greece and six lessons on Rome.

Michael then quickly introduces India (three days), China (three days), Sub-Saharan Africa (five days), the Byzantine world where he revisits Rome, the Mediterranean, and Christianity (four days), and Islam (four days). The African visit is longer than the others because Michael covers a much longer span of history. He begins with a lesson reviewing human migration out of the Rift Valley and concludes with a lesson on West African empires (Ghana, Mali, and Songhai) that covers from roughly 300 to 1600 AD. In other words, once the class leaves the ancient river valley civilizations, slightly more than half of the coverage – 17 of the next 32 lessons – is focused on European societies.

This pattern continues, but in an even more Eurocentric way, for the rest of the academic year. There are eight lessons on Europe in the Middle Ages (including the Crusades and the commercial revolution of the 13th and 14th centuries), seven lessons on the European Renaissance and Reformation, and nine lessons on the European Age of Exploration, and additional lessons, time permitting, on the development of absolute monarchies, the scientific revolution, and the start of the Enlightenment. These are interspaced with brief visits to Japan (to draw comparisons with European feudal society), Meso-America, and West Africa as it falls victim to European invaders and the trans-Atlantic slave trade.

National History Standards

The National Standards for World History developed by the National Center for History in the Schools (http://nchs.ucla.edu/standards/world-standards5-12.html, accessed June 4, 2010) with funding from the National Endowment for the Humanities, which is organized chronologically, has tried to address the problem of an overemphasis on European history by suggesting teachers examine topics and time periods broadly and include developments in non-Western societies. However, it does use the conventional Europe-based timeline, substituting BCE (before the common era) for BC (Before Christ) and CE (common era) for AD (Anno Domini, in the year of our Lord).

The standards divide history into the nine traditional eras: human beginnings through the agricultural revolution; early civilizations 4000 to 1000 BCE; classical traditions, major religions, and giant empires, 1000 BCE–300 CE; expanding zones of exchange and encounter, 300–1000 CE; intensified hemispheric interactions, 1000–1500 CE; emergence of the first global age, 1450–1770; age of revolutions, 1750–1914; half-century of crisis and achievement, 1900–1945; and the 20th century since 1945: promises and paradoxes.

These standards do not recommend a specific number of days for coverage of any time period or area of the world, which was one of the reasons why it was attacked by conservatives when first presented in the 1990s. Positive references to Third World civilizations and the diminution of

Western achievements drew special scorn. Albert Shanker, President of the American Federation of Teachers at the time, charged that according to these curriculum standards "Everything that is European or American, or that has to do with white people is evil and oppressive, while Genghis Khan is a nice sweet guy just bringing his culture to other places" (http://www.hartford-hwp.com/archives/10/009.html, accessed June 7, 2010). Lynne Chaney (http://www.hartford-hwp.com/archives/10/006.html, accessed June 7, 2010), chair of the National Endowment for the Humanities and the wife of future Vice-President Dick Cheney, argued, "If you look over history for the last 500 or 600 years, the rise of the West is the organizing principle, and the key to the rise of democratic standards." She charged that in the National World History Standards "everything is the same as everything else – gender relations under India's Gupta Empire, political and cultural achievements under Shah Abbas in Persia, and oh yes, the Magna Carta." According to Cheney, the authors saved "their unqualified admiration for people, places and events that are politically correct . . . African and Native American societies, like all societies, had their failings, but one would hardly know it from National Standards" (1994).

While most of the pundits, and they included Rush Limbaugh (http://www.hartford-hwp.com/archives/10/006.html, accessed June 4, 2010), were simply redirecting arguments they were already making against multiculturalism, Lynne Cheney did raise a serious criticism; that everything was presented with the same weight was a major problem with the standards. Rather than challenging the legitimacy of the single strand European narrative as the basis for teaching global history and offering an alternative way for organizing it, the standards just identified more information that needed to be included in the curriculum. It was like pigging out at an all-you-can-eat smorgasbord. Everything looks good, but in the end you have an awful stomachache.

Era 4 (300–1000 CE) includes the Christianization and division of the Roman Empire, its collapse in the west, the growth of Islam, the Tang Dynasty in China, the middle ages and feudalism in Europe, and the development of agricultural societies and new states in tropical Africa and Oceania, Mexico, and Andes, most of which are completely unrelated. All these developments are grouped together because they happened in the same 700-year period. In fact, one section of the standard does make it explicit that (A) during this period "no sustained contact existed between the Eastern Hemisphere and the Americas" and (B) for much of this period "Christian Europe was marginal" to these changes. The second point certainly did not endear the standards to the champions of Western Civilization.

Possibility for Revamping the Curriculum

The National Standards for World History does offer some genuine possibility for revising the global history curriculum, although it is largely buried in the avalanche of detail and a tentativeness resulting from fear of political rejection. In Era 4 (300–1000 CE) three broad patterns of change are "particularly conspicuous": the development of "networks" that promote more "intensive interchange and cultural creativity" partly based on the growing "sophistication of systems for moving people and goods"; the spread of major religions that "carried with them a variety of cultural traditions, aesthetic ideas, and ways of organizing human endeavors"; and "population growth, urbanization, and flowering of culture in new areas."

A genuine global history, as opposed to a European history with tangents, can be possible if social studies teachers organize the curriculum to encourage students to look for patterns of development, the ways systems work, factors promoting stability and influencing rates of change, and the causes of change over time, as well as similarities and differences between eras and regions. Examining global history this way, it makes sense to compare and contrast different societies – the Islamic world, sub-Saharan Africa, Tang Dynasty China, and medieval Europe – as part of the same unit of study. I believe, or maybe hope, that if classroom teachers take the lead in presenting history this way, historians, textbook companies, curriculum writers, test designers, and maybe even government officialdom will follow.

TEACHING IDEAS

The teaching ideas in this section are designed to stimulate debate. They are all available online at http://people.hofstra.edu/alan_j_singer. Activity 1 introduces students to the ten National Council for the Social Studies thematic strands and asks them to decide which factors play the greatest role in shaping human history. Teachers should list student ideas on the board and use them to promote a wide-ranging discussion of what is important to know about the factors that shape history – and why.

There are a series of pre-Columbian "world" maps available on Wikipedia (http://en. wikipedia.org/wiki/Early_world_maps, accessed June 4, 2010). According to the site all of their reproductions are in the public domain and available for copying and classroom use. Activity 2 asks students to explain why so many of these maps present the world as a flat disk and why so many societies place themselves at the center of human existence.

Activity 3 draws on student interest in sports betting and challenges the idea that the future is predetermined. Students are asked to place themselves in the year 1435 and decide which team (global region) will win the Historical Super Bowl.

Dig is an archeological magazine for elementary school children published by Cobblestone. The company produces a series of historical, social science, and scientific magazines including *Calliope,* which focuses on global history. Readers submit questions to "Dr. Dig" and they are published in the magazine or posted on the website. Activity 4 asks students to evaluate Dr. Dig's discussion of the historical notation of dates as BC and AD.

Activity 5 is related to the Historical Super Bowl activity. Students compare China's economic position in the 21st century with the economic dominance of Great Britain in the 19th century and the United States in the 20th century.

5

WHAT DOES A THEME-BASED GLOBAL HISTORY CURRICULUM LOOK LIKE? PART 1 – BC: BEFORE COLUMBUS

This chapter presents the first part of a theme-based global history curriculum, human history up until about 1500 AD, based on nine calendar areas of study that are roughly chronological. However, rather than following the European chronological narrative the central focus of the curriculum shifts between different areas of the world. The dividing line between Part 1 and Part 2 in this curriculum is the start of Western European oceanic voyages to discover a water route to Asia, a process that changed human history from regional to global. Selected topics are covered in depth and are used as "case studies" to illustrate broader historical trends. Some of the calendar areas of study include recommended websites.

I divide global history into nine roughly chronological calendar areas of study (CAS). Within each CAS are a series of more focused units; the number varies from area to area depending on what is known about the topics and how discussion of them helps to answer student–essential questions. The CAS are only roughly chronological, which is one way my approach to global history differs from most textbooks and the National Standards for World History, and why I call them areas, or areas of study, rather than eras, epochs, or ages. Certain societies, such as those in Meso-America, developed in different time frames than did the old world eastern hemisphere river valley societies. In addition, since the areas and units are designed to present history thematically, certain topics, such as the impact of Hellenization on the Mediterranean world, are discussed in some detail out of sequence when we examine the growth of trade networks and their role in cultural diffusion in the period from 300 to 1200 AD.

Within each CAS I suggest important themes based on the NCSS thematic strands, essential questions to address, unit topics, and some ideas for lessons. The "historical content" or main ideas do not differ significantly from the National Standards for World History. I think I am offering a more effective way of organizing the global history curriculum that will make it genuinely global in scope, but it is certainly not a radical reformulation that would require approval by governing bodies and new textbooks before being implemented.

Naming "calendar areas" is not a simple task because names usually define what gets included. Eric Hobsbawm, a historian of modern Europe mentioned in earlier chapters, titled his book on the French and industrial revolutions in Europe between 1789 and 1848 the *Age of revolution* (Hobsbawm. 1962), called the period between 1848 and 1875 the *Age of capital* (Hobsbawm, 1975), and described 1875–1914 as the *Age of empire* (1987). He named the "short" 20th century, 1914 to 1991, the *Age of extremes* (Hobsbawm, 1994). I have modified Hobsbawm's categories a bit. For example, CAS VII, which I call the Age of Global Transformation (1750–1914), includes Hobsbawm's ages of revolution, capital, and empire. However, I would argue that the revolutions in that period were only a first wave. A second wave of revolution, more global in its extent, swept the planet in reaction to imperialism and as a result of World War I and II. Because of this, I believe CAS VIII, which examines the 20th century, is more aptly named the Age of Reaction and Revolution.

The website "World History for Us All" (http://worldhistoryforusall.sdsu.edu, accessed June 7, 2010), a project of San Diego State University in cooperation with the National Center for History in the Schools at UCLA, has a similar focus to mine and is worth exploring in depth. It organizes the study of human history around nine "big eras" with essential questions and themes. Updated unit and lesson ideas and teaching materials are available for download. The site welcomes teachers and students with a video *History of the World in Seven Minutes* that gives a sense of the continuous acceleration in the rate of change of human civilization. The video is also available at http://www.youtube.com/watch?v=SbP6edA8H8E (accessed October 24, 2009).

The rest of this chapter examines CAS prior to the Columbian Exchange (circa 1500). It is the longest span of human history and represents the period before the European voyages of exploration, the colonization of conquered territories, and massive human migration, put the world on a path to one integrated historical narrative.

CAS I. The Human Experience – The First 100,000 Years

This CAS focuses on the emergence of biologically modern humans approximately 100,000 years ago and the initial development of culture as human bands responded to their environment, especially climate variation. It would conclude with the development of agriculture about 13,000 years ago and the beginning of the demographic shift from nomadic bands to sedentary communities. Major focal points in this CAS would be: establishing how scientists and historians learn about human life in the period before the advent of writing; distinguishing between biological and cultural change; the first cultural great leap forward about 50,000 years ago when humans developed new forms of stone tools (Diamond, 1997: 39–42); the social structure, belief systems, and daily life of nomadic human groups; how changing environments, particularly climate change, shape the human experience; and the impact of the discovery of agriculture. Some essential questions for consideration while students learn about this CAS are: What makes us human? What is the impact of geography on history and human societies? How do people interact with their environments? What is the impact of technological change on history and human societies? Why do people invent cultures? Are gender roles biologically predetermined?

Recommended Websites

Becoming Human (http://www.becominghuman.org, accessed May 19, 2010). This site, maintained by the Institute of Human Origins, addresses the course, timing, and events of human evolution. It includes interactive activities and provides news articles on evolutionary findings. The learning center includes classroom materials as well as games and activities. The bone box (http://www.becominghuman.org/node/building-bodies, accessed May 19, 2010) allows students to assemble human and chimpanzee skeletons.

Evolution; A Journey into Where We're From and Where We're Going (http://www.pbs.org/wgbh/evolution, accessed May 19, 2010). This PBS site is a great tool for both teachers and students. Seven major themes – Darwin, Change, Extinction, Survival, Sex, Humans, and Religion – are aligned with programs in a video series created by PBS. Each theme includes a multimedia library and activities designed specifically for students.

CAS II. Developing the Civilization Package – The Next 10,000 Years

Jared Diamond, in *Guns, germs, and steel: The fates of human societies* (1997) systematically traces the development of a civilization package. Not only is this the strongest part of his book, but his comparative approach provides a model for teaching about the next 10,000 years of human history. My suggestion is to replace the initial units in the traditional global history calendar that sequentially, and repetitively, examine the chronologies of early river valley civilizations in Mesopotamia (Tigris–Euphrates), Egypt (Nile), and maybe India (Indus) or China (Yellow), with an in-depth study of the development of the "civilization package" itself. Topics for lessons would include the impact on history and human societies of geography, technology, economy (work, trade, and money), religion, social structure, government (state formation, decision-making, and law), and regional interaction (cultural diffusion). Examples would be drawn from the different civilizations and comparisons can be made between the river valley civilizations in the eastern hemisphere, the Kush and Aksum kingdoms in Africa, and the Olmecs and Mayas in the Americas. AP World curriculum suggestions discussed in the previous chapter also recommend that these civilizations be compared so that students can identify similarities and differences although they did not occur at exactly the same historical time. This CAS would conclude with the evolution of kingdoms into stable regional empires. Essential questions addressed in this CAS include "Why do people believe in religion?"; "Does geography determine destiny?"; "Are technological changes always for the good?"; and "Does progress require social control?"

Recommended Websites

Amazing Worlds of Archaeology, Anthropology, & Ancient Civilizations (http://www.archaeolink.com, accessed May 19, 2010). Links and lesson plans for teaching about the early history of the entire world.

Ancient Web (http://www.theancientweb.com, accessed May 1, 2010). The site is a little elementary but is exhaustive in its scope including many more traditional cultures than most other sites (such as Armenia, Ethiopia, and New Zealand). It features interactive maps, link to books, as well as news articles and videos.

BBC – A History of the World (http://www.bbc.co.uk/history, accessed May 19, 2010). Includes a timeline of British history, links to documentaries, This Day in History, Ancient History In-Depth, Archaeology In-Depth, and an encyclopedia of famous people. Ancient History In-Depth looks at Egyptians, Greeks, Romans, Vikings, Anglo-Saxons, Ancient Indians, and the pre-historic British. The site also provides material on the ancient Americas, Asia, Africa, and the Middle East. An excellent resource for students.

Exploring Ancient World Cultures (http://eawc.evansville.edu/index.htm, accessed May 19, 2010). The site provides visitors with information about ancient civilizations and primary source material from the Near East, Egypt, Europe, China, Greece, Rome, and Islam. Teachers can use all these resources to have students compare different societies and make inferences about life in the ancient world.

Iron Age Farming (http://www.butserancientfarm.co.uk, accessed May 20, 2010). The Butser Ancient Farm is an archeological project that re-creates ancient farms. The site provides educators and students with information on farming during the British Iron Age from approximately 800 BC to 100 AD.

Mayans (http://www.mayaruins.com, accessed May 19, 2010). The site examines Mayan culture with pictures and maps of Mayan ruins in the Yucatan and Central America. An excellent reference site for students and teachers.

Mesopotamian Civilization: The Land between the Rivers (http://worldhistory1a. homestead.com/sumeria.html, accessed May 18, 2010). This site, created by a professor at the State University of West Georgia, provides an outline of Mesopotamian civilization and culture, pictures of artifacts, and a Cuneiform translator. An excellent reference site for teachers and students.

National Geographic – Mysteries of the Ancient World (http://www.nationalgeographic. com/history, accessed May 18, 2010). Includes an interactive map that allows students to select a civilization, videos, and pictures of ancient ruins and artifacts.

Women in the Ancient World (http://www.womenintheancientworld.com, accessed May 19, 2010). The site explores the status, role, and daily life of women in ancient Egypt, Rome, Athens, Israel, and Babylonia. The creator of the site admits that most of the information provided about women in the ancient world comes from the eyes of men, since very few women were able to read and write. Yet it is very interesting as one navigates through the site to see the differences in the value placed on women in each culture.

CAS III. Rise and Fall of Local States and Regional Empires, 750 BC–1600 AD

This is a relatively traditional unit of study except the primary focus would be on multiple causes and unanticipated effects as students try to discern why empires develop, are successful for long periods of time, and then decay and collapse. Mediterranean Greece, Rome, and Byzantium would be logical places to begin, especially as they come into conflict with Persia, the Phoenicians, Egypt, and Germanic, Slavic, and Islamic invaders. It is also a logical place to introduce war as a transformative force in human history. It makes sense to look at some societies in greater depth and to compare the rise and decline of Mediterranean regional empires with the Mauryan and Gupta empires in India, the Qin and Han dynasties in China, Ghana in western Africa, and the Aztec and Inca in the Americas.

In 1848, in the preamble to *The communist manifesto* (1964), Karl Marx and Frederick Engels proclaim "communism" a force for change emerging out of the dynamic element they see transforming all European societies throughout history, the struggle for supremacy between competing social classes. However, Marx and Engels, who were writing as Europeans with only second-hand knowledge of the rest of the world, tended to view Asian societies as much more static, with rigid hierarchies dominated by semi-theocratic aristocracies, and less likely to change from within. The different paths taken by societies, the reasons for those differences, and the possibility of dynamic social transformation are important topics to be explored in this CAS. Essential questions addressed in this CAS include "Is there only one right way?"; "Why do societies change?"; "Does human nature condemn us to perpetual war?"; "Are the mighty always destined to fall?"; and "If monarchy and dictatorship bring stability and peace, are they preferable to chaos and war?"

Recommended Websites

Eyewitness to History (http://www.eyewitnesstohistory.com, accessed May 18, 2010). Focuses on the ancient Mediterranean world and European Middle Ages and Renaissance. An excellent reference site for students.

Middle Ages (http://www.middle-ages.org.uk, accessed May 19, 2010). This site provides a timeline of the Middle Ages in Europe, descriptions of daily life for different social classes, and reports on the technology for warfare. Heavily laden with facts but interesting for students.

Medieval Siege (http://www.pbs.org/wgbh/nova/lostempires/trebuchet, accessed May 19, 2010). Based on the Nova series "Secrets of the Lost Empires," this site uses games and reenactments to explore the relationship between technology and war in medieval Europe.

Roman Empire (Illustrated History) (http://www.roman-empire.net, accessed May 18, 2010). Explores the history and culture of the Roman Empire. Includes a link describing the everyday life of a gladiator, videos of reenactments of Roman battles, and an image gallery of Roman ruins and artifacts. An excellent reference site for students and teachers.

CAS IV. Emerging Networks of Exchange, Mostly 300 AD–1200 AD

Michael Cook, *A brief history of the human race* (2003), mentioned in earlier chapters, tells much of the story of humanity from the perspective of the Islamic world and the regions it dominated. I like the idea of placing the Islamic world at the center in this CAS. The major focus is on networks of exchange, principally trade, cultural, literacy, and technological exchange, but also on war as a means of exchange and the spread of epidemic disease as a by-product. Students examine how Arab and Islamic forces fan out of the Arabian Peninsula, the reasons for their conquest of much of the Mediterranean world, the growth of cities, and the flowering of philosophy and legal systems in areas under their control. Important parts of this CAS are comparisons of the Arabs with other armed mounted forces that sweep through Europe and Asia, the Huns, Mongols, and Turks, and their competition with the Arabs for dominance. In this CAS, European feudalism moves to the periphery of global development where it belongs; however, it is discussed as students explore Christian Europe's resistance to Islam (in Spain from the 7th through the 15th centuries and Austria in the 17th century) and counter-offenses (such as the Crusades). Epidemics such as the Bubonic plague, which wiped out an estimated one-third of the population of Europe, are introduced as the consequences of war, trade, and cultural diffusion.

During this period, expanding trade and the development of trade networks play key roles in promoting the interaction of people and cultures and are a major focal point. The impact of geography on history, the notion of regional interdependence, and the role economics plays in social and political developments are introduced as major themes. Students revisit earlier trade-based networks, looking at the cultural impact of ties between Egypt and Crete, the impact of and resistance to Hellenization, and the role of Jews in the Roman Empire. They learn about the Silk

Road in Asia, the trans-Sahara gold and salt trade in Northwest Africa, the Hanseatic League in the Baltic region of Northern Europe, Venice's role in the Mediterranean, how the Inca Empire developed a numerical system but not a written language, and the emergence of merchant "castes" that facilitate trade and banking, the Jews in Central Europe, the overseas Chinese in Southeast Asia, and followers of Buddha in the Bay of Bengal and the Indian Ocean, as well as Arab merchants such as Abu Abdullah Muhammad Ibn Battuta (1304–1368/9 AD).

Ibn Battuta is a particularly important figure for understanding this period because he traveled widely and his journals recount visits to West Africa, India, and China (although there is some question whether he actually went to China). In 1352, Ibn Battuta traveled to the Sub-Saharan West African Kingdom of Mali, and his journals (http://www.fordham.edu/halsall/source/1354-ibnbattuta.html, accessed June 7, 2010) are an excellent primary source for the study of this West African society and of the Arab/Islamic trade network.

Mansa Kankou Musa governed Mali just prior to Ibn Battuta's visit (1312–1337). He was a Muslim and made the hajj, or religious pilgrimage to Mecca, in 1324. According to legend, Emperor Musa was accompanied on the hajj by 60,000 men including his personal retinue of 12,000 slaves, and 100 camels, each carrying hundreds of pounds of gold. The Arab historian al-'Umari, who traveled to Cairo 12 years after Mansa Musa, reported that residents of the city still told stories about the wealth of the African visitors.

The idea of including Mansa Musa and the Kingdom of Mali in the global history curriculum drew the indignation of opponents of multiculturalism in the 1990s. They disputed his historical significance and claimed he was only included so that students would be introduced to a Sub-Saharan African leader. I think they were right about why he was included in the curriculum, but wrong about Mansa Musa's historical importance.

The story of Mansa Musa and the Kingdom of Mali as a "case study" is worth a prolonged stop at this point in the global history curriculum because it helps students understand the expansion of Arab and Islamic influence through a region that stretched across Africa to Eurasia from the Atlantic to the Pacific. It was an "empire" held together by religious beliefs and trade, rather than by a shared language, culture, or government. In fact, the Islamic world, including so many different kinds of people, was ungovernable as a single entity.

By connecting into the Arab/Islamic trade network, the rulers of Mali brought the benefits of literacy and education to their kingdom and ensured that its capital city, Timbuktu, would play a major role in the trans-Saharan trade in gold, salt, ivory, and slaves. It is the role of the network, and the way it ties together far-flung kingdoms and people, that students need to understand. Mansa Musa and the trans-Saharan trade are an interesting part of the picture. They are important as well because they challenge the myth that Europeans brought civilization to Africa and Africans through imperialism and slavery.

Essential questions addressed in this CAS include "Are people and cultures fundamentally the same or different?"; "Why do culture and innovation spread?"; "Is cultural diffusion always a positive force?"; and "Who is an important historical actor?"

Recommended Websites

Decameron Web (http://www.brown.edu/Departments/Italian_Studies/dweb/the_project, accessed May 19, 2010). Organizes study of the Bubonic plague in Europe around the text of the book *Decameron*. Designed for college classes. Useful for teachers.

Islamic World (http://www.qma.com.qa/eng/index.php/qma/collections, accessed May 23, 2010). The site for Qatar's Islamic heritage museums. Artifacts presented on the site include weapons, armor, and art.

Silk Road (http://www.ess.uci.edu/~oliver/silk.html, accessed May 23, 2010). A useful illustrated history for teachers. Maps of the Silk Road are available at http://www.silkroadproject.org/tabid/177/defaul.aspx, accessed May 23, 2010).

Travels of Ibn Battuta (http://www.sfusd.k12.ca.us/schwww/sch618/ibn_battuta/Ibn_Battuta_Rihla.html, accessed June 7, 2010). A virtual tour with maps and photographs that allows students to follow the trips described in his journals.

CAS V. Regional Conflict and Growth (basically 1200 AD–1500 AD with extensions and comparisons on both ends)

It takes long periods of time to build the infrastructure (roads, institutions, networks) that makes possible an economic, political, or social take-off. It took thousands of years for the emergence of the "civilization package" (see Teaching Ideas below) after the initial development of agriculture and thousands of years more for it to spread around the world. Rates of transformation are so much faster in the computer age where our students live that it is difficult for them to comprehend the slow accumulative process that makes possible sudden rapid change. Grappling with this idea, and the possibility of alternative historical paths – the contingent nature of history – are an important part of this CAS. It compares different paths taken by societies in India, China, Japan, and Western Europe, not always by choice, and never with a full sense of the implications for the future.

Reactions to the expansion of Islam and Islamic control over trade between the eastern and western outposts of Eurasia and Africa led to challenges and the emergence of new centers of influence, at first in local regions, and then in an increasingly interconnected world. A major point of attention in this calendar area is a comparison between developments in the Indian subcontinent (Mogul Empire), in Pacific Rim Asia (Ming Dynasty in China and Shogun rule and the Tokugawa shogunate in Japan), and in Western Europe.

Between 700 and 1200 AD Islamic forces, first the Arabs and then the Turks, extended their control deeper and deeper into the Indian subcontinent. By the 13th century they were followed by central Asian "Mongol" armies led by Tamerlaine, who was also a Muslim, and by the start of the 16th century the Mongols had established an empire that controlled India for approximately 200 years. Mogul rule in India (Mogul comes from the Persian word for Mongol) points to one possible historical path. They brought political and economic stability to the region, public works, and artistic and architectural achievements (including construction of the Taj Mahal). However, Mogul stability left in place the Hindu caste system's rigid control over society, and oppressive conditions for the peasantry. In India, stability and control over internal and external destructive forces became an impediment to development and change, and by the 18th century the Indian subcontinent was vulnerable to domination by Western Europe.

In the 13th century, Mongol forces under the leadership of Genghis Khan and his successors conquered imperial China. For a time, this opened the door for the spread of Chinese goods, culture, and technology along the Mongol-controlled trade routes across Eurasia. Primary sources on China in this period and its ties with other societies include the journals of Marco Polo, a Venetian merchant who traveled to China at the end of the 13th century, and Bar Sauma, an ethnic Turk born in northern China in the first half of the 13th century. About 1275, Sauma traveled along the Silk Road on a pilgrimage to Jerusalem, which his group never reached. Sauma kept a journal of his experiences and reactions (http://www.aina.org/books/mokk/mokk.htm, accessed

October 24, 2009) and eventually arrived in Rome, where he met with Pope Nicholas IV, and Paris and Bordeaux, where he met with the Kings of France and England.

In the 14th century, a new ruling Chinese dynasty, the Ming, gained control, and they took a second historical path. In reaction to what they considered the "alien" Mongols, they closed China off to outside influence and reestablished traditional Chinese cultural practices and beliefs. Initially the Ming continued to support overseas trade and they sponsored the voyages of Zheng He in the Indian Ocean, including one that involved an estimated 300 ships. However, isolationist impulses won out and the expeditions of trade and discovery ceased. Essentially China remained isolated from the outside world, a self-contained empire until Western European incursions in the 19th century.

Japan, in this period, took yet another path. Japan is a mountainous archipelago with four major and over 4,000 smaller islands. It is located about 125 miles off the Asia mainland at the same latitude as the Korean peninsula. In discussions of the impact of geography on history, Japan is often compared to Greece, because it is mountainous, or Great Britain, because of its location off of the main continental mass. However, there are important physical differences that influenced the histories of all three areas. Greece is not an isolated island and it was an integral part of the cultural exchanges, trade, and wars of the Mediterranean world. Although Great Britain is an island, it is only 21 miles from the European mainland and much more integrated than Japan into the continental imperial battles and more subject to invasion, migration, and conquest.

While Japan imported agriculture, technology, and cultural practices from Korea and China, it was never subjugated by the mainland or subject to outside authority. In the 13th century it repelled two Mongol invasions. The island kingdom periodically broke up into warring feudal fiefdoms, and while these could be destructive, they also created space for cultural development and social change. Japan was effectively unified at the end of the 16th century and its rulers opted for isolation from foreign influences, especially European merchants and missionaries. The key difference between China and Japan was that while both chose isolation from a changing world, particularly Western Europe, earlier divisions allowed Japanese society to remain more open and conducive to experimentation and change even after governmental power was consolidated.

With the gradual collapse of the Roman Empire in the western Mediterranean, there remained no central governing body in Western Europe, a situation that continues into the current era. Small kingdoms and numerous principalities struggled against each other for control over territory and against divisive forces within their own boundaries. There were periodic threats from outside invaders (Norse, Arab, Hun, and Turk), occasional peasant uprisings, often expressed in religious

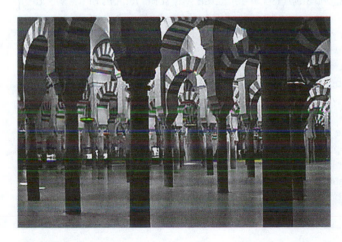

FIGURE 5.1 In Cordoba, Spain, a Roman Catholic cathedral is constructed around an Islamic mosque.

millenistic terms, civil conflicts fought between heavily armed feudal bands, and religious wars as state authorities both sought Roman Catholic Church support in their controversies and attempted to limit church political and economic influence.

Gradually, over the course of hundreds of years between roughly 600 AD and 1500 AD, and with repeated setbacks, Spain (which was finally unified in 1492), England (which was still negotiating its relations with Ireland, Scotland, and Wales into the 19th century), and France (not completely unified until the French Revolution and Napoleon) emerged as relatively stable, clearly defined, consolidated states and as the leading powers in Europe. However, none of the big three had the power to force its will on the rest of the region (although France under Napoleon and later Germany under Hitler would try) and establish a Western European empire.

The absence of central political authority led to a state of virtually perpetual war, but also, as it did in Japan, created openings for social, economic, and cultural change. Competition between trading centers, cities, and states, especially over the control of trade, spurred change in ways in which it did not, perhaps could not, occur in the other regions discussed in this calendar area of study. Italian city-states in control over the Mediterranean trade flourished, invested in the arts, and invented a European Renaissance that over the course of 300 years (roughly 1350 AD to 1650 AD) swept the continent and transformed technology, the transmission of knowledge, religious belief, scientific exploration, and artistic expression. The competition between states over trade also led to Portuguese exploration along the African coast in search of a water route to India and the decision by a newly unified Spanish crown to fund Columbus's voyages west.

Essential questions addressed in this CAS include "Why do societies take different paths?"; "Is the flow of history predetermined?"; "What stimulates change?"; "Why do rates of change accelerate, slow down, and even stall?"; "Why are some societies successful while others fail?"; and "Is competition essential for human progress?"

TEACHING IDEAS

Most students, including high school students, divide history into two epochs, BM and AM – Before Me and After Me – with the crucial watershed event being their birth. Everything before that moment is ancient history. Kerri Creegan Summers, a social studies teacher at Massapequa (NY) High School uses Activity 1 to help her students understand the defining features of historical eras in a more sophisticated way.

Jared Diamond in *Guns, Germs, and Steel* (1997) pondered why some regions of the world came to dominate while others became subservient. Much of history he attributes to geographical accident, particularly the concentration of the factors needed for agricultural development and the growth of civilization in a specific region. The "civilization package" starts with the availability of wild plants that can be transformed into crops, animals suitable for domestication, sufficient water supply, and fertile soil. The production of surplus food can lead to increased population density, work specialization with designated agricultural producers, craft workers, traders, soldiers, and government officials, both secular and religious, who exercise the power to appropriate wealth created by others. With all likelihood, institutions emerge that regularize the expropriation of labor and any surplus production and reinforce class hierarchies. They include a military, police, tax collectors, government bureaucrats, and organized churches. In some societies money, banking, and weights and measures, numeracy, and literacy are developed or are borrowed from other societies as aids to trade and taxation.

I use terms such as "can to lead to" and "with all likelihood" because all societies do not take these directions and adopt the "civilization package," either by choice, or because of geographic limitations. The problem these societies face is that they become vulnerable to neighbors, perhaps an expanding empire or even a highly effective nomadic military force such as the Huns or Mongols. Conquered and absorbed, they disappear as historical actors. Activity 2 examines the impact of different aspects of the civilization package.

Activities 3–8 are available online at http://people.hofstra.edu/alan_j_singer. A major topic in the National Council for Social Studies thematic strands is the impact of technology on history. Technological advances gave societies advantages over their neighbors, especially in warfare. A number of important developments changed the nature of weaponry in the ancient world and in the centuries prior to the Columbian Exchange (c. 1500 AD).

Bronze tools, developed across Eurasia after 3000 BC revolutionized warfare and then were replaced by iron weapons starting about 1200 BC. Four-wheeled animal-drawn vehicles were used in battle in Mesopotamia as early as 2500 BC. Horse-drawn, two-wheeled carts with spoked wheels may have been developed in Central Asia about 2000 BC, but they were certainly in use by the Hittites on the Anatolia Peninsula in the 17th century BC. Hyksos invaders from Southwest Asia were able to use chariots with spoked wheels to conquer and control Egypt in the 16th century BC. The catapult was invented in Greece about 400 BC and used in battles against Carthaginian fortifications in Sicily. It was probably based on earlier technology used in crossbows.

The longbow, which is usually about the height of a man, developed independently in a number of different locations, including among the Nubians, Kurds, Japanese, and Native Americans. During the European Middle Ages longbows could penetrate armor worn by mounted noblemen and played a crucial role in wars between England and France, including the Battle of Agincourt in 1415 during the One Hundred Years' War.

The Chinese invented gunpowder and may have started using it in weapons in the 11th century AD in bombs, cannons, and rockets. Knowledge about gunpowder arrived in Europe during the 13th century. Roger Bacon, an English scientist and philosopher, wrote about it in an essay dated 1268 AD. In the 15th century AD the Portuguese developed the carrack, a larger, three- or four-masted sailing ship that made possible cross-Atlantic voyages, including Columbus's aboard the *Santa Maria*.

One of the simplest and most interesting technological developments that revolutionized warfare was the stirrup, developed on the Central Asian plains around 1000 BC. The addition of leather loops as footholds on either side of a horse saddle led to greater control of mounts and enhanced horses as fighting engines. This contributed to the conquest of eastern, western and south Asian empires by warriors from otherwise less developed civilizations. Eventually defeated forces adopted the stirrup as well. Without this simple adaptation, heavily armored, mounted knights would not have been able to become the chief military force in Western European feudal societies. I have students look at the impact of technology on societies at different historical moments and also teach a comparative lesson where students select and defend the technological changes they believe had the greatest impact on history. Activity 3 lists fifteen scientific and technological developments between 975 AD and 1500 AD. The earliest developments move from the East to West. Later developments occur in Western Europe. I organize similar lessons for evaluating the impact of technological changes during other broad historical periods.

All change is not "progress." It is certainly not experienced as progress by the people who are its victims. In the Mediterranean world and Southwest Asia, the process of Hellenization, the spread of the Greek way of life by the armies of Alexander the Great (roughly 330–300 BC) is usually presented as a force for integrating the region, promoting trade and cultural diffusion, and as a spur to the advance of civilization. Ironically, some of the great freedom struggles in the Judeo-Christian tradition are fought against enforced Hellenization and later against Romanization. The story of Judah Maccabee of the Israelites is a battle against "Assyrians" and their local allies who want to integrate Judea (ancient Palestine) into the Greek world. Anthropologist Marvin Harris (1989) argues that in a similar way, the rebellion led by Jesus of Nazareth and other religious zealots in the same region was a struggle against forced assimilation into a Roman world. Activity 4 introduces students to these conflicts.

The Islamic struggle to repel European invaders between 1095 AD and 1270 AD, known in the Islamic world as the "Wars of the Cross," are generally presented to students from the European point of view as a series of religious Crusades to regain the mythical Christian Holy Land. Activity 5 is a scene from a play, "al-Hurab al-Salibiyya: An Islamic View of the Battle with Christendom," written by Michael Pezone for his global history classes at Law, Government, and Community Service Magnet High School in Queens, New York. It is designed to introduce students to these events from an Islamic perspective, and to challenge them to examine the course of history in different terms. Characters in the play include Abdul, the pigeon-keeper; Giovanni, an Italian merchant; Kareem, a resident of Cordoba; the Sultan, a member of the Ayyubid dynasty in Egypt; the Sultana; Farik, an Arab merchant; Abraham, a Jewish exile in Cordoba; advisors to the Sultan; Victor, a French nobleman; King Louis IX of France; Andrew, the King's advisor; Essahib, a Muslim poet; and Khailid, grandson of the pigeon-keeper. Scenes take place in Cordoba, Spain, King Louis's palace in Paris, a pigeon tower in Cairo, the Sultan's palace in Cairo, an outdoor café in Genoa, Italy, and a prison cell in Mansoura, Egypt. The entire play can be downloaded at http://nyscss.org/resources/publications/docket/docket-6-1.aspx (accessed March 26, 2010). Letters and poems contained in the play were taken from a translation of the Arabian manuscript "Essulouk li Mariset il Muluk" by Makrisi (http://www.fordham.edu/halsall/source/makrisi.html, accessed March 26, 2010).

The story of Mansa Musa is shrouded in legend. However, decades after Mansa Musa's hajj to Mecca, an Islamic merchant, Abu Abdullah Muhammad Ibn Battuta, visited the capital of the Kingdom of Mali and wrote about the trip in his journals. These journals provide a first-hand description of Mansa Musa's empire shortly after his death (Activity 6).

Just as Islamic and European Christian rulers and merchants were anxious to learn about East Asia and Sub-Saharan Africa, the rulers of China wanted to learn as much as possible about the power and wealth of other areas. Zheng He (1371–1435) was the admiral of the Chinese fleet who led a series of voyages into the Indian Ocean, perhaps as far as East Africa. Rabban Bar Sauma (1220–1294) was an ethnic Turk and Christian Monk who traveled from China to Europe prior to the travels of Marco Polo in the service of the Chinese emperor. According to his journals, edited and adapted in Activity 7, Rabban Bar Sauma met with the Roman Catholic Pope as well as the Kings of England and France (http://www.nestorian.org/history_of_rabban_bar_sawma_1.html, accessed November 20, 2009).

When examining the European Renaissance I try to engage students in two debates. We try to define the boundaries of the epoch (when does it begin and when does it end?) which is difficult because the Renaissance begins and ends in different parts of Europe at different times. I date the start of the European Renaissance with the decision to build the Basilica di Santa Maria del Fiore or "Duomo," an enormous domed cathedral in Florence, in the 1290s. The construction of this cathedral took over 100 years and marks the ascendance of commercial capitalism and banking power in Italy. It also stimulated science and the arts, as craftsmen had to invent the techniques and machines needed to erect its imposing dome. Many Italian Renaissance figures apprenticed working on the Duomo. Ironically, construction of a cathedral marked the emerging dominance of secularization in European society.

I have been less successful in identifying a meaningful end date or event for the Renaissance. I think the religious wars in Europe and the conquest and settlement of the Americas gradually shifted attention to new concerns and possibilities. By the beginning of the 17th century, even though wars continued to be fought in the name of religion, European rulers were much more secular and the acquisition of colonies and wealth had replaced more spiritual concerns at the center of European society.

The second debate I engage students in is over whether the European Renaissance was a rebirth of ancient Mediterranean Greco-Roman culture or was something new. Use of the term Renaissance, French for rebirth, to describe this period in Europe was actually started by historians in the 19th century, long after the events took place. People who champion the idea of a rebirth look toward the revival of classical studies in Florence by Petrarch in the middle of the 14th century. I tend to see the period as a break with the past, framed as a revival, to avoid condemnation of a secular movement by a still powerful Roman Catholic Church that actively persecuted heretics. At the start of the 13th century the Church launched the Albigensian Crusade to quash a Protestant-like heresy in southern France, leading to the execution of over 200,000 people.

I start discussion of the European Renaissance by having two students, close to the same height, lay down on the floor. They lay perpendicular to each other, with the head of one student near the waist of the other. The student whose head is by the waist puts out his or her arms and I ask the rest of the class to describe what they see. The class quickly realize that our arm span is approximately equal to our height, a relationship discovered by a Roman architect named Vitruvius Pollo in the 1st century BC and reaffirmed in a sketch by Leonardo Da Vinci c. 1487. While this relationship is obvious to anyone who looks, the key is that Da Vinci looked, saw, and recorded – properties that helped define the Italian Renaissance. It is also significant for our debate over rebirth that Vitruvius believed the proportions he described in his book *De Architecture* were precise and universal, while Da Vinci saw them as tendencies that had to be confirmed empirically.

One of my most successful lessons exploring the European Renaissance involves students in an examination of paintings portraying the Madonna and Child, all available online through Google image. Generally I focus on three paintings, Giotto's *Madonna and Child* (c. 1320), Da Vinci's *Madonna with a Flower* (c. 1478), and Raphael's *Small Cowper Madonna* (c. 1505). Students compare different aspects of the paintings, including color, dimension, portrayal of the girl/woman, and depiction of the baby Jesus. In Giotto's work, the picture is two-dimensional and monochromatic, the mother and child have physical halos, Madonna, shown as an adult, is ethereal, and Jesus is a miniature adult. Da Vinci's painting is three-dimensional, Madonna is a young girl on the verge of pubescence (something that probably got him into trouble with church authorities) and Jesus is a typical baby with an enlarged head. Both Madonna and child have distinct halos signaling their divinity. Raphael's painting is also three-dimensional, but it is an outdoor scene. Religiosity is virtually gone; the halos are mere shadows, the Madonna is pictured as a robust young woman, and both the mother and child are shown with the blond hair and light coloring of Germanic-looking northern Italians.

Activity 1. Defining Epochs

Instructions: There are defining points in everyone's life that mark changes in the way they live, relate to others, and think about the world. Think about defining points in your own life. Draw a timeline labeling each of these points. The periods between these defining points are like historical epochs. Think of a good name for each of these time spans or epochs in your life.

Activity 2. What Happens if You Don't Adopt the Package?

Background: In the 19th and 20th centuries a number of traditional peoples, including Native American tribes, the Maori in New Zealand, and the Aborigines of Australia, have tried to live according to their pre-agricultural cultural traditions. They resisted becoming settled and adopting the "civilization package." Often this meant war with more populous and technologically advanced invaders who wanted to control their tribal lands and resources. Generally, the traditional peoples were overwhelmed, their ways of life were destroyed, and they either died off or were absorbed by the dominant "civilization." According to National Geographic's Enduring Voices Project, by 2100 more than half of the world's more than 7,000 languages will disappear, along with the people who spoke them (http://www.nationalgeographic.com/mission/enduringvoices, accessed June 7, 2010).

Instructions: You are members of a team affiliated with UNESCO (the United Nations Educational, Scientific and Cultural Organization). You have been asked to develop a global policy to define the relationship between industrialized (modern) societies and traditional people in the 21st century. The question you must address is, "Should traditional people be allowed to live in traditional ways on protected reserves, even if this means denying their children access to medicine, education, technologies, and human rights available to children in more developed countries?"

6

WHAT DOES A THEME-BASED GLOBAL HISTORY CURRICULUM LOOK LIKE? PART 2 – AD: AFTER THE DELUGE

> This chapter presents the second part (the Columbian Exchange through the present) of a theme-based global history curriculum based on nine "calendar areas of study" that are roughly chronological. However, rather than following the European chronological narrative the central focus of the curriculum shifts between different areas of the world. Selected topics are covered in depth and are used as "case studies" to illustrate broader historical trends. Major focal points are the repercussions of the Columbian Exchange and capitalism as a transformative force in global history.

Whether students study global history for one year or two in high school, individual teachers or social studies departments need to split the curriculum calendar at some point. This helps keep all classes studying global history on pace to complete the full scope of the curriculum.

In New York State, where most students study global history in ninth and tenth grades and there is a standardized assessment (the New York State Global History Regents Examination) at the end of the second year, ninth grade usually ends, and tenth grade begins, with the European Scientific Revolution and the European Enlightenment. Note: while textbooks, curriculum guides, and teachers almost universally leave out the modifier "European," these are European, rather than global, phenomena.

This curriculum calendar split is convenient for organizing teaching time, but I think the logical historical break is the Columbian Exchange, which begins the transformation of the world and its history from multiple regions and histories into one world with a more or less integrated narrative. I believe this calendar division also makes it easier to show the connection between the conquest and European settlement of the Americas, the trans–Atlantic slave trade, the emergence of capitalism, and the development of the modern world. Unlike the Greek goddess Athena, who supposedly burst fully formed from the head of Zeus, the modern world was the product of these and other powerful historical forces.

Traditional Curriculum Calendar

I have had the privilege of working with many excellent high school social studies teachers. One of the best organized and most systematic is Jessica Cartusciello who helped develop the global history curriculum calendar for the Island Trees, New York school district, using the textbook *World History* (Upper Saddle River, NJ: Pearson Prentice Hall, 2007). Jessica's district provides teachers with ten Unit Topics and lists of content to be covered and skills to be emphasized in each unit that are aligned with the New York State Global History learning standards (http://www. emsc.nysed.gov/ciai/socst/pub/sscore2.pdf, accessed July 1, 2010). Teachers decide the focus of individual lessons and how many days to spend on each of the units.

One reason I chose to discuss the Island Trees curriculum calendar as an example of a traditional approach to global history is its honesty. It is linear and chronological with a focus on the European world without too many tangential side trips to Africa, Asia, and Latin America that teachers rarely make voluntarily. Eight of the ten units in the tenth-grade Island Trees global history curriculum, in fact the first eight, focus almost entirely on the history of Europe.

Students first learn about the (European) Scientific Revolution and the (European) Enlightenment and how ideas developed in France and England by Locke, Hobbes, Montesquieu, and Rousseau influenced the British North American colonies and other European thinkers. In the second unit they study the causes, consequences, and events of the French Revolution. The third unit is titled Latin America/Nationalism. After a brief detour to explore uprisings against the European colonial powers in Latin America and Haiti, the curriculum returns to Europe where students study nationalist movements in France, Italy, and Germany. Unit 4 is the study of the Industrial Revolution, primarily in England. As with most of the traditional chronological global history curriculum, it downplays the role of capitalism as a creative and destructive force generating industrial expansion, the emergence of new social classes, and broader global transformation.

In Unit 5, Imperialism, other areas of the world are introduced into the curriculum as European powers extend their tentacles around the globe, but these peoples are largely presented as passive victims, or as the fortunate beneficiaries, of European expansion, not as historical actors in their own right. Units 6 and 7 focus on the European origins of World War I and II, with some discussion of the Russian Revolution and the international role played by Japan. In Unit 8, the Cold War, the United States, a former British colony and the repository of the best of Western Civilization, and the Soviet Union, presented as heir to Europe's totalitarian "dark side," battle for global supremacy.

It is not until Units 9 and 10, the end of the school year when teachers are racing to prepare students for standardized exams, that students explore "Post-Colonialism: China, India, the Middle East, and Africa" and contemporary "World Problems," including genocide in Armenia, Cambodia, Bosnia, Rwanda, and the Sudan, deforestation and desertification in the Third World, environmental issues, nuclear proliferation, and terrorism.

I think the message to students in this traditional Eurocentric organization of the global history curriculum, while subliminal, is clear. Western Europe and its North American offspring did their best during the past 250 years to advance civilization. This was despite efforts by Eastern European powers (Germany and Russia/Soviet Union) to undermine their achievements and the "problems" that infest the rest of the globe and threaten to infect the West if it relaxes its defenses.

While individual teachers might give it a different twist, and I know that Jessica Cartusciello does, the way the curriculum is organized, students do not generally learn about the West's role in precipitating the horrific wars of the 20th century or that it has a major responsibility for the problems of the 21st century. These include genocides in societies where indigenous cultural, economic, and political institutions were systematically undermined by Western colonial powers. These things did not just happen, or only happen because of problems endemic to the Third World. In the theme-based calendar areas of study presented here, non-Western societies are presented as historical actors and the ongoing connections between the different regions of the world, especially the impact of and struggle against imperialism, are a constant focus.

CAS VI. Columbian Exchange, 1420–1763

I start this CAS in c. 1420 when Prince Henry the Navigator of Portugal began to sponsor expeditions along the coast of Africa in search of a water route to India. Columbus's voyages west were in response to these Portuguese efforts. The Portuguese set up trading fortresses and sugar plantations in West Africa that became the basis for the trans-Atlantic slave trade and the models for Caribbean sugar plantations. I complete the CAS in 1763 with the Treaty of Paris ending the Seven Years' War, which pitted England and Prussia against France, Spain, Russia, and the Austro-Hungarian Empire. Battles were fought in Europe, the Americas, India, and West Africa in what was essentially the first "world war." In United States history, this global conflict is remembered as the French and Indian War.

While the indigenous people of the Americas and Africa suffered catastrophically from the Columbian Exchange, during the course of the next 250 years Western Europe was transformed and emerged as the world's dominant economic, political, and military force. The wealth that was stolen or created financed the European Renaissance, the consolidation of states, the development of new world empires, and the building of the physical and fiscal infrastructure necessary for the Industrial Revolution.

It is a mistake to view this period in Europe as simply a progressive movement to modernity and global dominance. The Columbian Exchange led to hundreds of years of war, as monarchs and nations fought over territory in Europe and around the world. The Treaty of Tordesillas in 1494, where the Pope divided newly conquered lands between Spain and Portugal, virtually ensured schism within Christian Europe and the Protestant Reformation and religious wars as the English and Dutch had to break with the Roman Catholic Church to share in the loot.

In this period, as in all periods of transformation, there was tremendous dislocation for the majority of the population of Western Europe. Religious wars destroyed their homes and farms, and the taxes levied to finance war, exploration, and conquest impoverished them. Traditional village privileges were abrogated and people were driven off of the land, precipitating migrations to urban areas and to newly settled colonies, usually as bonded laborers.

Essential questions to be explored in this calendar area include "How can small events have such major repercussions?" and "Do the benefits of broad change justify the pain and dislocation that they cause?"

Recommended Website

Voyages of Discovery (http://www.ucalgary.ca/applied_history/tutor/eurvoya/index.html, accessed May 18, 2010). This site provides an in-depth examination of European voyages of exploration that led to the integration of the world and global transformation. Maintained by the Applied History Research Group at the University of Calgary. An excellent site for student research.

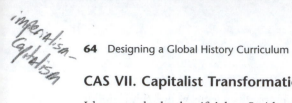

CAS VII. Capitalist Transformation, 1750–1914

I have no doubt that if Adam Smith, a champion of capitalism, and Karl Marx, its best-known critic, could have sat down for a public discussion somewhere, they would have agreed that capitalism was the greatest force transforming the world after the start of the Columbian Exchange. What distinguished chattel slavery from bondage in other historical eras was that in the capitalist marketplace people were redefined as commodities to be bought and sold with the goal of using their labor power to generate profits. In the capitalist world, free workers as well were increasingly viewed as a factor of production whose cost could be minimized through lower wages, longer hours, and the diminution of skill, and productivity could be increased with the introduction of new machinery, no matter the human cost. It was profit *über alles*, profit above all.

I argue that developments in global history between 1750 and 1914 were initially responses to instabilities in the colonial system that emerged from the Columbian Exchange. Periodic warfare between the European colonial powers bankrupted France and Spain, made Portugal and the Netherlands marginal political and economic actors on the world scene, and even left England, the dominant military and economic power at the time, vulnerable to colonial rebellions in North America and the Caribbean.

This CAS looks closely at and compares six "revolutions" that helped transform the post-Columbian world. The North and South American Wars for Independence left colonial elites in power in newly established independent states. The French civil war that toppled the ancient regime invented both nationalism and the idea of citizenship and precipitated similar movements on the European continent. In England, Luddite, Jacobin, and Chartist-inspired unrest between 1750 and 1850 seemed to have the potential to overthrow the social order. Rebellions led by enslaved Africans in Haiti and Jamaica contributed to ending both the system of chattel slavery and of colonialism.

Capitalism, transformation, and resistance are at the core of this CAS. Gradually at first, and then more rapidly, capitalism began shaping a new world order. It led to industrial development in England that spread across Europe and around the world, forcing societies to either adopt it or to succumb to the economic and military might of the capitalist imperialist powers. New industries of unprecedented scale emerged and concentrated wealth and power in the hands of a new economic elite. Displaced people, in record numbers, migrated in search of work. They moved to other countries and settled in new urban centers. New technologies meant new products and new weapons, further enhancing the position of the industrial powers, but also increasing competition for raw materials and markets. Competition between the European industrialized imperialist nations led to the division of Africa (in 1884) and of the Pacific Rim, and became the underlying cause of the Great War (1914–1918), now known as World War I.

I recommend, as a major case study in this CAS, the relationship between Great Britain and Ireland. Ireland, as Britain's first colony, was a proving ground for British colonial and imperialist policies in other areas. Schools were created to facilitate cultural assimilation, teaching was in English only and Roman Catholic children were required to read England's official Protestant version of the Christian Bible. It is in Ireland where capitalist free market ideology espoused by the British government allowed a potato crop failure caused by a fungal infection to become a famine leading to over a million deaths, the exodus of almost two million people, the halving of the island's population, and resistance to British authority that eventually led to independence.

I especially like focusing on Ireland because it is the one major instance where the colonized are White Europeans, which removes the issue of racial bias from the equation. There is an excellent online curriculum guide centering on the Great Irish Famine that was developed for New York State and received a National Council for Social Studies Program of Excellence Award (http://www.emsc.nysed.gov/ciai/gt/gif/curriculum.html, accessed May 23, 2010).

Every step in capitalism's advance generated internal and external resistance. At first, land-based aristocracy, challenged by new capitalist elites, struggled to hold on to state power. A new class of deskilled and increasingly impoverished workers in Europe, the proletariat, organized collectively for rights and power in many countries and helped found labor, socialist, and communist movements and political parties. In India (Sepoy Mutiny), China (Opium War and Boxer Rebellion), Sudan (Mahdist Revolt), the American West (Indian Wars), and southern Africa (Anglo–Zulu War), Cuba, and the Philippines, and in dozens, perhaps hundreds of other localities, indigenous movements resisted the transformation of their way of life from above and from outside and the expropriation of their lands and resources.

An important comparative study in this CAS is the alternative paths taken by India, China, and Japan in the 19th century. Between 1757 and 1857, first through economic concessions and then through military operations, Great Britain gradually increased its influence on the Indian sub-continent until it finally established full colonial control. Imperial China's monarchy and bureaucracy, despite occasional resistance, negotiated away authority to European powers over large areas of China in order to retain nominal political independence. Japan, after seeing what happened to India and China, embraced industrialization with the Meiji Restoration in 1866 and by the start of the 20th century was an economic and military power in its own right.

Once again, we want students to realize that the same forces can be both destructive and creative. Essential questions to be explored in this CAS include the relationship between capitalism and the movements to expand democratic participation and individual liberty during this time period and the relationship between capitalism and the knowledge explosion, especially scientific knowledge, that changed the way we see human history, the history of the planet, and the universe. Students should discuss whether societies, especially in the West, had real alternatives or whether historical events doomed them to follow particular paths.

Recommended Websites

French Revolution (http://chnm.gmu.edu/revolution, accessed May 20, 2010). "Liberty, Equality, and Fraternity" was developed by the Center for History and New Media and the American Social History Project. It features topical essays, images, timelines, a glossary, songs, maps, and over 600 primary source documents. Contemporary engravings depict events during the French Revolution. One of the most interesting features is the information the site provides on the Revolution in Haiti. An outstanding resource for both teachers and students.

Industrial Revolution (http://industrialrevolution.sea.ca/index.html, accessed May 20, 2010). An excellent site for students. The Industrial Revolution in England is examined through its impact on a small agricultural village called Bedlington and a fictional farmer named John Bumbleson.

Spartacus Educational (http://www.spartacus.schoolnet.co.uk, accessed May 19, 2010). Features include entries and documents on the Industrial Revolution, the British Trade Union Movement, Child Labor, and the history of the British Empire including its imperialist exploits.

Victorian Web (http://www.victorianweb.org, accessed May 19, 2010). Examines the 19th century through the lens of Victorian England. Very detailed discussion of a wide range of topics including women's suffrage, the condition of the working class, and the British Empire. An excellent resource for teachers.

CAS VIII. Reaction and Revolution, 1914–1989

(genocide)

The 20th century, what Eric Hobsbawm (1994) called the "Age of Extremes," is very much a reaction to the world created by industrial capitalism in the 19th century. In its second decade, competing imperialist powers plunged Europe and its overseas colonial empires into the Great War, later known as World War I. Sixteen million people, including almost seven million civilians, were killed and another 21 million were wounded. To prevent a similar conflagration from happening again, the victors, Great Britain and France, disarmed the defeated powers, harnessed them with a tremendous war debt, and reassigned their colonial outposts. They also broke up the Austro-Hungarian and Ottoman Turkish empires, creating new nation-states in Eastern Europe and the Balkans and new British and French colonies in Southwest Asia; attempted to overturn revolutionary rule in Russia; and established a trans-national organization, the League of Nations, to mediate disputes. Britain and France were so unsuccessful in these efforts that 20 years later Europe plunged the globe into a Second World War that left over sixty million people dead. At the end of this war, Western European economic and military power was spent, its colonial empires secured independence, and the United States and the Soviet Union, formerly Russia, emerged as the dominant global powers.

It is hard to comprehend, but the same Western European societies that invented political democracy and the Industrial Revolution and were responsible for some of humanity's grandest scientific and artistic achievements produced destruction on the greatest scale in human history. Hobsbawm believes the 20th century was "the most extraordinary era in the history of humanity, combining as it did unparalleled human catastrophes, substantial material improvement, and an unprecedented increase in our capacity to transform, and perhaps destroy, the face of our planet – and even to penetrate outside it" (vii).

As students study the 20th century they see continued efforts to support, reform, and control capitalism by the governments of the major industrial powers, individually through reforms such as the New Deal in the United States, and collectively through the efforts of trans-national organizations such as the United Nations, the World Bank, and the World Trade Organization. There are also efforts to overthrow the capitalist system by revolutionary parties in the name of the disposed, successfully, at least temporarily, in Russia, China, Vietnam, and Cuba, and unsuccessfully in Germany, Hungary, Greece, and Malaysia. There are democratic, primarily socialist, movements in a number of Western European countries that try to minimize the destructive impact of capitalism and to redistribute, at least partially, power and wealth. There are numerous independence movements in the Americas, Africa, and Asia as colonized peoples asserted the right to full and equal participation on the world stage. Mohandas Gandhi (India) and Ho Chi Minh (Vietnam) both believed that their colonized countries would be granted national rights and eventual independence by the Versailles peace conference at the end of World War I. When the rights of non-European people were ignored, they ceased cooperation with colonial regimes and became active revolutionaries seeking total and immediate independence.

I divide this CAS into four broad sub-topics: (A) Destruction, including World War I, World War II, and genocidal attacks on Armenians and Jews; (B) Reform movements in the industrialized societies including democratic socialism, the labor movement and labor parties, and campaigns for women's rights; (C) Revolution in Russia and the Third World; and (D) Reorganization and Cold War. The impact of technology on human history is a major focal point in each of these topics.

CAS IX. Emerging World Order, 1989 to Present

In the Island Trees curriculum calendar this unit is named "World Problems," but I think focusing on the problems that emerge or reach fruition during this time period puts the emphasis on the result, rather than the underlying historical forces that shaped the conditions. I considered calling this CAS "Capitalist Globalization," because globalization is driven by capitalism, just as was the case with the transformation discussed in CAS VII. The process, however, is neither complete nor preordained. The idea of "emerging" recognizes that things are changing and new patterns are developing, while acknowledging that the future remains unclear. In historical terms we are discussing a very short time period and it is difficult to predict what the new global balance or world order will look like. Prior to 1989, few, if any, historians predicted the collapse of the Soviet-style communism.

In a 1990 speech to Congress, United States President George H.W. Bush described his vision for the post-Cold War years. Instead of "a world divided – a world of barbed wire and concrete block, conflict and cold war . . . there is the very real prospect of a *new world order*" (http://www.c-span.org/executive/transcript.asp?cat=current_event&code=bush_admin&year=0391, accessed June 13, 2010) based on justice, fair play, freedom, and respect for human rights. Bush did not actually invent the phrase "new world order"; it has been attributed to a 1940 book by H.G. Wells, where he argued for the possibility of a world without war. A good organizing idea for this CAS is to have students discuss what they believe a "new world order" would, or should, look like.

In this CAS I revisit the essential questions identified by students at the beginning of our course of study (and periodically revised as they study global history). In Chapter 1, I discussed an activity where students in Adeola Tella's ninth-grade class came up with a series of questions including "Why do people keep having wars?"; "Who is a terrorist?"; "Are national borders still important in today's world?"; "Why are some people so poor and others so rich?"; "Does global trade make the world better or worse?"; "Does our great wealth cause them to be poor?"; and "How come the things that people need to live are too expensive for them to buy?"

As classes attempt to answer these questions more directly based on student knowledge of history and of current events they will touch on the pressing issues of the 21st century that need to be included in this CAS. These include capitalist globalization; democracy and human rights; the threat of war; environmental issues such as global warming, oil depletion, availability of fresh water, and population growth; technological change; the quality of human life (health, housing, education, work conditions, etc.); and the possibility for global cooperation and social justice.

Capitalism continued to be the driving economic force in a globalized world, especially with the collapse of the Soviet Union as an alternative model for a state-controlled, centralized, command economy. China's leadership, formerly communist, has embraced a state-sponsored authoritarian form of capitalism that places government planners in partnership with entrepreneurs to promote rapid industrial growth. Some leftwing critics see it as reminiscent of the corporate–government partnerships that defined fascism in Germany, Italy, and Japan prior to World War II.

Meanwhile the free market variant of capitalism, widely touted by both liberals and conservatives in the United States and Western Europe, was quickly abandoned as governments rushed to bail out banks, brokerages, insurance companies, and industrial corporations driven to the brink of bankruptcy (or over) by a sharp economic decline starting in 2007. An important question for students to explore is whether the world, particularly the North Atlantic region, is looking at a temporary economic downturn brought about by market fluctuations and management miscalculations, or a deeper structural crisis in the way capitalism works.

A primary concern in this CAS, as it was in the initial exploration of human origins and the development of civilizations, is the relationship between the environment and history. Global warming, the availability of fresh water, unchecked population growth, the depletion of fossil fuel reserves, are trans-national problems that cannot be effectively addressed by individual countries. Ending environmental destruction will require international cooperation and new levels of economic, social, and political integration.

While I was writing this chapter, world leaders, including U.S. President Barack Obama, were meeting in Copenhagen, Denmark to develop new guidelines to combat, and hopefully reverse, the impact of climate change caused by industrialization. The question, whether the United States, Western Europe, and the industrializing world (especially China and India) have to choose between the environment and economic development, is not easy to answer, and I do not expect a major breakthrough at the conference or a significant shift in government policies. Former Vice–President Al Gore, who was awarded the Nobel Peace Prize for his efforts, believes global warming can be reversed without major structural changes, if we have the necessary willpower. I am not as hopeful as Gore. I believe this question, and others related to environmental concerns and global cooperation, need to be carefully examined and furiously debated in this area of study.

TEACHING IDEAS

I use the Columbian Exchange to focus student attention on some of the essential questions introduced earlier and some new ones: How can a small event or development impact on a much broader world?; Should decisions and actions be evaluated based on short-term or long-term consequences?; Do events that benefit one group or region of the world always benefit everyone else?; and Do ends justify means? Europeans justified what they did in Africa and the Americas, by claiming they were bringing Christianity and civilization to the native peoples they conquered.

I usually begin discussion of the Columbian Exchange (Activity 1) by having students discuss the short-term and long-term impact of agricultural products "shared" by the different regions of the world including maize (corn), potatoes, and tobacco from the Americas and cotton and sugar cane from Africa and Eurasia. For this activity students write down the product they think had the greatest short-term and long-term impact and the reason why they made this selection. Sugar cane was the most important and profitable crop during the initial conquest and settlement of the Americas, but it was eclipsed by cotton during the Industrial Revolution. Maize (corn) is increasingly important in the manufacture of artificial sweeteners, animal feed, and bio-fuels. Two excellent books about the Columbian Exchange, useful as teacher resources and as sources of material for students are *Rethinking Columbus, 2nd edition* (Bigelow and Peterson, 1998) and *Seeds of change: The story of cultural exchange after 1492* (Davis and Hawke, 1992).

Activities 2–10 are available online at http://people.hofstra.edu/alan_j_singer. The ill-treatment of the Native Americans by European conquerors contributed to a demographic catastrophe; within a century of the European invasion the indigenous population of the Valley of Mexico suffered a 90% decline. In Activity 2 students read excerpts from Bartholomé de las Casas's report on the treatment of Native people by the Spanish Conquistadores. A Spanish priest, de las Casas, wrote a book protesting against their enslavement and detailing the methods used by Spanish conquistadors to conquer, torture, and kill. The book, which was illustrated by Théodore de Bry, describes people being burned alive, babies fed to dogs, forced relocations, beatings to make people work, and people having their hands amputated if they failed to deliver a monthly quantity of gold to their European conquerors. De Bry was a Flemish Protestant who had been driven into exile by Spain. Students should discuss whether his personal experiences invalidate his work. Images by Théodore de Bry are available at a number of Internet sites including http://www.floridahistory.com/de-bry-plates/de-bry-biography-mirror.htm and http://www.infoamerica.org/museo/expo_bry/bry000.htm (accessed June 13, 2010).

As a student teacher in the turbulent early 1970s, I opened a lesson on the Protestant Reformation in Europe by involving my sixth-grade students in a mock political protest demanding religious and political reform. We yelled, sang, made posters, and posted our own theses on the classroom door à la Martin Luther on the Castle Church in Wittenberg Germany in 1517. It was only years later that I learned that while Luther was willing to use theological arguments, pamphlets, and debates to challenge the ecclesiastical authority of the Roman Catholic Church, he was not a social leveler and spoke out against more radical reformers who sided with peasant demands to eliminate both church and political hierarchies (http://www. historyguide.org/earlymod/peasants1525.html, accessed December 16, 2009).

The political demands of the German peasants were best expressed in the Twelve Articles of the Christian Union of Upper Swabia, also known as the Twelve Articles of the Black Forest, which were disseminated in 1525 (http://www.marxists.org/archive/marx/works/1850/ peasant-war-germany/ch0e.htm, accessed December 16, 2009). Many historians consider promotion of the Twelve Articles to be the first organized campaign for human rights in world history.

The peasant uprising in Germany during the European Reformation provides teachers with the opportunity to introduce a number of major historical themes. Events, as seen in Germany, can spiral out of control as challenges to authority take on a dynamic of their own. There were similar developments during the French Revolution and most movements that successfully overturned the old way of doing things. This uprising helps show that the human desire for political freedom was not born in one place at one time, Enlightenment England in the 17th and 18th centuries, but when circumstances are favorable, has burst out in many places around the world including Soweto, South Africa and Tiananmen Square in Beijing, China. It also illustrates the importance of struggles for social change and the ability of ordinary people to shake the foundations of the system in power when they organize collectively. Students should examine the brutal institutional responses to peasant protests and why demands for political reform are often expressed in religious terms as they were in 17th-century Europe and as they are in Islamic movements in the 21st century. To facilitate these discussions, Activity 3 has students examine an edited version of the Twelve Articles.

When global history teachers teach about the French Revolution and the anti-colonial wars in British and Spanish America at the end of the 18th and the beginning of the 19th centuries they rarely spend much, if any, time on Haiti. The standard strategy is to present the United States and France as revolutions built on Enlightenment ideals, although France takes a wrong turn with the "Reign of Terror" and Napoleon's ascendancy. Students are encouraged to compare these developments with the Latin American wars for independence led by Bolivar and San Martin, but these are not presented as part of the main historical narrative.

Michael Pezone (2002) has three goals when teaching about a complex series of events like the French Revolution: to "reduce" difficult history to a few fundamental themes and concepts; to help students become actively engaged in learning; and to promote public-speaking and literacy skills. He created a play that presents several important issues, including the causes of revolution, conflict between social classes, and political violence. The performance involves all students, who find it both enjoyable and informative. The project culminates in a cooperative learning activity, in which groups of students rewrite the play in their own language, and then perform the new plays. Activity 4 is one scene from the play.

There are a number of reasons that Haiti receives little attention in the traditional global history curriculum. I argue that not only should students study the Haitian Revolution, but as an exercise in historiography (the study of how history is written and what gets included), they need to discuss why Haiti has frequently been ignored.

Until the 1930s and the work of C. L. R. James, a Trinidadian journalist living in England, little attention was paid to the Haitian Revolution by European and North American historians. James (1963) argued that the Haitian Revolution was actually a seminal event in global history because the Haitians, under the leadership of Toussaint L'Ouverture, were able to defeat French, Spanish, and British forces, including the army of Napoleon and helped to precipitate the end of slavery in the Americas (Activity 5). They demonstrated that Africans were as intellectually and physically capable as Europeans and that they could be just as brutal and amoral in warfare.

However, because James was Caribbean; lacked prestigious academic credentials; identified as a Marxist; was an active member of a political faction allied with the supporters of Leon Trotsky; and probably because of racism as well, his work received little recognition from mainstream historians. Haiti also received little attention because while an independent United States gradually emerged as a world power and France continued as an important historical actor, Haiti after independence remained isolated, agricultural, and impoverished. A last reason is that the United States and the European nations wanted to minimize the significance of the Haitian Revolution, initially because they were concerned about the spread of slave rebellions, and later because they were engaged in other wars suppressing independence movements. One of the few academic websites with a great deal of information on the Haitian Revolution is http://www.webster.edu/~corbetre/haiti/history/revolution/revolution.htm (accessed May 20, 2010).

From 1750 on, technological change increased at an accelerating pace. An excellent website for units on technology and on industrialization is Spartacus Educational (http://www. spartacus.schoolnet.co.uk/IndustrialRevolution.htm, accessed December 13, 2009). It is both an encyclopedia and a collection of primary source documents. Topics within the section on the Industrial Revolution in England include the pre-industrial domestic system, the development of the textile industry, inventors and inventions, factory conditions, biographies of textile entrepreneurs and factory workers, debates over child labor, and the development of the railroad. Because of the quality and reliability of its information, it is an excellent site for an independent online student webquest (Activity 6). One activity on the site assigns each student in a class a specific person. They must discover details about the life of their character and their views on child labor. They then write a brief biography and prepare a speech for a parliamentary debate over legislation making it illegal for children under the age of 12 to work in textile factories (http://www.spartacus.schoolnet.co.uk/Twork.htm, accessed December 13, 2009).

I was fortunate to work with a number of outstanding scholars and teachers developing a curriculum guide for New York State on the causes, impact, and results of the Great Irish Famine (1845–1852). The entire curriculum guide is available online at http://www.emsc.nysed.gov/ciai/gt/gif/curriculum.html (accessed December 16, 2009).

We developed the curriculum to answer a series of questions, including: What was Ireland like before the famine? Was the Great Irish Famine an act of nature? How did the Great Irish Famine change Ireland and the world? What is the legacy of the Great Irish Famine?

The curriculum is very much organized to promote a social studies approach to global history. One of its primary goals is to promote access to plentiful and nutritious food as a fundamental human right. Throughout the curriculum students are asked to compare events in Ireland to events taking place in other countries in other eras, including 20th-century famines and genocides in Europe, Asia, and Africa. It is a fourth-grade through twelfth-grade curriculum. Younger students often focus on how people lived in Ireland before, during, and after the famine. High school students examine the famine as a product of England's colonial and laissez-faire capitalist government policy. The British often experimented in Ireland with policies they would deploy in other colonies. Students are accustomed to thinking of exploitation in relationship to color or race. One of the striking things in this case is that both the British and the Irish are European and White. Activity 7, which is based on a similar activity in the curriculum guide, asks students to discuss whether the Great Irish Famine was an act of nature or of man, and if it was an act of man, did it constitute genocide?

The United States has been at war in Afghanistan since 2001. In 2009 President Barack Obama announced an escalation in U.S. troops and at least another 3 years of involvement. In its November/December 2009 issue of *Social Education*, the National Council for the Social Studies published an excellent article with lesson ideas preparing students to debate continued U.S. military operations in Afghanistan. Council members can download the article, lesson ideas, and activity sheets at http://www.socialstudies.org.

Bayard Faithfull, the author of "Lesson Plan on Afghanistan," reported that at Beacon High School in New York City they used a two-week in-depth examination of policy alternatives in Afghanistan to introduce students to a range of social studies themes, including the impact of geography and technology on history, culture and cultural diversity, and the impact of the past on the present. The project promotes written, oral, and technological literacies, the mastery of map-reading skills, and involves students in document-based research and the work of the historian as they prepare their own policy statements for discussion.

The current international debate over Afghanistan, whether it can be conquered, pacified, democratized, neutralized, or even unified under its own government, and the need to know more about this region of the world, suggests that we examine its history at different points in the curriculum calendar. Logical places would be: (1) Afghanistan as an invasion route into the Indian subcontinent by the forces of Alexander the Great (c. 330 BC) and repeatedly through the Khyber Pass by warriors from the Asian steppe; (2) the role of the Silk Road as a trade network connecting east and southwestern Asia; (3) British imperial policy during the 19th century; and (4) the war in Afghanistan that helped undermine the Soviet Union and precipitated its collapse and the end of the Cold War at the end of the 20th century. Significantly, in each case Afghanistan was more important as a route to somewhere else than it was for itself and it was essentially unconquerable.

Activity 8A provides primary source documents for a discussion of the First Anglo–Afghan War (1839–1843). Activity 8B is based on *New York Times* coverage of the Second Afghan War (1878–1880). Activity 8C is an excerpt from a secret U.S.S.R. report prepared prior to sending Soviet troops into Afghanistan in 1979.

The demands for the protection of human rights and for greater democracy were important rallying cries in the 20th century, although as we saw with the Twelve Articles of the Black Forest, they have been raised in the past as well. "Charter 08" is a manifesto signed by thousands of Chinese intellectuals and human rights activists to promote political reform and democratization in the People's Republic of China. It was published in December 2008, the 60th anniversary of the Universal Declaration of Human Rights. It argues that the "New China" established in 1949 is a "people's republic" in name only because it is under the control of a ruling power that monopolizes all political, economic, and social resources. The signers want a Chinese government based on the principles of Freedom, Human Rights, Equality, Democracy, and Constitutionalism. The document (Activity 9) presents seventeen steps to achieve this goal including the election of public officials, separation of powers within the government, and freedom of association, assembly, expression, and religion. Liu Xiaobo, who was awarded the 2010 Nobel Peace Prize, is one of China's best-known dissidents. He is the principal author of Charter 08 and has been arrested a number of times for pro-democracy activities. In 2009, he was sentenced to 11 years in prison for writing and disseminating the manifesto. The entire document is available online at http://www.hrichina.org (accessed December 12, 2009).

The spread of the McDonald's restaurant franchise around the world (Activity 10) has been proposed as a measure of globalization. The first McDonald's opened in San Bernardino, California in 1940. The first Asian outlet opened in Tokyo, Japan in 1971. In 2009, India and Pakistan each had only twenty-five McDonald's restaurants. Belarus had only one. The only McDonald's in Bolivia closed in 2002. As of this writing, there is still no McDonald's in Afghanistan.

In 2009, there were nineteen countries with at least two hundred McDonald's restaurants. Thomas Friedman in *The Lexus and the Olive Tree* (1999) claimed, "No two countries that both had McDonald's had fought a war against each other since each got its McDonald's" (195). Unfortunately, the statement is not true.

Useful websites for finding or creating lessons about contemporary issues include http://www.lifeaftertheoilcrash.net (accessed May 19, 2010) for information about the world's dependence; http://www.sociology.emory.edu/globalization/debates.html (accessed May 19, 2010), a site that engages students in the current debate over the impact of globalization on developed and developing nations; and Teachable Moment: A project of the Morningside Center for Teaching Social Responsibility (http://www.teachablemoment.org, accessed May 19, 2010), which provides teachers with a large selection of lesson plans and primary source documents.

Activity 1. Columbian Exchange

Instructions: Select which Columbian Exchange crop you believe had the greatest impact on world history. Be prepared to defend your claims in the course of class discussion.

The Columbian Exchange Crops

Columbian Exchange crop	Area of origin	Original use and short-term impact	Current use and long-term impact
Maize (Corn)	Mexico	food for people and animals	corn syrup sweetener, animal feed, food for people, and bio-fuel
Cotton	Mexico, Andes, West Africa, India	clothing	clothing
Potatoes	Andes	food for people and animals	food for people and animals

Columbian Exchange crop	Area of origin	Original use and short-term impact	Current use and long-term impact
Tobacco	Americas	hallucinogenic, stimulant, hunger suppressant, nasal desensitizer	stimulant, hunger suppressant, nasal desensitizer
Sugar cane	Southeast Asia	sweetener, liquor	sweetener, liquor, bio-fuel

After reviewing the chart, students assign a value of importance to each product on a scale of 1–5, with 5 being the highest, for each century. Below is a sample chart that we then translated into a line graph.

Sample Chart Showing Value of Importance for Each Century

Century	Cotton	Potato	Maize/corn	Tobacco	Sugar cane
1600–1700	1	2	3	4	5
1700–1800	3	4	2	1	5
1800–1900	5	3	4	1	2
1900–2000	3	2	5	1	4

Sugar cane started as the highest valued product according to students, declined in importance in the 19th century, and then increased in importance in the late 20th century because of its use in the manufacture of ethanol. Maize also increased in importance during the 20th century because of its use as animal feed, a sweetener, and in the manufacture of ethanol.

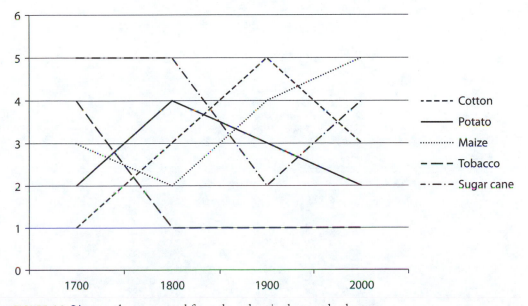

FIGURE 6.1 Line graph constructed from the values in the sample chart.

PART II

Debating Global History

7

THE GRAND NARRATIVE OF
WESTERN CIVILIZATION

This chapter critiques the "grand narrative" of Western civilization that places the start of
civilization in ancient Greece and argues for its continuous development from that point to
the present. An earlier version of this chapter appeared as "Are We Teaching 'Greek Myths'
In The Global History Curriculum?" in *Social Science Docket, 2* (1), Winter/Spring 2002.

In March 2001, *The New York Times* (Broad, 2001: F1) reported that a submerged robot, searching
the bottom of the Mediterranean Sea off of the island of Cyprus, found the remains of an ancient
Greek vessel. The research team identified it as a Hellenistic trader carrying a shipment of wine
between Rhodes and Alexandria. They estimated that it sank 2,300 years ago in the era of Alexander
the Great.

The discovery supports the idea that in the ancient world the Mediterranean Sea was a giant
highway for transporting products, peoples, and cultures from one site to another. This assisted the
process of cultural diffusion and contributed to the growth of early empires. In *The Odyssey*, Homer
claimed that the Greek hero Odysseus sailed a similar route from Crete to North Africa. That
voyage would have taken place about 1300 BC. The Greeks were not the only prolific sailors of
this era. During the thousand-year period before the consolidation of the Mediterranean world
under Roman rule, the Phoenicians regularly sailed between the Middle East and Carthage in
present-day Tunisia, and as far as Spain.

This find is of historical significance because the isle of Rhodes is about 200 miles north of the
wreck, near the coast of present-day Turkey. Alexandria, Egypt is 200 miles south in North Africa.
The trip necessitated navigating across open water away from the sight of land.

The research team is continuing to search the region, hoping to uncover a Minoan shipwreck.
The Minoans were seafarers who ruled an empire in the eastern Mediterranean and Aegean Seas
from the island of Crete between 2500 and 1200 BC. This period is known as the Bronze Age in
the Mediterranean region because bronze, an alloy of copper and tin, was the primary metal used
to make tools and weapons. No Minoan ship from this period has ever been found.

The subheading of *The New York Times* article was "Accidental Find Lends New Credence to
Greek Tales of Sailing Feats." This statement is the crux of the issue that I address in this chapter.

Do social studies teachers present a distorted view of the past when our starting point is Greek accomplishments? If the Mediterranean was truly a highway in this period, then the likelihood is that it was dominated by the era's military, economic, and cultural superpowers, Egypt on the Nile River and Sumer or Babylon in Mesopotamia (the Fertile Crescent). Greece, at best, would have been a peripheral trading partner. If Greece was at the margins and Egypt and Mesopotamia were at the center of cultural and technological advancement in this period, social studies teachers may be presenting "Greek myth" as history when they attribute the origin of "Western Civilization" to ancient Greece.

The Nile and Fertile Crescent

The significance of the Nile and Fertile Crescent civilizations in early human cultural development and the power of cultural diffusion are well established. To cite an example, Jared Diamond in *Guns, Germs, and Steel* (1997) shows that agricultural and animal husbandry emerged in the Fertile Crescent, and spread to the Nile River Valley, over 10,000 years ago (8500 BC). Eventually this "food package," and a sedentary way of life based on it, spread throughout the Mediterranean world. Diamond traces a similar route for the spread of writing systems. Starting about 5,000 years ago (3200 BC), they developed in Mesopotamia and Egypt (later, but independently, in China, 1300 BC and in Meso-America, 600 BC), and diffused across the region. Other cultural developments in the ancient Mediterranean world followed a similar pattern of dispersion. Pottery first appeared in the Nile Valley and Mesopotamia about 7000 BC; metallurgy about 4000 BC; formal governments about 3700 BC; and iron tools about 900 BC. Since the historical record makes it virtually impossible to decide whether a development first emerged in Egypt or Mesopotamia, they are considered as a single point of origin.

Given the early achievements of Mesopotamia and Egypt, why the unbalanced focus on ancient Greece in history textbooks and social studies classrooms? There are three general answers to this question. The first is that historians and teachers often focus on ancient Greece because they perceive Greek civilization as fundamentally different from the civilizations that preceded it or existed at the same time, as somehow more "Western," and they believe these differences produced the modern world as we know it.

Historian Peter Burke (1998) calls this view the "'Grand Narrative' of the rise of Western Civilization: a triumphalist account of Western achievement from the Greeks onwards in which the Renaissance is a link in the chain which includes the Reformation, the Scientific Revolution, the Enlightenment, the Industrial Revolution, and so on" (2). Within this framework, Houghton Mifflin's high school text, *History of the world* (Perry et al., 1990), stated, "The earliest civilizations that grew up on the Greek islands developed a unique culture. Although these people were conquered by foreign invaders, many of their traditions endured. Greek ideas would come to have a powerful influence on the politics, thought, and art of Europe and the Western Hemisphere. For this reason, Greece is known as the 'cradle of Western civilization'" (71).

In a more recent secondary school global history textbook published by Bedford St. Martin's, *A history of world societies, 8th edition* (McKay et al., 2009), the authors argue, "The people of ancient Greece developed a culture that fundamentally shaped the civilization of the western part of Eurasia much as the Chinese did for the eastern part. The Greeks were the first in the Mediterranean and neighboring areas to explore most of the questions that still concern thinkers today" (77). While the second statement makes more limited claims for the contributions of ancient Greece, it still places Greece at the center of future developments in the West.

Can We Document Continuity?

Diane Ravitch and Abigal Thernstrom (1992) edited a collection called *The democracy reader* that includes classic and modern speeches, essays, poems, declarations and documents on freedom and human rights. In this book, Ravitch and Thernstrom support a thesis championed by Harvard sociologist Orlando Patterson (1991), who argues that we can trace the history of democratic ideals as an essential component of Western philosophy from ancient Greece to the modern world. But an examination of the table of contents raises an interesting problem. The book contains no documents for the 1500-year period between Aristotle's *The Politics* (written c. 320 BC) and Thomas Aquinas' *Summa Theologia* (written c. 1250 AD). Even if the ancient Greek city-states possessed a system with recognizably democratic elements, it is exceedingly difficult to establish a direct political or intellectual connection between societies separated by over 1,500 years of history. In fact, Greek texts were largely unknown in Europe prior to the Crusades, and only survived because they were preserved by Arab scholars.

Myth of continuity?

A second explanation for the unbalanced focus on ancient Greece is that modern societies can see themselves in their art, literature, philosophy, and ideologies. Classical Greek sculpture appears realistic rather than symbolic or exotic. Socrates and Plato, as presented in the textbooks, sound as if they could be giving interviews on C–SPAN. Athens seems the model for democratic society, while martial Sparta reminds some of 20th-century totalitarian societies or *Star Trek*'s Klingon Empire. Even their Gods, with soap opera-like battles and love affairs, remind us of our own passions and conflicts.

But are we reading more into their culture and history than can actually be supported by the historical record? Are we seeing what is there, or what we want to see? Let me offer two examples that illustrate what I mean. The first is an example of seeing what is not there – an ancient philosopher championing modern democratic values. The second is an example of ignoring what is clearly there – a different attitude toward sexual mores.

The popular conception is that Socrates was a Greek philosopher and teacher persecuted, and then executed, by an authoritarian government for questioning leaders and pursuing the search for truth. Unfortunately, the historical record is not so clear-cut. In *The trial of Socrates* (1988), I. F. Stone concluded that Socrates was actually involved in an attempt by the oligarchy to undermine efforts to broaden representation in Athenian government.

A second issue, rarely addressed because of our culture's homophobia, is the Greek attitude toward same-sex sexual relationships. According to M. I. Finley (1963: 123–125), Aristotle believed that true friendship was only possible between intellectual and social equals, hence impossible between men and women. Bisexuality was common, especially among the upper class, where men and women were expected to seek both physical and spiritual companionship from people of the same gender. Sexual relations between adult men and younger boys were a feature of military elites in Sparta and Thebes and among the nobility in Athens. This aspect of ancient Greek culture is missing from the high school textbooks I am familiar with.

Celebrating Greek Democracy

Probably the most comprehensive effort to read the present into the past is the celebration of Greek "democracy." According to Houghton Mifflin's *History of the world*, "Democracy, which had been developing in Athens over many years, reached its peak under the leadership of Pericles. He opened all political offices to any citizen. He paid jurors so that poor citizens as well as the wealthy could serve. Athens had a direct democracy – that is, all citizens had the right to attend the Assembly and cast a vote." In the next paragraph, however, we learn that "Athenian democracy was far from complete. Citizens had time for public service largely because they owned slaves . . . Most residents of Athens were not citizens and had no say in government . . . Women, too, had no political rights" (86–87).

In fact, during the era of Pericles, the population of Athens was about 450,000 people, and less than 10% were adult male citizens with the power to vote. About 18% of the population was foreign-born with no legal rights, and 55% of the residents of Athens were enslaved (Linder, 1979: 95). Athenian "democracy" was so restricted in scope and in time (the age of Pericles lasted for 32 years) that students should consider whether Athens should legitimately be labeled democratic at all.

Eurocentrism?

A third explanation for the focus on ancient Greece as the source of Western Civilization is Eurocentrism – the effort to center history on European societies and to minimize the contributions of non-European "others." For example, the debate over the relationship between Egypt, Mesopotamia, and Greece in the ancient world is highly charged. Claims by Afrocentric authors that Egypt was the source of Greek civilization, that ancient Egyptians were "Black Africans," and that this history has been hidden by mainstream "White" institutions in order to strip people of African ancestry of their proper place in history, have been challenged by essays in most of the major historical and archeological journals (Lefkowitz, 1992: 440–460; Pounder, 1992: 461–464; Lefkowitz and Rogers, 1996).

I want to sidestep the debate over whether ancient Egyptians were "Black Africans" because I believe it takes us away from the more important issue of Egyptian influence on Greek culture and development. We may never know for certain the skin color or genetic heritage of ancient Egyptians. Their art is largely symbolic and I suspect the colors used to portray people were selected from pigments available to artists, not because of the skin color of subjects. Most likely, since ancient Egypt was a crossroads civilization, it was a genetically and culturally blended society with diverse people who probably did not place the same significance on race as we do in the United States today.

Much of the debate over the relationship between Egypt, Mesopotamia and Greece is in response to the work of Martin Bernal (1987, 1991, 2001, 2006), who published a three-volume collection called *Black Athena: The Afroasiatic roots of classical civilization*. Bernal marshaled extensive evidence to present a detailed case for Egyptian and Semitic (Middle Eastern) contributions to Greek culture during the Bronze Age (prior to 1100 BC) based on an examination of religion, art, mythology, language, and artifacts. Among other things, he provides powerful arguments for the origins of the Hercules legend and the Sphinx in ancient Egypt.

The ancient world is not my area of expertise as either a teacher or historian, so I cannot evaluate Bernal's documentation. What I find most interesting are the concessions made by his opponents. Among his more vocal critics, Molly Myerwitz Lefkowitz (1992; Lefkowitz and Rogers, 1996) accepted some of Bernal's claims about Bronze Age influence, but argued that they were not at the core of what we identify as classical Greece – its art, politics, and philosophy.

Contributions of Ancient Egypt

In an essay titled "Did Egypt shape the glory that was Greece?" John Coleman, a classicist from Cornell University, presents an alternative historical scenario to Bernal's and concludes that "recognizing that Greek civilization was influenced from abroad and made use of previous advances in mathematics and science . . . is a far cry from asserting that it had 'Afroasiatic roots'" (Coleman,

1996: 281). Coleman claims that all scholars recognize the contributions of Egypt and the Middle East to the ancient Greek world, especially to Minoan or Cretan civilization, and argues that the dispute with Bernal is primarily a matter of degree.

According to Coleman's narrative, cultural contact between the Aegean and Egypt started in the early Bronze Age, around 2100 BC, as a result of migration and trade. Crete needed to import tin, a major ingredient in the manufacture of bronze, which was lacking in the Aegean world. The widespread diffusion of pottery from 2100 to 1725 BC shows increasing contacts between Greece and Egypt. During this period, Minoan culture, which was shaped by its contacts with Egypt, exerted a powerful influence over the developing mainland Greek societies. Later, with the decline of Crete, Mycenaeans (mainland Greek societies) took over the trade connections with Egypt.

We know less about Greece between 1100 and 750 BC, but after 750 BC Greek soldiers were used as mercenaries in Egypt and, according to Coleman, there is a "flood of influence on all Greek arts and crafts from Egypt" (296). These conclusions are supported by an exhibit I visited, "Crete–Egypt: Three Millennia of Cultural Interactions" at the Heraklion Archaeological Museum in Crete. It contains 527 artifacts that demonstrate interaction between the two Mediterranean peoples. Some of the exhibit can be viewed at the museum's website (http://www.cretefinder.gr/english/iraklio/hermuseum.htm, accessed March 28, 2010).

I find Coleman's statement balanced and reasonable, and believe it establishes a significant relationship that was ignored before the Bernal work. It is in sharp contrast to what is usually taught in secondary schools. Houghton Mifflin's *History of the world* section on Minoan civilization reports that they were "seafaring traders, exporting wine, honey, and olive oil to Egypt, Asia Minor, Syria and Greece" (71), but ignores any Egyptian influence over Crete or Greece. After the collapse of Crete, Egypt plays no further role in Greek history until it is conquered by Alexander the Great. The chapter on ancient Egypt (34–42) recognizes that Egypt traded with other civilizations in the Mediterranean region including Crete, but does not identify the Greek world or discuss any cultural exchange between the two civilizations.

In this case, the Bedford/St. Martin's *A history of world societies* does an even poorer job. Egypt is covered in five pages in an umbrella chapter on "Early Civilization in Afroeurasaia, to 450 BCE" and is briefly mentioned as a trading partner with the Minoans (78) in a much more extensive chapter on "The Greek experience" (76–101). McDougal Littell's *World history, patterns of interaction* (Beck et al., 2005), another widely used secondary school global history textbook, hardly does any better. It has two chapters on ancient Egypt, "Pyramids on the Nile" (35–43) and "the Egyptian and Nubian Empires" (89–94), but neither chapter mentions broader Egyptian influence over the Mediterranean or Greek worlds. While Egypt gets a combined 13 pages, "Classical Greece" is covered in five chapters and 31 pages. Egypt is mentioned twice in these chapters, when it is discovered by Mycenaean traders sailing the eastern Mediterranean and when it is conquered by the armies of Alexander the Great. Its influence on Greece and Western Civilization is completely ignored.

The spread of Greek culture through Alexander's conquest of the Mediterranean world, known as Hellenization, is presented in the Houghton Mifflin, Bedford/St. Martin's, and McDougal Littell texts as a major accomplishment of ancient Greece that stimulated trade, science, philosophy, and cultural diffusion. The Bedford/St. Martin's text points out that the Greeks did learn from the "more sophisticated" cultures that they encountered (90).

But should conquest and forced assimilation into the Greek world be presented uncritically? Would similar conquests and assimilations be viewed that way if they took place today? The much celebrated Hebrew revolt under the Maccabees (the story of Hanukah) about 170 BC was a response to efforts by Greek rulers to enforce Greek culture, law, and religion in ancient Israel (Johnson, 1987: 102–107).

Rome and Christianity

From Greece, Western Civilization marched on to Rome and then directly to the modern world, at least according to the textbooks. McDougal Littell opens the chapter on the Roman Republic with a picture of the Roman Senate showing Cicero, "one of ancient Rome's greatest public speakers" as he addresses fellow members of the Roman Senate, who are seated in a semicircle on wooden benches and wearing long white togas (154). The problem with this very dramatic scene is that the image is a painting by an Italian artist who lived 19 centuries after Cicero. The painting is fanciful and historically inaccurate. The Roman Senate did not meet in the building where the scene places it and Cicero, who was in his early forties when the events depicted in the picture occurred, is portrayed as a wise old man.

For our purpose, the crucial chapter in the McDougal Littell text is the fifth, or last, chapter on Rome – "Rome and the roots of Western Civilization" (178–185). In this chapter students learn that Rome borrowed and adapted culture from Greece; however, the "Romans created a great civilization in their own right, whose art and architecture, language and literature, engineering, and law became its legacy to the world" (178). Over and over again the chapter explains that Rome inherited something from the Greeks, but they adapted and created rather than copied. It is this Greco-Roman culture that the text defines as classical civilization.

A full-page student activity sheet in this chapter titled "Analyzing Key Concepts" defines Western Civilization as the heritage of ideas that spread to Europe and America from ancient Greece and Rome (180) and provides a timeline that purports to show the direct connections. According to McDougal Littell, in 509 BC, "Rome developed a form of representative government" and in the 5th century BC "Greece implemented a direct democracy." Two thousand years later in the 17th century AD, "England became a constitutional monarchy" and in 1776 AD, "The United States declared independence from England and began building the republican democracy we know today."

Similarly, philosophy leaped from Aristotle (4th century BC) to Thomas Aquinas (13th century AD) to Immanuel Kant in 1781 AD, while literature jumped from Homer (9th century BC) to Virgil (70–19 BC) to James Joyce (1922 AD) to the Coen brothers movie *O Brother, Where Art Thou?* (2000 AD). In a box below the timeline labeled "Connect to Today," students are asked to hypothesize why "ancient Greek and Roman culture have had such a lasting influence on Western civilization" and to provide other examples of their culture evident in the modern world.

Once everything is summarized so clearly, what else is there to learn? You wonder why the textbook goes on for another thousand pages.

Rome did leave a lasting legacy. However, I do not believe it is their architecture and engineering which largely crumbled, their art and philosophy, or even their forms of government that disappeared and had to be discovered fresh by new people in different eras. Today, more than 800 million people are native speakers of Romance languages that evolved from Latin. But probably the most important legacy of Rome is the Roman Catholic Church; with over a billion members, and despite the twists and turns of history, it maintains an institutional connection with the ancient world. This connection is minimized in the text, probably because during the past 2,000 years the Church has often represented autocracy (papal infallibility), dogmatism (heresy and interdict), mysticism (miracles and relics), fanaticism (crusades and inquisitions), and bigotry (treatment of the Jews and women and support for slavery), which are not the qualities of Greece, Rome, and Western Civilization that the textbooks are promoting.

Henri Pirenne (1937) was one of the most prominent historians in the 20th century to write about the European Middle Ages and the transformation of Europe into a more modern society. Although he generally identified with what I have described as the "grand narrative," his work also suggests some of the problems with this conception of history. Pirenne believed that the "barbarian kingdoms, founded in the 5th century on the soil of Western Europe, still preserved the most striking and essential characteristics of ancient civilization, to wit, its Mediterranean character" (1). He argued they maintained an economic life that was "simply a continuation of that of the ancient world" (2). However, Pirenne also believed that the growth of Islam after the 7th century undermined these economic relationships by closing Christian Europe out of the Mediterranean trade, altering the course of European history. The second great discontinuity was the Crusades at the end of the 11th century, which again opened the Mediterranean Sea to European merchants. As a result, mercantile wealth began to replace land-based wealth as a source of power and influence in European society, and laws that had restricted trade and finance began to be rewritten. Things changed a third time in the 14th century because of the Black Plague and internecine religious wars, disasters that while they initially stifled economic growth, also created space for innovation. While Pirenne's work largely focused on what he saw as the internal dynamic of European development, the growth of towns, fairs, trade networks, and supportive institutions, he recognized that these changes were often in response to outside forces.

European Renaissance and Enlightenment

The celebration of the roles of ancient Greece and Rome within the "grand narrative" of the Western world is reinforced in standard interpretations of the European Renaissance presented in high school global history classes, which define the era as a rebirth of classical Greek and Roman civilization (Thompson, 1996). According to Burke (1998), "the major innovators of the Renaissance presented – and often perceived – their inventions and discoveries as a return to ancient traditions after the long parenthesis of what they were the first to call the 'Middle' Ages" (2).

Houghton Mifflin's text credits Italian humanists, especially Petrarch of Florence, with reading ancient texts and "rediscovering knowledge that had been lost or forgotten" (327). Francesco Petrarch (1304–1374 AD) was a Florentine poet, essayist, and correspondent who, during travels across Western Europe, collected ancient documents. He believed that he and his compatriots had rediscovered the knowledge of the Roman world and disparaged medieval Europe as the "dark ages." Petrarch is frequently quoted as writing, "Each famous author of antiquity whom I recover places a new offence and another cause of dishonor to the charge of earlier generations, who, not satisfied with their own disgraceful barrenness, permitted the fruit of other minds, and the writings that their ancestors had produced by toil and application, to perish through insufferable neglect. Although they had nothing of their own to hand down to those who were to come after, they robbed posterity of its ancestral heritage" (http://www.mlahanas.de/Greeks/LX/Petrarch.html, accessed April 17, 2010).

But even if Renaissance innovators believed that social change was a result of the rediscovery of ancient traditions, it does not mean that it actually happened that way. In *Worldly goods: A new history of the Renaissance* (1996: 12), Lisa Jardine presents a very different materialist interpretation of the period. She argues that the celebrated culture of the European Renaissance was the result of a "competitive urge to acquire" stimulated by the growth of trade, cities and a new affluent, secular, elite. She believes that Early Renaissance works of art which we admire today "for their sheer representational virtuosity were part of a vigorously developing world market in luxury commodities" (19).

If Jardine is correct that economic development was the primary cause of the European Renaissance, and I believe she is, then trade, war, and cultural interaction between medieval Europe, the Islamic world, Africa, and China play a much greater role in the emergence of the modern era than do ancient Greco-Roman civilizations. For example, Fernand Braudel (1992: 115), in his epic histories of the Mediterranean world, suggests that Islamic and Jewish merchants in the eastern Mediterranean had pioneered many of the economic innovations that would become the basis for commercial capitalism. He also details the way that prior to the Columbian Exchange and the infusion of wealth from the Americas, Sub-Saharan gold from the Sudan, and West African kingdoms such as Mali, provided the Mediterranean world and the rest of Europe with the specie needed to facilitate internal commerce and trade with East Asia (1966: 466–467).

To help students understand the European Renaissance and Jardine's proposition, I focus on the role of the Italian city of Florence as a commercial, banking, political, and artistic center starting with the 11th-century "commercial revolution" in Europe. Visiting this small somewhat isolated city today (pop. 367,589) it is hard to imagine that it was so prominent in the changes taking place in Europe from 1300 to 1500 AD. Even then, its population was only about 60,000. At the time, in China there were cities with over a million people.

While I know it is an exaggeration, I present the case that the Florentines "invented" the European Renaissance as they grappled with building the cathedral of Santa Maria del Fiore. Construction of Il Duomo, as it is commonly known, began in 1296 and was interrupted during the middle of the 14th century by the Bubonic or Black Plague. The cathedral was not completed until 1436 because of difficulty in designing and erecting its large octagonal dome without using an internal wooden frame for support. Il Duomo remains the largest brick dome in the world. Among the apprentices who worked on different aspects of its design and construction was a young Leonardo da Vinci. *Brunellechi's dome* by Ross King (2001) is an excellent popular history of the cathedral and its impact.

Florence's position in the transition from the medieval period to Renaissance was based on its role as a leading producer of wool cloth and as the primary banking center in Western Europe (Goldthwaite, 1982). Its industrial economy (wool was cleaned, finished, dyed, and exported through the Florentine-controlled port at Pisa) gave the city and its elite economic advantages over competing Italian cities.

The Medici Bank of Florence had close ties to the papacy and the Roman Catholic Church and was in a position to provide financial assistance to European monarchs in return for political influence. As Florentine bankers and merchants established branch offices across Europe its currency, the gold florin, emerged as the semi-official currency of European trade, similar to the British pound in the 19th century and the American dollar today. As the city grew wealthier, its leading families, anxious to establish their legitimacy in a world that still honored feudal trappings, became patrons of the arts, sponsoring many of the great artists of the period, and starting the European Renaissance.

The idea that the changes taking place in Italy and Florence represented a Renaissance or rebirth of classical civilization (*rinascita* in Italian) was first put forward by Giorgio Vasari (1511–1574), a painter, architect, and art historian, who was a contemporary and friend of Michelangelo. Vasari, who worked in Florence and Rome under the patronage of the Medici family, was also one of the earliest Italian authors to use the word *concorrenza* or economic competition to explain social development. He believed Florentine artists especially excelled because of fierce competition for commissions.

In *The lives of the artists* (1550), Vasari acknowledged the greatness of Rome, but was critical of the quality of art produced in the ancient world, especially in Greece. He believed Florence and the Italian province of Tuscany had achieved a much higher level of artistic achievement.

Why would this increasingly affluent, secular world claim spiritual and intellectual descent from classical Mediterranean civilizations? The answer, I believe, is related to the power of religious authority in that era. The Roman Catholic Church, threatened by competing religions (Islam, Orthodox, and Christian heresies) and new worldviews, brutally resisted change. In Florence, prominent religious figures initially attacked the study of "pagan authors" as an impediment to salvation and humanists were forced to defend the ancient texts as compatible with church teachings

(Burke, 1998: 31–32). However, in the end, Church and secular authorities preferred to credit Aristotle and Ptolemy with the origin of civilization, rather than acknowledging the role of contemporary Muslims and Jews.

For political thinkers, as well as for artists, framing new ideas and discoveries as a rebirth of knowledge from classical Greco-Roman and biblical eras ensured the survival of both them and their work. Debates over ideas during the European Renaissance were not just intellectual exercises. In the early 13th century, Pope Innocent III launched a Crusade to crush heresy in southern France that resulted in the slaughter of tens of thousands of people, all Christians (O'Shea, 2000). Spain's Roman Catholic monarchs established the Inquisition to uncover non-believers and expelled Jews and Muslims. Under Torquemada, the third Grand Inquisitor, over 2,000 people were burned at the stake for suspicion of rejecting Catholic religious orthodoxy (Thompson, 1996: 509).

Noted Renaissance artists and scholars were not immune from suspicion or attack. In 1516, Leonardo Da Vinci, whose actions and work were frequently impious, and who made no pretense of connection with classical antiquity, fled the Italian peninsula and sought sanctuary from King Francis I of France (Thompson, 1996: 147–158). In 1633, Galileo was tried for heresy by the Holy Office of the Inquisition in Rome for challenging the Ptolemaic system and asserting that the Earth traveled around the sun (Sobel, 1999: 273–278).

Another explanation for claiming that the European Renaissance was a rebirth of classical civilization is simple proximity. Europeans claimed that Greece and Rome were their source of knowledge because ruins of those societies are there and clearly visible. In an interesting parallel, the Navaho of the American Southwest honor local ruins as remnants of their ancestors and roots of their civilization, although the Navaho are relatively recent migrants into the area and the ruins and artifacts were left behind by other unrelated people.

European Enlightenment

During the European Enlightenment in the 17th and 18th centuries, there was a similar revival of interest in Greco-Roman civilization. Again, to establish their credibility, thinkers attributed what were essentially new ideas to the ancient Mediterranean world. For example, Baron de Montesquieu (1689—1755) of France, whose best-known work is *The spirit of the laws* (Cohler, Miller, and Stone, 1989), attributed his ideas on the need to balance conflicting forces in government and society as a protection for liberty with his understanding of ancient Roman government and his interpretation of the English Constitution. Many of Montesquieu's ideas were later incorporated into the United States Constitution when it was written in 1787.

In the United States, whose official history as a nation does not begin until 1789, the "grand narrative" has become especially entrenched. Prominent founders, including George Washington and Thomas Jefferson, were enamored with the Greco-Roman world, albeit based on very limited historical knowledge. In his correspondence, Jefferson referred to Greece as the first civilized nation and claimed,

> The Greeks and Romans have left us the present models which exist of fine composition, whether we examine them as works of reason, or of style and fancy . . . that to read the Latin and Greek authors in their original is a sublime luxury; and I deem luxury in science to be at least as justifiable as in architecture, painting, gardening, or the other arts.
>
> (Bergh, 1907: 146–147)

Washington was compared to the Roman General Cincinnatus when he said farewell to his troops at the end of the American Revolution to return to his life as a simple farmer, which he never had been before and never would be. The United States Capitol building was intended to reflect the design of the Parthenon in Athens, and according to the White House Museum website, the White House is supposed to "echo classical Greek Ionic architecture" (http://whitehousemuseum, accessed April 18, 2010). To commemorate the centennial of George Washington's birth, Congress commissioned a statue for the Capitol Rotunda. Now exhibited in the Smithsonian, the statue depicts Washington as Zeus-like and wearing a toga. There are also a number of busts of Washington from this era where he appears to be wearing Roman garb. Michael Pezone, a high school social studies teacher who made a number of contributions to this book, argues somewhat sarcastically that the founders of the United States identified with ancient Greece and Rome because all three societies combined a pretense of democratic institutions with slavery.

Where does this leave social studies teachers? We need to re-conceptualize both the "grand narrative" of Western Civilization presented in global history and the way we teach social studies. Instead of presenting the past as a series of facts and truths to be memorized and celebrated, teachers should engage students in a critical examination of different explanations of the past and present. The global history curriculum can be organized so that students explore essential historical questions (Wiggins and McTighe, 1998: 28–32; Singer, 1999: 28–31), including: What were the origins of Western Civilization? Was there only one origin? Was Athens or any ancient society democratic? Does conquest make a leader (Alexander) great? What are the costs of cultural diffusion and assimilation? How does democracy emerge? How do societies change? Why do societies accept and promote myths about their past?

TEACHING IDEAS

Activities 1 and 2 are general activities that involve students in examining the ancient Mediterranean world and whether Greece and Rome represent the start of Western Civilization. In Activity 1, students are presented with a timeline of the ancient Mediterranean world that largely predates Greece and Rome. They are asked to identify the three developments they feel had the greatest impact on the ancient Mediterranean world and to explain their selections. Activity 2 is a webquest that has students evaluate the proposition that Greece and Rome are "the cradles of Western Civilization."

Activities 3–10 are available online at http://people.hofstra.edu/alan_j_singer. Activities 3, 4, and 5 specifically look at ancient Greek and Roman society. Activity 3 provides students with a demographic breakdown of Athens during the Age of Pericles and asks students whether a stratified society can be considered democratic. In Activity 4 students read and evaluate a selection from *The Peloponnesian War* by Thucydides where Pericles discusses Athenian government. In Activity 5, Cicero explains the principles underlying the Roman republic.

The trial of Joan of Arc (Activity 6) challenges simplistic notions of progressive rationalism in European society. In France, the Maid of Orleans is condemned by the Roman Catholic Church and burned at the stake for heresy and witchcraft at the same time that European Renaissance arts and ideas are starting to flourish in Italy.

Activities 7 and 8 provide different perspectives on the origin of the European Renaissance. Activity 7 traces Renaissance-style scientific innovations to the Islamic world. In Activity 8, Giorgio Vasari (1511–1574), a contemporary and friend of Michelangelo, describes changes in the arts taking place in Italy during this period. In Activities 9 and 10 students examine the philosophical debates and contributions of the European Enlightenment through the works of Thomas Hobbes, John Locke, and Montesquieu.

Activity 1. Timeline of the Ancient Mediterranean World, 5000 BC–500 BC

Source: Grun, B., ed. (1975). *The timetables of history*. New York: Simon & Schuster, 2–10.

Instructions: Examine the chart below. Identify three developments that you feel had the greatest impact on the ancient Mediterranean world and explain your selections. Greece and Rome are often called "the cradles of Western Civilization." Evaluate that statement based on the information in this chart.

The Ancient Mediterranean World

Years	Events
5000–4000 BC	Egyptians develop 360-day calendar; earliest Mesopotamian cities.
4000–3500 BC	Sumerians settle on the site of the future city of Babylon and develop writing on clay tablets; Copper, silver and gold work by Egyptians and Sumerians; Ships sail Mediterranean.
3500–3000 BC	1st and 2nd dynasties unify Egypt; Egypt develops numerals, plowing, and fertilizing of fields; Sumerian cuneiform evolves; Sumer develops wheeled vehicle.
3000–2500 BC	Pyramids and the Great Sphinx built in Egypt; Sumerians develop metal coins; Systematic astronomical observations recorded in Egypt and Babylonia; Initial settlement of Crete.
2500–2000 BC	Pharaohs rule Egyptian empire; Egypt develops philosophy and the first libraries, discovers use of papyrus; Earliest Egyptian mummies.
2000–1500 BC	Egypt controls Crete and the Aegean Islands, develops symbolic alphabet; Hammurabi reunites Babylon and develops legal code; Palace of Minos is built on Crete; Greeks migrate from Caspian Sea region to eastern Mediterranean.
1500–1000 BC	Beginning of the Iron Age; Egyptian empire extends to the Euphrates; Destruction of Troy; First Greek alphabet.
1000–500 BC	Persian empire defeats Egypt, dominates the Middle East; Greek city-states periodically unified by Athens or Sparta; Spread of Greek settlement and culture across the Mediterranean; Initial settlement at Rome.

Activity 2. Webquest: Ancient Mediterranean History

Task: You have been invited to participate in an historical debate about the origins of "Western Civilization" in the ancient Mediterranean world. A group of historians will be presenting evidence for Egypt, Greece, and Rome as points of origin. You will be assigned to present the case for one of the three, using information from the website http://library.thinkquest.org/10805/index.html (accessed April 19, 2010). Not only should you marshal your evidence, but you should also be prepared to counter the arguments presented by other historians. You should prepare a written statement of approximately 500 words and a PowerPoint presentation with between 10 and 12 slides.

8

IF CHINESE HISTORIANS WROTE THE GLOBAL HISTORY CURRICULUM

In Chapters 4 and 6, I argued that in most cases the standard global history curriculum is the history of Western Europe and British North America (Western Civilization) with tangents. Imagine if the global history curriculum and textbooks were written by Chinese historians who placed China at the center of world events. Their global history would certainly look very different from the traditional global history taught in the United States, with different epochs, heroes, and tragedies, but it would not necessarily be any less, or more, valid. While the content information would definitely be different, teachers could introduce students to the same themes and address the same essential questions. At the end of every chapter in the textbooks focusing on China, there would probably be a section titled "Meanwhile in the Rest of the World."

This is my effort to organize a global history curriculum with areas of study based on the chronology of Chinese history with attention to main ideas and recurring historical themes. Although I present it as an alternative approach that illustrates how much the current curriculum is affected by a Eurocentric bias, it might actually be interesting to teach global history this way.

Until the 20th century, history written in China served the interests of ruling groups. It focused on dynastic politics with one dynasty following another in a "cycle of ascent, achievement, decay, and rebirth under a new family." This focus on dynasties continues to be at the core of most secondary school global history textbook coverage of China. The Library of Congress's online Country Study of China (http://lcweb2.loc.gov/cgi-bin/query/r?frd/cstdy:@field%28DOCID+cn0012%29, accessed March 31, 2010), on the other hand, identifies important themes in Chinese history that illustrate many of the main ideas we want students to understand about global history. They include "the capacity of the Chinese to absorb the people of surrounding areas into their own civilization" through conquest, colonization, and assimilation. It attributes their success to China's written language, the superiority of its technology and political institutions, its "artistic and intellectual creativity," and the "sheer weight of their numbers." Another recurrent theme in the history of China (as well as in the history of the Roman Empire and of pre-Columbian Meso-

American empires) is "the unceasing struggle of the sedentary Chinese against the threat posed to their safety and way of life by non-Chinese peoples on the margins of their territory in the north, northeast, and northwest."

The Chinese placed themselves at the center of the universe, which was reflected in their traditional Chinese name for the country, "Zhonghua" or Middle Kingdom. The Chinese believed they were surrounded by culturally inferior barbarians (as did the ancient Greeks). This China-centered view of the world continued into the 19th century, when China, unable to adjust to changing global circumstances, was "humiliated militarily by superior Western weaponry and technology and faced with imminent territorial dismemberment."

Geography played a major role in the history of China and the development of this worldview. As a result of mountains and deserts, China was relatively isolated from the other Afro-Eurasian river valley civilizations (Egypt, Mesopotamia, and the Indus/Ganges), although trade networks started to be established during the era of the Roman Empire in the Mediterranean world. The mountain and desert barrier also helped China maintain a relatively homogenous and unified society. While there are 56 recognized ethnic groups in China today, the Han is by far the largest and makes up over 90% of the current population. One result of relative isolation is that China has maintained a unique form of logographic or pictographic writing with a separate symbol for each word. This was a unifying influence in the history of China. People who speak different regional dialects that are virtually independent languages can all read the same texts.

Prior to the 18th century, physical China was significantly smaller than the current territory of the People's Republic of China, which includes Tibet, parts of Mongolia, Turkestan, and Manchuria. For most of recorded history, these areas were not inhabited by ethnic Chinese nor were they governed by Chinese rulers.

What we know as civilization and the civilization package (agriculture, permanent settlement, specialization, state formation, organized religion, and literacy) initially developed in China at small settlements in the Yellow and Yangtze river valleys, although there were parallel developments in other parts of the world at about the same time. There is physical evidence of writing on pieces of bone and turtle shell dating back to approximately 1500 BC. Classical Chinese culture emerged during the Zhou Dynasty between 1045 BC and 256 BC. This period produced the great philosophical schools identified with Confucius, Doaism, and Legalism.

Unified imperial government supported by military might and an elaborate bureaucratic system developed around 200 BC and governed China more or less effectively, despite intermittent breakdowns, into the 20th century AD. At the start of this period, the Chinese began construction of the Great Wall of China as a defense against northern invaders. For centuries, Chinese culture, industry, technology, philosophy, and governmental organization was more advanced than the civilization of its neighbors and any other region of the world. Because of these developments, by 1100 the population of China probably exceeded 100 million people, which was more than the population of all of Europe.

By the 19th century, the conquest of the Americas by Western European nations, followed by industrialization and imperialism, created a powerful military and economic rival that was able to dominate, but never conquer China. At the end of the 20th century, a newly unified and invigorated China emerged out of a century of civil war, war against rival regional powers, and competition with the United States, Western Europe, and the Soviet Union (Russia), to once again challenge for global primacy.

The major calendar areas of study (CAS) in this curriculum would be:

CAS I. Beginning of Civilization in China (12000–2000 BC)
CAS II. Chinese River Valley Civilization (2000–1066 BC)

CAS III. Classical Chinese Civilization (1066–221 BC)
CAS IV. Imperial China (221 BC–618 AD)
CAS V. Golden Age I (618–1305)
CAS VI. Golden Age II (1368–1450)
CAS VII. Dark Ages (1450–1911)
CAS VIII. Reemerging World Power (1912–1989)
CAS IX. Chinese Century (1989 to the Present)

In the rest of this chapter I present content and conceptual summaries of the first eight CAS. Too much is happening as I write for me to address the present (and future) in an adequate way. For example, on April 5, 2010, an article in *The New York Times* suggested that a prolonged drought in southern China may have been caused, and certainly was exacerbated, by the overdevelopment of agriculture and industry in the region that has depressed the water table to the lowest level on record (http://www.nytimes.com/2010/04/05/world/asia/05china.html?ref=world, accessed April 5, 2010). Geography, climate, and population pressure may yet prevent China from emerging as the dominant world superpower in the 21st century as many commentators are predicting (http://www.nytimes.com/2004/07/04/magazine/04CHINA.html?ex=1246680000&en=127e3 2464ca6faf3&ei=5088&partner=rssnyt&pagewanted=1, accessed April 7, 2010).

CAS I. Beginning of Civilization in China, 12000–2000 BC

Stone tools discovered at Chinese sites show that pre-humans arrived in the area that we now call China over a million years ago. One Chinese site has evidence of the earliest use of fire by Homo erectus. Archaeologists have also discovered very early examples of pottery in China that was made between 16500 and 19000 BC. According to Chinese mythology, civilization began with Phan Ku, the great creator who burst from an egg and then sacrificed himself to create the universe. His skull became the sky, his body the soil, his blood the rivers and seas, his hair plant life, and his body vermin became humanity. While Phan Ku died from his efforts, he left behind emperors and heroes who taught the Chinese to communicate with each other and how to survive and prosper (see Chapter 3, Activity 1).

Agriculture and semi-permanent human settlements started in the Yellow (Huang He) and Yangtze (Chang Jiang) river valleys between 12000 and 10000 BC, although the oldest solid evidence for grain-based agricultural communities producing millet is from about 7000 BC. The Yellow River Valley where millet and later wheat were the dominant crops is further north and suffers from periodic drought. The Yangtze River Valley is warmer and wetter and more easily navigable. In this region, rice-based agriculture, which may have spread there from further south, dominates. In both river valley systems, pigs, dogs, and cattle were domesticated by 3000 BC. While dogs were primarily work animals in other parts of Eurasia, genetic evidence suggests they may have first been domesticated in southern China about 15000 BC where they were probably used as a food source (http://news.nationalgeographic.com/news/2009/09/090904-dogs-tamed-china-food.html, accessed March 31, 2010).

With agriculture and settlement came the civilization package. Population increased, communities were able to store and redistribute crops, and they could support, either willingly or unwillingly, craftspeople, soldiers, religious leaders, and rulers. Settlements were often surrounded by fortified walls, which suggests that food surpluses and craft products had to be protected from enemies. In northwest China, thousands of cave carvings and paintings have been discovered that probably date from 6000–5000 BC, although Chinese authorities claim they are even older. They depict characters such as the sun, moon, stars, and gods, and activities such as hunting and grazing, and may be the earliest known examples of Chinese pictograph writing (http://www.china.org.cn/english/culture/117261.htm, accessed March 31, 2010). Distinctive pottery emerged in different areas between 5000 and 3000 BC. Archeological sites from this era show elements of cultural diffusion, especially in religious and burial rituals.

This CAS would conclude with comparison of the shift from hunting/gathering bands to agricultural communities in China with shifts taking place in other regions of the world. The focus would be on similarities and differences in geography, climate, available resources, rates of change, and culture.

CAS II. Chinese River Valley Civilization, c. 2000–1066 BC

Our knowledge of life and institutions in the earliest Yellow River Valley civilizations is very sketchy. One of the world's oldest bronze smelters was unearthed in this area and dated at approximately 2000 BC. Sima Qian, an early Chinese historian, writing about 100 BC, told of a Xia Dynasty founded about 2100 BC, although the accuracy of his accounts has been questioned. Sima Qian can be seen as a Chinese composite of Homer and Thucydides from ancient Greece. According to mythology, the Xia Dynasty ended around 1600 BC at the epic Battle of Mingtiao. The Xia emperor lost support because of his extravagance and disrespectful treatment of his advisors and palace workers. The Shang clan from the eastern lower reaches of the river and its allies defeated his forces.

Written records and larger numbers of artifacts survive from the Shang Dynasty (c. 1700–1066 BC) that followed. Writing developed, bronze metallurgy flourished, and religious belief and ritual were formalized during this period. Evidence from royal tombs suggests that funeral rites for emperors and other royalty were similar to those practiced in Egypt. When royalty died they were buried with articles of value to use in their afterlife and accompanied by their servants or slaves who were buried alive.

Similar to the Egyptians, Greeks, and Romans, the Shang Chinese were polytheistic, but generally believed in a supreme God who ruled over the other gods. Belief in Shangdi, the Chinese supreme god evolved into belief in a natural force called "tian" or Heaven that granted divine authority, or the Mandate of Heaven, to the rulers of China. Natural disasters and political upheaval were seen as evidence that the authority granted by the gods had been withdrawn from a ruler or dynasty. There is also evidence that the Shang Chinese believed deceased parents and grandparents had divine qualities and each family worshiped its own ancestors.

This CAS would conclude with a comparison of river valley civilization in China with river valley civilizations in Mesopotamia, Egypt, and India and early non–river valley civilization in the Americas and Sub-Saharan Africa. The focus would be on identifying the components of the "civilization package" and how the different components were related.

CAS III. Classical Chinese Civilization, 1066–221 BC

The Zhou Dynasty was founded by a frontier region chieftain who overthrew the Shang, which illustrates the principle that change often comes from the periphery. The Zhou shared the language and culture of the Shang and gradually extended the empire into the Yangtze River Valley until it included most of what would later be known as China Proper.

During the Zhou Dynasty, which was the longest in Chinese history, China eventually developed into a semi-feudal society. Power became decentralized and local military leaders asserted authority over different regions. There were hundreds of relatively independent states similar to Western Europe after the collapse of the Roman Empire. By the 5th century BC the Zhou emperor was only a figurehead and seven warring states vied for actual control over China. These developments were partly in response to a series of invasions from the north that weakened the central Zhou administration. They were accelerated by new military strategies made necessary by the invention of the crossbow around 350 BC and the adoption of armor as a counter-measure.

Decentralization contributed to a diversity of ideas known as the Hundred Schools of Thought and the emergence of the philosophies of Confucianism, Daoism, and Legalism. Many of the teachers identified with these schools of thought were itinerant intellectuals employed by local rulers as advisors on governing, war, and diplomacy. During this period, trade expanded, supported by the introduction of coinage and technological improvements. Iron replaced bronze in the manufacture of weapons, tools, and farm implements. It was a period marked by massive public works projects including walled fortifications, flood control, irrigation, and canals. A new social class of wealthy merchants and industrialists emerged during this period and began to acquire influence.

Confucius (551–479 BC), also known as Kong Zi or Master Kong, is considered the premier thinker of this period. As with Socrates in Greece, his teachings were recorded by his disciples. He believed the early days of Zhou rule provided a model for an ideal social and political order where people accepted their roles in society. According to Confucius, authoritarian government and social stratification were facts of life to be accepted because they supported the proper functioning of society. People should obey rulers just as sons were obligated to obey fathers. However, he stressed that government and family should be based on virtue. One of his disciples, Mencius or Meng Tzu (372–289 BC), modified Confucian teachings, arguing that humanity was essentially good, and that a ruler could not govern without the tacit consent of people. The penalty for unpopular, despotic rulers was the loss of the "mandate of heaven." Together, Confucius and Mencius provided traditional Chinese society with a comprehensive framework ordering every aspect of life.

Another Confucian disciple, Xunzi (c. 300–237 BC), took a very different intellectual path. He disagreed with Mencius and taught that people were innately evil. Xunzi believed this justified authoritarian government. His ideas were eventually formulated as the doctrine of Legalism by Han Feizi (c. 280–233 BC) and others and became the philosophic underpinning for imperial government into the 20th century. The Chinese schools of thought with their relationships between teachers and pupils are reminiscent of ancient Athens, while the debate between Mencius and Xunzi over human nature and its implications for government presages the European Enlightenment debate in England between John Locke and Thomas Hobbes.

CAS IV. Imperial China, 221 BC–618 AD

The short-lived Qin Dynasty (221–206 BC) successfully reunited the core of the Han Chinese homeland under a highly centralized authoritarian regime. It stressed a Legalist doctrine government of strict adherence to legal codes and the absolute power of the emperor. Nobles were forced to leave their lands and relocate to the capital, a governing strategy later employed by Louis XIV in France. Local officials owed their positions to the emperor and had no hereditary right to office.

The Qin initiated major construction projects including a road system, similar to the one built by Rome, to facilitate the movement of troops. Their attention to detail included making the size of cart axles uniform, which also assisted in the growth of trade. They also mobilized hundreds of thousands of bound or unfree workers to begin construction of the Great Wall. Reforms included efforts to standardize language, measurement, and currency. At the same time political opponents were banished or executed and Confucian texts that questioned Legalism were burned. Qin policies ended the turmoil and warfare that plagued the late Zhou Dynasty, but their brutal enforcement practices raise the question of whether ends justify means.

The Han Dynasty (202 BC–220 AD) that followed the Qin lasted for over 400 years and ushered in an era of relative internal peace and outward expansion including ventures into Vietnam and Korea. Unlike the Qin, Han emperors emphasized a commitment to Confucian teachings. Officials, who were drawn from landowning families and had a measure of economic independence, were now encouraged to question unfair policies.

This period saw the opening of the "Silk Road," a land-based network of roads that opened trade and communication with the West, the arrival of Roman emissaries in China, the development of a system of tributary states on the borders of China, and the population of China growing to almost 60 million people. Other major accomplishments during the Han Dynasty were the invention of paper and porcelain, advances in iron making, the start of a civil service examination system, and the first comprehensive history of China written by Sima Qian.

The last years of the Han Dynasty were marked by excess, incompetent administration, internal division, and civil war. Eunuchs (castrated males) were increasingly used as officials in the palace and court. It was believed they would be loyal to the interests of the emperor because they could not produce their own heirs. In 184 AD a millenarian religious group launched a massive uprising known as the Yellow Turban Rebellion. The rebellion and the response led to the end of the Han Dynasty and the breakup of the Chinese empire into regions governed by competing warlords. One result of this division was that areas of China became vulnerable to domination by non-Chinese invaders, especially in the 4th and 5th centuries. Rather than transforming Chinese life and culture, these groups were "Sinotized" and became Chinese. In some ways, this is similar to Germanic invaders of the Roman Empire becoming Romanized and Christian.

During this period of political instability, Buddhism spread rapidly across China. It posed no threat to the social order and for the lower classes it offered hope of a better life after reincarnation. Monasteries became important social and economic centers, offering men and women who joined safe haven and simple, but adequate, livelihoods. There also continued to be technological advances including the invention of gunpowder, which was first used to make firework displays, and the wheelbarrow.

After completing this CAS on Imperial China (221 BC–618 AD), students could do a side trip to look at the Roman Empire, particularly in the West. In Europe, there are important parallels with the rise and decline of the Han Dynasty, invasion and domination by groups from the fringes of the empire that were formerly considered barbarians, and the spread of monastic life after its collapse. Students could examine similarities and differences in the spread of Buddhism and Christianity.

CAS V. Golden Age I, 618–1305

Dynastic periods in Chinese history are reminiscent of the biological theory of punctuated equilibrium; long periods of evolutionary stability are followed by relatively short periods of rapid change. In this case, the Tang, Song, and Yuan Dynasties were interspaced with tumultuous events. At the end of the 6th century, China was reunited after nearly four centuries of political fragmentation. The start of the Tang Dynasty (618–907) precipitated a wave of prosperity and innovations in the arts, especially poetry, and technology. The population of the largest city, Chang'an, was more than two million, and its streets were laid out in a rectangular grid pattern. During this period, trade with other regions flourished, and foreign merchants were allowed to settle in China. Buddhism became the predominant religion in China and was even adopted by the imperial family.

During the Tang Dynasty, Wu Zetian was the only woman to be emperor of China. A former child concubine, Wu became empress in 656 and first exercised power through her husband – and after he died through her sons. In 690, she declared herself Emperor, claiming she was a Buddha reincarnation in feminine form. Wu Zetian was an effective, albeit ruthless ruler, who held the throne until she died in 705. Students should compare her reign with other female monarchs in history, most of whom had symbolic, rather than real authority.

The Song Dynasty (960–1279), which followed the Tang after a 50-year period of political disunity, governed for approximately 300 years, although during their reign they were sometimes forced to share power with a dynasty based in the north. This was a period of great technological achievement that included the development and use of gunpowder in weapons, advances in metallurgy, and the maintenance of a permanent standing navy for the first time in Chinese history. The design of the compass and of ships dramatically improved and Chinese traders began to challenge Indian and Arab merchants for dominance in Southeast Asia and Indian Ocean ports.

Trade was facilitated by the first government-issued paper money in the world, which was commented on by Marco Polo in his journals. The expansion of trade led to increased specialization, the growth of merchant guilds, and the formation of "companies" with partners and shareholders. Block printing on printing presses had been invented during the Tang Dynasty. Continued innovation under the Song Dynasty led to the development of movable type 400 years before it appeared in Europe.

Rice cultivation expanded in south and central China and with the increased food supply so did population, which probably reached 100 million by 1100. Farmers increasingly produced for the market, which allowed ordinary people to share in China's growing prosperity. Affluence also had a negative impact on Chinese culture, especially women. Concubinage increased, women had no say in the disposal of family property, and the practice of foot-binding to keep a girl's feet small and "attractive" spread among the elite.

A government official during the Song Dynasty named Shen Gua was a "Renaissance man" in the mode of Leonardo da Vinci and may well have "discovered" the idea of scientific explanation. His best-known written work is *Dream Pool Essays* (c. 1088). Shen Gua developed three-dimensional relief maps, oversaw the construction of waterworks and fortifications, lobbied for the adoption of a solar calendar, argued that medical practice should be based on clinical observation, and wrote about the use of petroleum. In a study of petrified bamboo he hypothesized climate change over long periods of time and he demonstrated that changes in ocean tides correlated with lunar cycles rather than with the rising and setting of the sun.

The Song were eventually defeated by Mongols from the north, who were initially led by Genghis Khan. Kublai Khan, one of his grandsons, adopted Chinese customs and established the Yuan Dynasty (1234–1305) with Beijing as the capital. The Mongols improved road and water travel in China, built a system of granaries for protection against famine, and rebuilt Beijing, adding new palace grounds with artificial lakes, hills, and parks. However, a long period of warfare led to a dramatic decline in the population of China from an estimated high of 120 million people to approximately 60 million in 1300. The population continued to decline for most of the 14th century because of epidemic disease, especially the Bubonic or Black Plague.

Following completion of this CAS, students could examine the way war, technology, trade, food production, and disease impacted on cultures in other parts of the world. This is also a good place to examine in depth how and why the position of women changed in different societies.

CAS VI. Golden Age II, 1368–1450

Confucian teachings argued that recurrent natural disasters such as plague signal that rulers had lost the "mandate of heaven" to govern. The natural disasters in the 14th century eventually led to a revolt against Mongol rule by ethnic Chinese led by a former peasant and Buddhist monk. The Yuan Dynasty was replaced by the Ming (1368–1644), ushering in a new "Golden Age." This period saw new waves of agricultural and commercial expansion, the extension of the Grand Canal (which promoted internal trade), repairs and additions to the Great Wall, urban growth, and a rise in population. Iron production increased, books were published using movable type, and in Beijing, the imperial palace was completed in the "Forbidden City."

Under the Ming, Chinese merchants and government-sponsored voyages explored the Indian Ocean and reached East Africa. Between 1405 and 1433, Chinese Admiral Zheng He led seven voyages that included among their goals acquiring new scientific knowledge, a better understanding of geography, and obtaining products from other parts of the world, as well as establishing Chinese domination in areas that would produce tribute. His first fleet had 317 ships and thirty thousand men. The life and achievements of Zheng He, who was a devout Muslim, taken prisoner as a boy and castrated before being placed in the service of a Chinese prince who later became emperor, deserves special attention in the curriculum and textbooks.

The Ming maritime expeditions stopped abruptly after 1433 and the reasons are still debated by historians. There was growing concern at the time with defending the empire against a possible new invasion by Mongols from the north. There may also have been opposition from advisors with roots in agriculture who did not want state support of commercial ventures and some belief that China, with its advanced civilization and robust economy, had little to learn from the rest of the world. After 1474, the largest ships in the Chinese fleet were actually broken up and the lumber was reused.

CAS VII. Dark Ages, 1449–1911

Between 1449 and 1644, the Ming Dynasty faced repeated threats to its sovereignty from the North. Its authority was also threatened by Japanese incursions into Korea and attacks by Japanese "pirates" on Chinese coastal cities. The end of the Ming Dynasty was "foretold" by the Shaanxi earthquake of 1556, a sign that their "mandate of heaven" had ended. The earthquake killed over 800,000 people and is considered the deadliest earthquake in human history.

In 1644, the Manchus or Manchurians invaded China from the North, captured the Ming capital of Beijing, and established the Qing Dynasty (1644–1911). While the Manchus kept the government structure intact, unlike previous northern invaders they forced their own customs on the Han Chinese, including hairstyles and clothing. Han Chinese were prohibited from migrating into Manchuria, and intermarriage between the two groups was forbidden. During the 18th century, the Manchus consolidated control over China proper, by pitting different ethnic and religious groups against each other, and by absorbing outlying areas such as Tibet, Mongolia, and Taiwan.

At the same time as these events were taking place, Western European merchants, explorers, and Christian missionaries from Portugal, Spain, Great Britain, France, and the Netherlands were establishing footholds in China and other parts of East Asia and an expansionary Russia was consolidating control over Siberia. After initial efforts to rebuff European commercial inroads, the Qing approved limited and managed trading. However, by the 19th century, China faced a new challenge – attempted domination by European imperialist powers strengthened by wealth stolen from the Americas, profits from the trans-Atlantic slave trade and slave-produced commodities, and the capitalist industrial revolution.

Open conflict between the Qing Dynasty and European powers followed Chinese efforts to stop the export of opium to China from Britain's colony in India. After a decade of unsuccessful anti-opium campaigns, the Qing implemented a series of laws against the opium trade. Enforcing the new laws, imperial agents confiscated and destroyed opium owned by Chinese dealers and

British importers and temporarily detained the entire foreign community in the port city of Guangzhou. The British responded with military actions known as the First Opium War and easily defeated Chinese forces. The Treaty of Nanking (1842), signed on board a British warship, was a national humiliation for China. It forced them to cede control over Hong Kong to Britain, granted British nationals in China exemption from Chinese laws, opened additional ports to British residence and foreign trade, capped tariffs, ended other restrictions on European trade with China, and forced China to pay an indemnity to cover British expenses during the war. Victor-imposed indemnity payments were standard practice until onerous payments saddled on Germany at the end of World War I became an underlying cause of World War II.

The Treaty of Nanking and other predatory agreements during the second half of the 19th century established an unequal relationship between Europe and China that undermined the domestic authority of the Qing Dynasty and exacerbated tensions with ethnic minorities and a Han majority that bridled under Manchu rule. The 19th-century conflict with European imperialist powers came at a time when China was faced with serious internal economic problems. By 1800 the population of China was over 300 million, but economic development had failed to keep up with population growth. A shortage of arable land and lack of work led to a breakdown in law and order. There was widespread rural discontent and urban pauperism as people migrated into the cities. Secret societies were formed that combined anti-Manchu political activities with banditry, and local revolts periodically erupted against Manchu rule.

During the decades following the Opium War, China was rocked by a series of civil wars. The Taiping Rebellion lasted from 1851 to 1865 and at one point almost a third of China was under the control of a quasi-Christian religious movement that proclaimed the founding of the Heavenly Kingdom of Great Peace. The new order promised a classless society in which peasants would own and farm the land in common and that slavery, concubinage, arranged marriage, opium smoking, foot-binding, and unfair judicial practices would be abolished. This rebellion was savagely repressed by the imperial army with support from European powers who feared a class-based revolution in China. The death-toll is estimated to be as high as 30 million people. During this same period Qing authority was challenged by the Nien Rebellion (1851–1864), the Punti-Hakka Clan Wars (1855–1867), and a series of Muslim-led insurrections including the Panthay Rebellion (1855–1873).

In response to external and internal threats, a faction within the government, with support from the emperor, tried to modernize education, government administration, and the military. It instituted a Self-Strengthening Movement that was similar to Meiji-imposed reforms in Japan. Schools were opened where students could study Western science and languages. Arsenals, factories, and shipyards were reorganized according to Western models and there was investment to develop a modern economic infrastructure for China, including the expansion of railroads, coal-mining, steamship navigation, and telegraph lines. The reformers, however, were met with sharp opposition. Bureaucracy and traditional practices remained firmly entrenched, and modernization was largely unsuccessful. Foreign encroachments, including Russian advances into Manchuria and the French occupation of Vietnam, continued to threaten the integrity of China. The "modern-ized" army was soundly defeated in the Sino–French War (1883–1885) and the Sino–Japanese War (1894–1895). The Treaty of Shimonoseki with Japan forced China to cede Taiwan to Japan, pay another huge indemnity, permit the establishment of Japanese industries in Chinese cities, and recognize Japanese control over Korea. In addition, during this period Great Britain, Japan, Russia, Germany, France, and Belgium each established "spheres of influence" in China where they effectively ruled.

At the start of the 20th century, a nationalist movement known as the Boxers led a rebellion against foreign influence which hoped to restore China to its previous position as the world's leading power. The Boxers especially targeted Christian missionaries and Chinese who had converted to Christianity. When the Boxers placed the capital in Beijing under siege, an Eight-Nation Alliance invaded China. This consisted of troops from Britain, Japan, Russia, Italy, Germany, Austria–Hungary, France, and the United States. The Qing tried to repeal the foreign invaders but both the Boxers and government forces were defeated. The Protocol of 1901 once again imposed humiliating conditions on the Chinese. The Qing agreed to the execution of ten high government officials and the punishment of hundreds of others, stationing of foreign troops in China, and a war reparations payment that was double the annual revenue of the Chinese government. By 1911, the Qing Dynasty had collapsed, ending 4,000 years of imperial rule.

In this CAS students discover how 450 years of internal division and resistance to change left China exceedingly vulnerable to incursions by outside forces. At the completion of this CAS, students would examine the Colombian Exchange, slavery and the trans–Atlantic slave trade, capitalist industrialization, and imperialism – the factors that allowed the allied forces of Europe to surpass China as a world power and bring it under their domination.

CAS VIII. Reemerging World Power, 1912–1989

In this CAS students discover how European conflicts that led to two horrific world wars and severely weakened imperialist empires, and the ability of the Chinese to adapt selected European ideas and economic practices, made it possible for China to reemerge as a major world power in less than a century. Three leaders played crucial roles in this transformation. Sun Yat-sen (1866–1925) was a nationalist who helped China move from monarchical to republican government at the beginning of the 20th century. Mao Zedong (1893–1976) led a peasant-based communist revolution that drove foreign military and economic forces out of China, defeated regional warlords, restored national political unity, and mobilized the Chinese people in support of a fundamental economic and social transformation of their society. Deng Xiaoping (1904–1997), a more pragmatic communist than Mao, engineered economic reforms that reintroduced capitalist practices to China while keeping the economy under centralized state management. As a result of the Deng reforms, according to some measures, by the beginning of the 21st century China had the world's second largest economy (http://www.economywatch.com/economies-in-top, accessed April 5, 2010).

From October 1911 through March 1912, a military uprising challenged the Qing Dynasty. The revolt ended with the creation of the Republic of China, with Sun Yat-sen as President. However, the new government faltered. Sun was supplanted by a military leader, there were unsuccessful attempts to establish a new dynasty, and regional warlords began to dominate different sectors of the country.

World War I brought additional humiliation for the Chinese. Japan, which fought on the Allied side, seized German holdings in Shandong Province and even threatened to make China a Japanese protectorate. While China was able to resist this demand, it acquiesced to the Japanese control over Shandong, southern Manchuria, and eastern Inner Mongolia.

When the Paris peace conference that defined post–war national boundaries confirmed these arrangements, student demonstrations shook China and led to the May Fourth Movement, a new resistance struggle led by Sun Yat-sen, and the beginnings of Chinese communism. Sun established a military base in southern China with the goal of reuniting the fragmented nation. After his death from cancer in 1925, Chiang Kai-shek took control of Sun's Nationalist (Kuomintang) Party and by 1927 brought most of China under its rule. At that point Chiang and the rightwing nationalists turned against communists and other radical reformers in the Kuomintang and attempted to exterminate them.

The communists under the leadership of Mao Zedong regrouped in the Chinese interior where they led successful resistance to an invasion and a 14-year-long occupation by Japan. At the end of World War II communist military forces were stronger than the rightwing nationalists and had more popular support. By 1949, the communists ruled all of China except for a nationalist enclave in Taiwan.

The great strengths of the Chinese communists in securing victory under Mao were their ideological vision and discipline. These also turned out to be two of their greatest problems when governing. After acquiring power, the communists confiscated the land holdings of the landlords and richer peasants and redistributed them to 300 million poor peasants and landless agricultural workers. Prostitution and drug use were stopped, private enterprise was abolished, education became a national priority, and women were granted full legal equality with men. The communists also developed 5-year economic plans intended to promote a "Great Leap Forward." They were based on models developed in the Soviet Union and supposed to rapidly industrialize the nation. The plan was also to collectivize agriculture in order to produce enough food to feed a population of over 580 million people.

On the agricultural communes people would work collectively and live communally, similar to the vision promoted by mid-19th-century utopian rebels. The communes were envisioned as self-supporting units, producing food and providing communities with their own small-scale industries, schools, and self-governance. Peasants, who preferred to live and work on independent family-owned farms, vigorously resisted. Ideologically determined efforts at centralized planning produced food shortages, widespread hunger, poor-quality goods, mismanagement, and disaffection with communist leadership.

In response to these problems, Mao and his supporters within the governing Communist Party launched the Socialist Education Movement (1962–1965) and the Great Proletarian Cultural Revolution (1966–1971) with the goal of reviving revolutionary ideals, exposing the internal enemies of socialism, and where possible, reeducating "capitalist-roaders" in the government, schools, military, and the broader society. In retrospect, these movements are seen as largely disruptive of Chinese development, and since the early 1980s they have been officially condemned by the government of China and the Communist Party.

Probably the most prominent member of the Communist Party or government leadership to be driven out of office during the Cultural Revolution, reeducated, and then rehabilitated, was Deng Xiaoping, who was reinstated as a vice premier and appointed to the party's Central Committee in 1973. Deng, a political pragmatist, is credited with the statement, "I don't care if it's a white cat or a black cat. It's a good cat so long as it catches mice" (http://en.wikipedia.org/ wiki/Seek_truth_from_facts, accessed April 7, 2010). He was strongly identified with the "Four Modernizations," a program emphasizing modernization of the economy over ideological struggle and democratic political reforms. Despite setbacks, by 1978 Deng solidified his position as the principal leader of both the Communist Party and Chinese government. As a signal of his ascendancy, leaders of the Cultural Revolution, derisively referred to as the "Gang of Four," were driven from party and government positions, convicted of major crimes, and imprisoned. Deng and his supporters, while promoting private economic ventures and a managed market economy, kept a firm rein on political dissent. In 1989, over a million protesters gathered in Tiananmen Square in Beijing and demanded the end of martial law and the expansion of democratic rights in China. After seven weeks, the protests broke up and the government launched a campaign to arrest protesters and their supporters. The foreign press was barred from covering events and local news coverage was strictly controlled.

In this CAS students examine the role of individuals and social movements in shaping the 20th-century history of China. As a comparison, they can look at the impact of other 20th-century individuals and social movements, including Vladimir Lenin and Leon Trotsky and the Bolsheviks in Russia, Adolph Hitler and the Nazi Party in Germany, Mohandas Gandhi and the Indian independence movement, Gamal Nasser of Egypt and pan-Arab nationalism, Nelson Mandela and the anti-apartheid movement in South Africa, and Rigobertu Menchu and the campaign for the rights of indigenous people in Central America. Other comparisons can be drawn between revolutionary movements and economic development in different regions in the 20th century. An important essential question is: Why are some revolutionary movements successful while others fail? In the case of China, students should examine whether it was social conditions, leadership, ideology, the failure of opposition groups, or some combination of factors. Interesting questions to discuss include whether a communist communalist philosophy and authoritarian governance were accepted by the masses because they were seen in some ways as compatible with traditional Confucian values and whether China will be able to continue to effectively utilize Western notions of economic liberalization while denying political and cultural freedom to its population.

TEACHING IDEAS

Historical maps of China from the Neolithic era through the contemporary era are available online at the website of the University of Washington. This site also provides excellent slides illustrating Chinese civilization in different historical periods (http://depts.washington.edu/chinaciv/timeline.htm, accessed April 10, 2010). Asian Topics in World History (http://afe.easia.columbia.edu/chinawh, accessed May 21, 2010), maintained by Columbia University, compares the histories of Europe and China from 1500 to today. It includes background information and video mini-lectures.

I would have students conduct research projects on the history, culture, and geography and on current social, political, and economic issues using the following websites: Library of Congress Country Studies (http://memory.loc.gov/frd/cs/cntoc.html, accessed April 10, 2010); UNESCO's World Heritage Sites (http://whc.unesco.org/en/statesparties/cn, accessed April 10, 2010); and CIA World Factbook (https://www.cia.gov/library/publications/the-world-factbook/geos/ch.html, accessed April 10, 2010). By directing students to these sites, and by limiting students to them, you ensure that the sources are reliable and make it less likely that they will just download reports.

Activities 1–12 are online at http://people.hofstra.edu/alan_j_singer. Activity 1 looks at the transition from semi-nomadic hunting/gathering societies to sedentary agricultural societies by focusing on the domestication of dogs in China. In Activity 2, students learn about the Grand Historian of the Han court who helped define the craft of the historian.

Confucius (551–479 BC) or Master Kong is considered the most influential thinker in Chinese history. According to Confucius, authoritarian government and social stratification were facts of life to be accepted because they supported the proper functioning of society. People should obey rulers just as sons were obligated to obey fathers. However, he also stressed that government and family should be based on virtue. In Activity 3, students analyze Confucian teaching about the qualities that produce successful monarchs. In Activity 4 they examine the teachings of Mencius or Meng Tzu, a Confucian disciple who developed a philosophy based on the idea that humanity was essentially good and that a ruler could not govern without the tacit consent of the people.

Most Confucians believed the subservience of women to men was natural and proper and part of the harmonious organization of the universe. During the Han Dynasty, a woman named Ban Zhao was imperial historian and an advisor to the Empress. Despite her own achievements,

Ban accepted the inferior status of women. In Activity 5, students examine Ban Zhao's writings on the nature of women and their role in society.

Activity 6 introduces students to the life and writings of Shen Gua, a Chinese official who was a "Renaissance man" during the Song Dynasty (960–1279). Activity 7 presents three primary sources describing life in Ming Dynasty China (1368–1644).

Activities 8, 9, and 10 are about Chinese responses to European imperialism. Emperor Qianlong ruled China for much of the 18th century. Activity 8 concerns a 1793 letter from Emperor Qianlong to King George III of England denying a British request for special trading privileges in China. In 1839, the Emperor of China issued an edict outlawing the importation of opium and spelling out the penalties for violating the law. Activity 9 includes a copy of the law and a letter to Queen Victoria from a Chinese commissioner requesting support in suppressing the trade. Activity 10 is a secret edict issued by Qing Empress Dowager Tzu Hsi in 1899 calling on the Chinese to resist efforts by European nations to seize control over Chinese territory.

Activities 11 and 12 are excerpts from speeches by 20th-century Chinese revolutionary leaders Sun Yat-sen and Mao Zedong.

9

WHO AND WHAT GETS
INCLUDED IN HISTORY?

> Global history textbooks are still largely organized around the "great" men of history with
> a few women mixed in to add diversity. This chapter explores other approaches to organizing
> a global history curriculum, including: one that focuses on packages, take-offs, and turning
> points; another that compares social institutions across time and place; and a social history
> approach that emphasizes the lives and struggles of ordinary people.

"The history of the world is but the biography of great men," argued the 19th-century Scottish
historian and essayist Thomas Carlyle in *On heroes and hero worship and the heroic in history* (1841)
(http://www.gutenberg.org/files/1091/1091.txt, accessed May 9, 2010). While few historians
would make this claim today, this idea, expanded to include "great women," continues to be the
primary organizing principle behind most secondary school global history textbooks and curricula.
They offer students lists of heroes and villains, rulers and religious figures, with occasional
philosophers, scientists, and artists sprinkled in to broaden our perspective.

In McDougal Littell's *World history: Patterns of interaction* (Beck et al., 2005), the index, under
letter "A," lists Abbasid, Almohad, Almoravid, and Andhra dynasties; rulers Abbas the Great of
Persia, King Gustavus Adolphus of Sweden, Emperors Akbar and Aurangzeb of India, Alexander
the Great of Greece, Russian czars Alexander II and III, Alfred the Great of England, Ashurbanipal
of Assyria, Askia of Songhai, Atahualpa of the Inca, Attila the Hun, and Augustus of Rome; Queens
Ahhotep of Egypt, Amina of west Africa, and Anastasia of Russia; and religious figures Abraham,
Caliph Abu-Bakr, Thomas Aquinas, Athena, Saint Augustine, and Allah. Even teachers obsessed
with names and dates would be hard pressed to justify including almost any of these names. The
rest of us, of course, are but bit players in someone else's story.

Within this fact-based top-down approach to global history, students are lucky if they come to
realize that other people even existed, or that many of the same people (Kublai Khan, Julius Caesar,
Mansa Musa, Mustafa Kamal Attaturk, Joseph Stalin, or Mao Zedong) are considered both heroes
and villains, depending on the side you were on at the time events took place or on the point of
view of the person who is writing history.

I opened Chapter 1 by referring to the poem "A Worker Views History" by Bertolt Brecht (http://www.cs.rice.edu/~ssiyer/minstrels/poems/1406.html, accessed April 24, 2009). At that point I was defining a social studies approach to global history and was most interested in Brecht's focus on questions. But Brecht is also challenging historians and teachers to reconsider views about who is important to include in the historical record. In Brecht's case, he wanted the lives of ordinary people, what the Judeo-Christian Old Testament in Joshua 9:27 refers to as "hewers of wood and drawers of water," given more attention.

During the 1980s, self-affirmation movements in minority communities championed the idea that the ancestors of American Blacks had been princes and princesses in Africa. While I understand the motivation behind these assertions, the reality is that for most of us, our ancestors were peasants. Mine lived in small villages in what is now Poland and Byelorussia where they helped make history in their own way by participating in the great migration from Eastern Europe to the United States at the start of the 20th century.

Other Approaches

There are approaches to studying history, writing textbooks, and organizing the curriculum, that do not just look at individual historical actors. These include focusing on packages, take-offs, and turning points; comparing social institutions; and examining collective struggles by the poor and disposed to hold on to the little they have or to secure a better life for themselves as a group. I do not advocate expunging the "greats" from the historical narrative, but recognizing that the achievements they are credited with were dependent on many other things and people.

Packages, Take-offs, and Turning Points

In *Man makes himself*, archaeologist and historian V. Gordon Childe (1951) described nineteen early breakthroughs that transformed civilizations and led to the vast expansion of human populations. According to Childe these crucial developments included irrigation and the use of the plow for agriculture, harnessing animal power on land and wind power on water, wheeled vehicles, orchard husbandry, fermentation, the production and use of copper, bronze, and iron, building with bricks and arches, glazing, the solar calendar, writing and numbers, and the construction of aqueducts for transporting water to urban centers. No names or individuals are associated with any of these developments. Yet high school global history textbooks focus overwhelmingly on the few names that survive from the past. Inevitably they are rulers and military leaders with an occasional thinker and inventor. But there are few clues about everyone else.

The developments described by Childe, what Jared Diamond (1997) in *Guns, germs, and steel* and others labeled the "civilization package," provide the infrastructure that makes possible an agricultural surplus, increased population, differentiated work, and the invention of civilization. Focus in global history classes on the development of conditions supporting the civilization package including agriculture, animal husbandry, state formation, religious institutions, literacy, numeracy, metallurgy, and trade (which promotes cultural diffusion) makes it possible for students to examine major forms of historical explanation including the difference between underlying and immediate causes, the likelihood of multiple causation, and the impact of similarities and differences on historical development. Students should examine why some river valleys – Tigris-Euphrates, Nile, Yellow, Yangtze, Indus, and Ganges – supported the civilization package, while others – Amazon, Mississippi, Congo, Niger, Rhine, and Danube – did not. They can also discover problems that develop when civilizations such as the Mayan in the Yucatan are geographically isolated and lack key ingredients of the civilization package including iron and a river. As part of this area of study students also investigate key social studies themes including the impact of geography and technology on history and the role of government, economic systems, culture, and religion in defining societies.

While the development of river valley civilizations is probably the most dramatic example of the package, it is not the only one. During human prehistory nomadic bands developed new forms of stone tools that changed how they lived and rapidly, for that time, spread to other groups. The Commercial Revolution in Europe that brought feudalism and the Middle Ages to an end and helped create the modern world required that a number of factors be in place. Following the collapse of the Roman Empire in the western Mediterranean it took hundreds of years for these conditions to emerge. There needed to be a sufficient agricultural surplus to support differentiated production, population growth, the growth of towns, and trade. There also needed to be new markets and products such as woolen goods, spices and silks, capital to invest in development, technological improvements to promote transportation, laws to protect those engaged in trade, and a measure of political stability. As the Commercial Revolution progressed there were battles over territory, trade routes, and prerogatives that contributed to the rise of more centralized and powerful states. Within these states, new classes increased in importance, particularly commercial groups and guilds within the towns, and new technologies, such as the printing press, led to a much more rapid and accurate exchange of information (Lopez, 1971).

In a similar way, the presence of coal and iron reserves, short rapid waterways, a canal system for internal transportation, a workforce displaced by the enclosure of agricultural lands, capital generated by slavery and the slave trade, an available supply of raw materials (first domestic wool and then imported cotton), an already existing overseas trade network of markets, and relative political stability made possible the emergence of an industrialization package in late 18th-century England. Other countries developed more slowly or not at all because they lacked one or more of these attributes. In the 19th century, the leaders of Germany and Japan recognized the power of the industrialization package and made conscious decisions to adopt it, later emerging as industrial and military rivals to England.

When packages are in place, or at least the rudiments of them are, a relatively rapid transformation of society becomes possible. What appears to be a sudden change in direction is usually described as a turning point or a take-off, although I prefer the idea of a take-off. European voyages to the Americas and the establishment of colonial empires that exploited American resources and African labor built on infrastructure that developed during the Commercial Revolution. After the "discovery" of America there was a take-off in European economic, political, and military development that transformed the world. Among other things, the battle over potential empires in the Americas fueled the Catholic/Protestant schism and 100 years of warfare. The Commercial Revolution also created the conditions for the European Renaissance and a take-off in Florence once it was established as a trade and financial center.

At the start of the Industrial Revolution in England, textile production was the initial "take-off" industry that provided the capital, labor-discipline model, factory system, technology, and demand for industrial growth that other industries later emulated. In the 19th century a similar role was played by the railroad, which required new machinery, iron, coal, and wagons. It also stimulated the organization of some of the first trade unions. The pattern was replicated in the first half of the 20th century by the automobile industry, which generated demand for petroleum, window glass, steel, rubber, asphalt, roads, bridges, repair shops, and roadside services. The arms race between the United States and the Soviet Union in the second half of the 20th century had a similar take-off effect. Efforts to develop missile technology led to a space race, pressure for miniaturization, and the computer and technology revolutions.

One of the best examples of a take-off made possible by a package is the spread of the moveable and reusable type printing press (see http://www.hrc.utexas.edu/exhibitions/permanent/

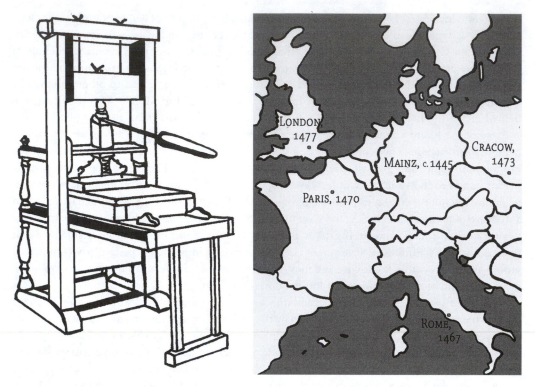

FIGURE 9.1 The spread of the moveable and reusable type printing press, from its first European development in Mainz, Germany.

gutenberg; http://www.britaininprint.net/introtoprint/spread.htm; and http://en.wikipedia.org/wiki/History_of_printing, accessed May 24, 2010). Block printing using a single carved or etched piece of wood originated in China in ancient times and spread very slowly. The earliest printed material that still survives is cloth from about 200 AD. Sometime during the next 200 years printing also developed in Egypt, possibly independently or perhaps through cultural diffusion. It was not until the 11th century that moveable and reusable type was invented in China employing ceramic pieces for each character. Moveable and reusable metal type was later developed in Korea in the middle of the 13th century. The idea of printing using moveable and reusable symbols probably spread west along the Silk Road. Johannes Gutenberg of Mainz, Germany, possibly with some awareness of Chinese innovations, but certainly without seeing a press or drawings of one, developed the first European moveable and reusable type printing press in about 1439 and completed printing the first Christian Bible in 1455. During the next 50 years, moveable and reusable type printing presses appeared in a number of European cities and then radiated outward from each locality like exploding fireworks. There was a printing press in Rome, Italy in 1467, Paris, France in 1470, Cracow, Poland in 1473, and London, England in 1477. By 1481 there were printing shops in twenty-one cities and towns in the Netherlands and forty each in Italy and Germany. By 1500 there were probably as many as 1,000 printing presses in Western Europe. *The Atlas of Early Printing* (http://atlas.lib.uiowa.edu/, accessed May 24, 2010) has an interactive map illustrating the spread of printing in Western Europe and animation showing how the early presses worked.

Trade, conquest, and Christian missionaries spread the moveable and reusable type printing press around the world. There was a printing press on the West African island of São Tomé and Príncipe in 1494, one in Thessaloniki, Greece in 1515, one in Mexico City sometime between 1539 and

1544, and one in Moscow, Russia in 1553. Jesuit priests brought this form of printing to India in 1550 and Japan in 1590. The first moveable and reusable type printing press in British North America was in Massachusetts in 1638.

As I said earlier, I prefer the idea of take-off to turning point, which I find overrated in global history and in the social studies curriculum. The New York State global history and geography core curriculum guidelines (http://www.emsc.nysed.gov/ciai/socst/pub/sscore2.pdf, accessed May 24, 2010) require that students know and are able to analyze the impact of "critical turning points in history," and specifically list the introduction of agriculture (6), the Turkish conquest of Constantinople (10), the voyages of Columbus (15), the American, French, and Latin American Revolutions (18), World War I and II (23), the Russian Revolution (23), and the collapse of the Soviet Union (29).

However, unless these turning-point events contributed to the transformation of material conditions within society they had little long-term impact. Generally they are the result of underlying forces, rather than causal agents. For example, the destruction of the Spanish Armada off the Atlantic coast of Ireland in 1588 is seen as a turning point in the battle between England and Spain for colonial empires and as a crucial event in England's eventual domination of the seas and world trade. However, Spain was already headed in the wrong direction because of its history, geography, and culture. Between the 8th and 15th centuries the Iberian Peninsula was a battleground between Christian Europe and Muslim North Africa. The expulsions of Muslims and Jews at the end of the 15th and the beginning of the 16th centuries as part of national consolidation left Spain trapped in landed and religious feudalism without a merchant and banking class capable of utilizing wealth looted from the Americas to generate greater economic development and, with it, military power. The sinking of the armada only sealed Spain's second-class status in a rapidly changing world.

Battles are often cited as turning points, but again, their results often represent underlying historical currents or geographic conditions. The Battle of Tours in southern France in 732 is presented as a turning point in the struggle between Christianity and Islam for control over Western Europe. However, the Arab world never had sufficient population to expand further north, and even in Spain (al-Anduslasia), which it controlled for centuries, it left a very light footprint. A similar argument has been made for the importance of the defeat of the Ottoman Turks (Muslim) by the Austro-Hungarian Empire (Christian) at the Battle of Vienna in 1683. But in many ways this was a feudal war fought between imperial houses, neither of which would have much further impact on global history. The result of this war maintained a stalemate in Eastern Europe that continued until both empires collapsed during World War I.

Former Yankee manager Joe Torre used to argue that the regular season in baseball had to be viewed as a "marathon, not a sprint" (http://www.cigaraficionado.com, accessed May 25, 2010) and teams with better players, deeper benches, and wealthier owners generally made the play-offs. The play-offs, on the other hand, are a short season when contingent factors such as injuries and an individual getting "hot" perform a much greater role. In the short term in history, contingent factors such as a war, superior leadership, and blind luck are always important, but in the long term, packages and take-offs trump turning points.

Social Institutions

A social institutions approach requires identifying the key institutions, broadly defined, that shape human history, and comparing developments between different regions and different time periods. Its strengths are that it adjusts for the differences in chronologies and rates of development in the different regions of the world and that it focuses on life as lived by most of the world's people. Key institutions to study would include family, clan and tribe; food production; organized religion; state

FIGURE 9.2 Alhambra in Grenada, Spain, the last Islamic stronghold on the Iberian peninsula.

formation, government, and national identity; legal and economic systems; education, literacy, and philosophy; work; and caste, class, and gender hierarchies.

Nel Noddings (1992: 230–241) argues that a completely reconceptualized social studies curriculum could focus on women's culture and institutions, the realm of the home and family, women's work, women as community builders, and women as international peacemakers. This would be very different from efforts to add more women to global history textbooks without a major reorganization of the curriculum. Current additions tend to be limited to upper-class women because they are the ones who leave behind documentary records.

The Many-Headed Hydra

As a college student in the 1960s my teachers introduced me to the work of historian Edward (E. P.) Thompson. His book, *The making of the English working class* (1963) was an inspiration for my generation of historians. Thompson argued that one of his goals was to:

> rescue the poor stockinger, the Luddite cropper, the "obsolete" hand-loom weaver, the "utopian" artisan, and even the deluded follower of Joanna Southcott, from the enormous condescension of posterity. Their crafts and traditions may have been dying. Their hostility to the new industrialism may have been backward-looking. Their communitarian ideals may have been fantasies. Their insurrectionary conspiracies may have been foolhardy. But they

lived through these times of acute social disturbance, and we did not; and if they were casualties of history, they remain, condemned in their own lives, as casualties.

(Thompson, 1963: 12–13)

These people and their movements (Southcott was a self-professed prophet of peasant origin who envisioned a utopian society and had a strong rural and worker-class following in England during the Napoleonic wars) have largely been erased from historical memory. However, that they lost their battles against industrial transformation and powerfully ruling groups does not mean their struggles did not take place or influence their times. In fact, their struggles were an important part of the dynamic that shaped the world to come, and in some places similar struggles were at least temporarily successful. Thompson reminded his readers of something that was true in the 1960s and is still true today:

> The greater part of the world today is still undergoing problems of industrialization, and of the formation of democratic institutions, analogous in many ways to our own experience during the Industrial Revolution. Causes which were lost in England might, in Asia or Africa, yet be won.

(Thompson, 1963: 13)

Edward Thompson, who I had the opportunity to meet at a presentation he did for a working-class, largely minority audience in Brooklyn, New York, was a political activist as well as a historian. His belief that study of these 18th- and 19th-century movements has a bearing on the way people might understand and respond to contemporary movements for social change or the preservation of traditional rights is very much consistent with what I have called a social studies approach to global history.

I had always described Thompson's approach as social history with a focus on social struggle. The idea of calling it "the many-headed hydra" comes from a book by Peter Linebaugh and Marcus Rediker (2000) on what they call the "hidden history of the revolutionary Atlantic." The image of the hydra originates with the Greek (or perhaps Egyptian) legend of Hercules (2). Linebaugh and Rediker argue that in 17th-century Europe the effort of Hercules to cut off the hydra's heads, which both regenerate and multiply, was seen as an allegory describing the difficulty of imposing order on the disruptive forces inhabiting an increasingly globalized world. Thomas Hobbes (1588–1679), the British Enlightenment philosopher best remembered for *The Leviathan* (1651), where he advised rulers that force must be deployed to control human passions, used the hydra metaphor when describing the 1640 "May Day" street riots and attacks on prisons by "sailors, mechanics, watermen, apprentices, the lowly and the base" (Linebaugh and Rediker, 2000: 69–70).

The Columbian Exchange, when coupled with the widespread expropriation of communal village lands by landlords and nobility anxious to increase their holdings and wealth, led to the displacement and impoverishment of European rural populations, migration into urban areas ill-equipped to absorb the new population, social unrest, and the creation of the many-headed hydra. By the end of the 16th century there were twelve times as many property-less people in England as there had been only 100 years earlier (17). Elites and governments responded with repressive measures including imprisonment, execution, forced mobilization into the military, and deportation to overseas colonies. Turmoil-fueled expropriation, resistance, and repression produced the 19th-century English working class described by Edward Thompson in much the same way as capitalist imperialism in the 19th century and current-day globalization produced and continues to produce new social movements all over the world. My proposal is to move these tensions and movements to the center of the global history curriculum.

Struggle Against Slavery

One of the most significant struggles of the 18th and 19th centuries was the battle to end the trans-Atlantic slave trade and chattel slavery in the Americas. If you asked most Americans, they would say Abraham Lincoln ended the enslavement of Africans when he signed the Emancipation Proclamation in 1862. British students would probably recognize William Wilberforce, who led a campaign in Parliament for 26 years until the passage of an act outlawing British involvement in the slave trade in 1807. Wilberforce was also a founder and parliamentary spokesperson for the Anti-Slavery Society that was founded in 1823. He died in July 1833, three days after learning that the passage of the act abolishing slavery in the British Empire was assured. In Brazil, however, where 3.6 million Africans arrived in bondage (at least a third of the American total) Isabel, the Imperial Princess Regent, is celebrated as the liberator for signing the *Lei Áurea* or Golden Law in 1888. What these three people share in common is that they were Whites of European ancestry and members of the governing class. By crediting them and their actions with ending slavery, despite the fact that the institution of chattel slavery was already unraveling, global history teachers minimize the struggles of hundreds of thousands of enslaved Africans that actually precipitated the overthrow of the slave system in the Americas.

The history of slavery in the Americas is also the history of resistance (Genovese, 1979). In Pernambuco, Brazil in the early 17th century, over ten thousand Africans rebelled against European control and enslavement and established the independent African Republic of Palmares in Brazil. It was not until 1697 that they were finally defeated by Portugal with the support of European allies. In the early 18th century, Jamaican Maroons, living in the interior of the island, battled British forces and in 1739 they were declared legally free forever. In the early 19th century there were major slave rebellions in Barbados, Guyana, and Brazil. In Barbados in 1816, twenty thousand Africans from over seventy plantations drove Whites off the plantations during "Bussa's Rebellion." In Guyana in 1823 the East Coast Demerara Rebellion was fueled by the belief among enslaved Africans that the planters were deliberately withholding news of the impending freedom of the slaves. In Bahia, Brazil there were repeated rebellions led by African-born Muslims from the West African Hausa nation. The largest, in 1835, involved hundreds of enslaved Africans who fought a pitched battle with Brazilian soldiers and White colonists for control over the city of Salvador. After their defeat, five hundred rebels were sentenced to death, imprisonment, brutal physical punishment, or deportation. These revolts led to a wave of repression, but also opened debate in Brazil over the future of slavery and the slave trade.

The two most important slave rebellions, the ones that did the most to topple the institution of chattel slavery in the Americas, took place in the French colony of St. Domingue (Haiti) between 1793 and 1804 and in British Jamaica during the winter of 1831/1832. They should be treated as major historical events and given a prominent place in the global history curriculum; however, generally they are not even included. In McDougal Littell's *World history: Patterns of interaction* (Beck et al., 2005), Haiti is briefly mentioned twice in sections on Napoleon (665) and Latin American revolutions (682). Jamaica and Sam Sharpe, the leader of the insurrection that brought down slavery in the British Empire are never mentioned. They receive a similar lack of coverage in Bedford/St. Martin's *A history of world societies* (McKay, 2009).

The importance of these struggles was recognized in the 19th century, especially the role of Toussaint L'Ouverture. In 1862, abolitionist Wendell Phillips gave a speech at the Smithsonian Institute in Washington DC marking the end of the first year of the American Civil War. Phillips prayed that the United States would avoid an all-out slave insurrection on the Haitian model and "raise into peaceful liberty the four million [enslaved Africans] committed to our care." He concluded by comparing Toussaint L'Ouverture to Napoleon Bonaparte, Oliver Cromwell, and

George Washington, and claiming that L'Ouverture was their superior as a soldier, statesman, and martyr (Clavin, 2010: 2).

In *The suppression of the African slave trade to the United States, 1638–1870*, first published in 1896, W. E. B. DuBois (1969) argued, "The role which the great Negro Toussaint, called L'Ouverture, played in the history of the United States has seldom been fully appreciated." DuBois credits L'Ouverture with creating a "Negro 'problem'" that defined the anti-slavery movement and precipitated the "final prohibition of the slave-trade by the United States in 1807" (70).

Haiti, at the end of the 18th century, was the world's largest producer of sugar and coffee and the richest colonial possession. The island's wealth was produced by the labor of over half a million enslaved African men and women. Conditions on the island were so cruel and dangerous that 40,000 newly enslaved Africans had to be brought there every year. Under the leadership of Toussaint L'Ouverture, the African population of Haiti took advantage of weakened authority caused by the French Revolution to rebel, declare independence, and abolish slavery. They then defeated efforts by France, Great Britain, and Spain to reestablish European control (Katz, 2007: 30–31). The Louverture Project (http://thelouvertureproject.org, accessed May 25, 2010) is an excellent web resource for both teachers and students that "collects and promotes knowledge, analysis, and understanding of the Haitian revolution of 1791–1804."

Toussaint L'Ouverture certainly qualifies as a "great man" who shaped history. He demanded that European Enlightenment and French Revolutionary ideas be applied to his people. As a military leader, he led by example and was wounded seventeen times in battle. He shifted alliances to pit European colonial powers against each other. He pioneered mobile guerrilla warfare, attacking the coastal plains and then retreating into the interior mountains to evade capture and regroup. He was a master at waiting for seasonal tropical diseases to weaken his opponent before launching an assault.

According to historian William L. Katz (2007), the Haitian Revolution sent shock waves throughout the Americas. Stirred by events in Haiti, enslaved Africans and Native Americans, with the support of some Whites, organized to overthrow slavery in New Orleans. Gabriel Prosser mobilized hundreds of enslaved Africans in 1800 to attack Richmond, Virginia. In Jamaica, the British governor warned that enslaved Africans were composing songs about Haiti's uprising and he was "preparing for the worst." In Dominica, a British officer warned, "the Bomb was ready to burst in every quarter," and the colonial governor reported that slaves were learning about the "Idea of Liberty" from nearby French islands. In Trinidad, the governor feared that a dancing festival would be used to plot "the diabolical scene which led to . . . St. Domingo" (31).

Orlando Patterson (1969), a sociologist and historian originally based at the University of the West Indies in Jamaica, argued "with the possible exception of Brazil, no other slave society in the New World experienced such continuous and intense servile revolts as Jamaica" (211). Patterson believed this was because of a number of reasons. Jamaica has an inaccessible mountainous interior. There was a high proportion of Africans to Europeans, between 10 and 13 to 1, on the island. There was an unusually large number of enslaved people, approximately 50%, who were born free in West Africa and raised in a highly militaristic environment in what is now Ghana and the Ivory Coast. He also cited the general ineptitude of the planter caste and their high rate of absenteeism. It is significant that these were very similar to conditions in Haiti prior to its revolution. An excellent online source for exploring Caribbean history in general and slavery in the Caribbean in particular is the British National Archives (http://www.nationalarchives.gov.uk/caribbeanhistory/default.htm, accessed May 19, 2010).

The 1831 slave rebellion in Jamaica that shook the British Empire and led to the abolition of slavery in British colonies was centered in the area around Montego Bay in the northwest portion of the island. It is variously known as the Baptist War (because its leaders were members of Baptist evangelical churches), the Christmas Uprising (because it was timed to take place following the

Christmas holiday break from work), or the Great Jamaican Slave Revolt. Its principal leader was Samuel Sharpe, a literate man and Baptist lay preacher, who was born in Jamaica rather than in Africa. The rebellion never spread to other parts of the colony and was largely suppressed within two weeks, although troop actions against suspected rebel strongholds continued until the end of January 1832.

Samuel Sharpe and his followers believed, mistakenly, that emancipation had already been approved by the British Parliament, and that local planters were refusing to obey the law. They used their church connections to organize a general strike demanding that they be paid wages to work. Reprisals by plantation owners transformed the work stoppage into a slave rebellion. Twenty thousand enslaved Africans attacked over two hundred plantations in the Montego Bay area. They burnt down plantation houses and warehouses full of sugar cane, causing over a million pounds worth of damage. Nearly 200 Africans and 14 British planters or overseers died in the fighting. Hundreds of the rebels were captured and over 750 were convicted of insurrection. Of those convicted, 138 were sentenced to death, either by hanging or firing squad. The rest were brutally punished and/or deported to other islands. Sharpe was captured and publicly executed in May 1832 in Market Square at Montego Bay. Before he was hung, Sharpe is reported to have said, "I would rather die in yonder gallows, than live for a minute more in slavery."

Two parliamentary inquiries were launched to determine the causes of the insurrection and a week after Sharpe's execution, the British Parliament appointed a committee to consider ways of ending slavery in the colonies (The Abolition Project, http://abolition.e2bn.org/index.php, accessed May 9, 2010). In August 1833, the Slavery Abolition Act was approved, formally ending slavery in British America. A provision of the act was that plantation owners would receive compensation for the loss of their slaves. No provision was made to compensate enslaved Africans for years of bondage and unpaid work.

TEACHING IDEAS

Activity 1 asks students to read and evaluate a passage written by former historian Howard Zinn where he argues that ordinary people have the "creative power" to change the world. Activities 2–10 are available online at http://people.hofstra.edu/alan_j_singer. As noted earlier, most early documents written by or about women focus on elites. Activities 2 and 3 give insight into the lives of upper-class women in ancient Greece, Rome, and Egypt, and feudal Japan. In Activity 4, Egyptian Workers Put Down Their Tools, students investigate the first documented strike in human history.

The transformation of any society produces social tension and can lead to class conflict as rules, expectations, and mechanisms of social control change. The three documents in Activity 5 examine lower-class uprisings in France, Italy, and England during the 14th century. They provide insight into the impact of the decline of European feudalism. Expert groups can examine one of the documents and report their findings to the class. The Putney Debates, examined in Activity 6, represent the emergence of new democratic forces in 17th-century England. In this activity, students prepare statements to include in the debate.

Activities 7 and 8 document slave rebellions in Haiti and Jamaica during the late 18th and early 19th centuries that led to the end of the trans-Atlantic slave trade and the overthrow of the slave system in the Americas. Activity 9 is a poem about the slave trade written by a Brazilian abolitionist. Activity 10 is a song from the Mexican Revolution at the start of the 20th century. It is a song about violence that introduces students to the reality of revolutionary struggles.

Activity 1. A Power Governments Cannot Suppress

Instructions: Howard Zinn (1922–2010) was a United States historian and political activist best known for the work *A people's history of the United States* (New York: Harper Perennial, 1995). This quote is from an essay, "If History is to be Creative," written in 2006 (http://www. zcommunications.org/if-history-is-to-be-creative-by-howard-zinn, accessed May 26, 2010). In the essay, Zinn argues that historians and citizens should know about the "creative power of people struggling for a better world." Read the quote and write a response to Zinn explaining your view on this topic.

> To omit these acts of resistance is to support the official view that power only rests with those who have the guns and possess the wealth. I write in order to illustrate the creative power of people struggling for a better world. People, when organized, have enormous power, more than any government . . . Our history runs deep with the stories of people who stand up, speak out, dig in, organize, connect, form networks of resistance, and alter the course of history . . . I don't want to invent victories for people's movements. But to think that history-writing must aim simply to recapitulate the failures that dominate the past is to make historians collaborators in an endless cycle of defeat . . . If history is to be creative, to anticipate a possible future without denying the past, it should, I believe, emphasize new possibilities by disclosing those hidden episodes of the past when, even if in brief flashes, people showed their ability to resist, to join together, and occasionally to win.

10

RELIGION IN HUMAN HISTORY

This chapter examines the role that religious beliefs and religion as a social institution have played in human history. It is critical of most textbook coverage and of national standards. The teaching activities are designed to stimulate students to question their own assumptions. An earlier version of this essay appeared as "Are We Teaching Religious Myth Instead of the History of Religion?" in *Social Science Docket*, *8* (2), 8–13.

Although I am an atheist, or perhaps because of it, when I travel to other countries and continents I always visit churches – big ones, little ones, ornate, and plain. On hot days they are cool. On cold or rainy days they offer shelter. I find the atmosphere in churches calming and sometimes I sit in on services. I have even quietly and inconspicuously attended weddings and funerals.

European churches, including churches in former European colonies, are often majestic structures and each has its own history, characteristics, and idiosyncrasies. Among my favorite buildings and artifacts are the Cathedral of Notre Dame on the Île de la Cité in Paris with its external buttresses and gargoyles; the stained glass windows of Chartres; the castle-like abbey of Mont St. Michel overlooking the English Channel in Normandy; the testaments to British imperialism in the Anglican Protestant St. Patrick's Cathedral in Roman Catholic Dublin; the ruins of the fortified medieval Glendalough monastery in County Wicklow, Ireland; the Duomo in Florence where they invented the European Renaissance; 600-year-old Grote Kerk (Great Church) in Breda in the Netherlands where my wife and I participated in the town's anniversary celebration; the small Greek family shrines alongside cart and hiking paths on Aegean islands; the mummified body of Pizarro in the Roman Catholic Cathedral in Lima; gold leaf on the walls behind the altar in the Cathedral in Seville; and the remains of an Islamic Mosque in the middle of the Roman Catholic Cathedral in Cordoba. I once arrived by bus in Cuzco, the ancient Inca capital in the Andes, at four o'clock in the morning. The elevation of the city is over 11,000 feet. My friends and I were freezing and spent the hours until dawn hovering over the memorial candles in the Cathedral located on the Plaza de Armas.

However, my favorite "church" remains the medieval cloisters in Fort Tryon Park on the northern end of Manhattan where I bring student groups at least once a year. The New York City

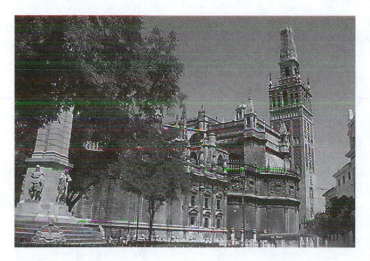

FIGURE 10.1
The Cathedral in
Seville, Spain.

Cloisters are a branch of the Metropolitan Museum of Art and a gift to the city from oil magnet and banker John D. Rockefeller, Jr. The Cloisters were built from the ruins of European religious communities in France and Spain and remnants of different churches, including the church of San Martín at Fuentidueña in Segovia, Spain, the Benedictine monastery of Saint-Michel-de-Cuxa located on the French side of the Pyrenees, and the Pontaut Abbey Chapter House from French Gascony. Most were destroyed or went into decay as a result of the French Revolution's attack on established religion because of the alliance between the *Ancien Régime* and the Roman Catholic Church, but they have been resurrected as part of the Cloisters (http://www.metmuseum.org/cloisters, accessed June 16, 2010).

The Cloisters has original archways, doors, statues, icons, mosaics, paintings, and the world-famous Unicorn Tapestries, seven wall hangings that are an allegorical retelling of the legend of the crucifixion and resurrection of Jesus of Nazareth. Little is known about the early history of these tapestries except that they were woven in Brussels about 1500. It is believed they were commissioned by Anne of Brittany to commemorate her marriage to Charles VIII of France.

I bring teachers to the Cloisters and then they bring their own students. My tour focuses on religion as a defining aspect of life and culture in the European "Middle Ages" and reading the artifacts to uncover the history. Most of the teachers are still wrapped up in a mythical Camelot/Robin Hood version of history that emphasizes the nobility of feudal chivalry (except for a few bad eggs like the Sheriff of Nottingham) and the purity and piety of the lords and ladies. I present a much darker world where peasants and townspeople struggled for survival and feudal nobles were anything but noble. They were military marauders who seized control over territory from rival gangs and forced local inhabitants to work without payment to support them in luxury.

At the New York Cloisters students "feel" the way that stone, arch, light, and vaulted high ceilings could be awe-inspiring for people living in mud and wood hovels, and would reinforce the belief that the established hierarchy and social inequality were ordained by a powerful supreme being. The thickness of the stone walls and iron reinforced doors, the arrow slots for windows, the interior herb and medicinal gardens, and the pillars with iron tethering rings for animals show that these buildings served multiple functions, as fortifications, pharmacies, and trading posts, as well as their primary purpose as religious communities. Stained glass images of the nativity and the Stations of the Cross as well as tapestries, paintings, and statues that illustrate biblical tales substitute for the written word in what is, for most of its members, a pre-literate society. Students "see" different depictions of Jesus of Nazareth and Mary and we talk about how the images reflect particular cultures. They also view artwork with symbolism that is either Islamic or pre-Christian, which adds complexity to their views about that time and place, and challenges notions they hold of a monolithic church.

Cloistered Life

One question that puzzles many of my students (whether they are high school students or teachers) is why someone would voluntarily enter a cloistered life. It is a very difficult decision for them to understand, especially given our culture's valuing of individual freedom and sexual expression. What religious communities offered in an insecure and dangerous world were very practical and material things such as community, safety, work, food, clothing, shelter, health, literacy, the possibility of advancement unavailable in the outside world, as well as the opportunity to participate in religious rituals, honor deities and their representatives, avoid practices deemed sinful by the rest of society such as homosexuality, and potentially secure salvation in the afterlife. For these reasons, families had to purchase places for their children in the more popular and comfortable religious communities.

The point here is that we cannot understand medieval European society, or really any society, without examining the beliefs of its people and their relationship with one of its most important institutions. Because of this, I am a strong advocate of greater attention to the role of religion in history. What I want to see included in the global history curriculum, however, is significantly different from what is currently there and is very different from what religious advocates would like to see taught.

Church and State

Many social studies teachers have interpreted the tradition of separation of church and state in the United States to mean they should not talk about religion in the classroom. But this eliminates one of the major forces shaping human history. Other teachers – and this is a serious problem in the sciences as well as social studies – shy away from the topic of religion because they fear repercussions from supervisors, parents, and even students, who may be unhappy when the historical record does not support religious dogma. For example, fundamental aspects of Judeo-Christian religious belief probably originated in other, more dominant, cultures in Southwest Asia and North Africa, and were adopted by Jews and Christians. There is no evidence of Noah's flood in ancient Judea and in all likelihood the story was imported into the Old Testament from the Babylonian Epic of Gilgamesh. Judeo-Christian monotheism can be traced to Egyptian belief in Ra the Sun God as the principal God and his evolution into Aton the only God under Amenhotep IV (1364–1347 BC). There is also no independent historical verification of the existence of Jesus of Nazareth to support accounts later incorporated into the New Testament by Christian believers. The officially accepted Christian gospels offer an edited version of the story codified by church leaders 300 years after what they believe was Jesus's miraculous incarnation, birth, crucifixion, and resurrection.

NCSS Thematic Strands

National Council for the Social Studies (NCSS) Thematic Strands include a discussion of religion in an anthropological examination of culture and in efforts to promote respect for cultural diversity, but not in their historical strands. According to the NCSS, the "study of culture prepares students to ask and answer questions such as: What are the common characteristics of different cultures? How do belief systems, such as religion or political ideals of the culture, influence the other parts of the culture? How does the culture change to accommodate different ideas and beliefs?" Unfortunately, it also anticipates an answer, "we all pray to the same god but in different ways," that is neither interrogated nor substantiated.

I have a number of disagreements with this way of presenting religion in a social studies classroom. It is ahistorical. It assumes that religion has meant the same thing and religions have functioned the same way throughout time. It is not analytical. Students are directed to look for cultural similarities, common characteristics, but not substantive differences in either time or place. It is uncritical. It assumes the universality of religion rather than examining why it develops. It is misleading. Because the focus is on culture, including theology (ideas) and ritual (practices), students never question the actual role organized religion as an institution played within different societies during the past and present. And finally, it is proselytizing. The result of this approach is that the existence of God is assumed. In effect, we teach religion when we do not question it.

There are similar problems with the National History Standards for Global History (NHSGH) developed by the National Center for History in the Schools (http://nchs.ucla.edu/standards/worldera6.html, accessed June 16, 2010) and in most high school global history textbooks. In both the NHSGH and textbooks, religious beliefs and practices are a major focus in discussion of traditional societies and the ancient world (1000 BCE–300 CE). According to the NHSGH, "The classical civilizations of this age established institutions and defined values and styles that endured for many centuries and that continue to influence our lives today. Six of the world's major faiths and ethical systems emerged in this period and set forth their fundamental teachings." Other faiths, such as Islam, are introduced to students in a similar way at the chronologically appropriate moment. Yet given the lack of later coverage of religion in the NHSGH, it is as if once the world's "major faiths" were founded, they ceased to be of importance.

Textbook Coverage

McDougal Littell's *World history: Patterns of interaction* (Beck et al., 2005) is one of the major textbooks used in global history classes. Its index clearly shows the ongoing importance of religion in global history. Yet despite the breadth of coverage, detailed examination is concentrated in few areas, and while religion is continually mentioned, its role in history, or in individual societies, is rarely analyzed. The major discussion of religion is in a sixteen-page supplement (282–297) called "World Religions and Ethical Systems" that focuses on similarities and differences in six major religious traditions (Buddhism, Christianity, Hinduism, Islam, Judaism, and Confucianism). It includes excellent maps and charts, more than two dozen pictures of gods, rituals, and celebrations, but almost no text. A quote from historian Karen Armstrong's *History of God* (1993: xix) included in the supplement betrays the bias of the text. Armstrong asserts, "Human beings are spiritual animals. Indeed, there is a case for arguing that Homo Sapiens is also Homo religious. Men and women started to worship gods as soon as they became recognizably human" (297). Students are then asked, "With which of the following opinions would Armstrong probably agree?" The only possible choice, selection A, is that "People are naturally religious."

The biggest problem with this textbook is the lack of analysis. Students are told that in Ur, "Rulers, as well as priests and priestesses, wielded great power" (22), but not how or why. In Sumer, the earliest government was supposedly controlled by temple priests because of the superstitions of the farmers who believed the priests were go-betweens with the gods. How this might have come to be is never discussed. States in many parts of the world and at different times claimed the "mandate of heaven," yet comparisons are not made or used to discover explanations. Flood stories from Mesopotamia, and Hebraic and Hindu beliefs are juxtaposed, but the questions and activities ignore the role of river flooding in early agricultural societies. Mostly we read engaging stories about exotic rituals such as mummification in Egypt (38) and colorful individuals like Siddhartha Gautama (68).

The role of Confucian ideas in cementing state authority in China and of the Roman Catholic Church in the Roman Empire provide ideal opportunities for exploring the material basis for religious belief and the institutional role of religion in empires, but the textbook largely ignores them. Confucianism is cited as the "foundation for Chinese government and social order," but the assertion goes unexplained (105). A chapter on "The Rise of Christianity" (168–172) argues that this religion grew in the Roman world because it emphasized a "more personal relationship between God and people" that Romans found attractive and because its followers were strengthened by their "conviction" that their religion's founder had "triumphed over death." The existence of Jesus of Nazareth and his life story are cited as historical fact recognized by historians, but no references are provided. Curiously, chapters on "The Fall of the Roman Empire" and "Rome and the Roots of Western Civilization" have almost no mention of Christianity. Meanwhile, the savagery and brutishness of the Christian Crusades are described as part of an "Age of Faith" (379).

The "Rise of Islam" merits its own chapter (263–268), as do "Islam Expands" (269–272), and "Muslim Culture" (273–281), with detailed discussions of the life of Muhammad, the "beliefs and practices" of the faithful, and cultural contributions. But the role of Islam, in promoting literacy and integrating an empire based on trade, shared language (Arabic), and a relatively simple, demystified, belief system, is missing.

The one instance where the integral relationship between state and religion is directly presented is in discussions of New World Aztec and Inca societies (462). But these are brief discussions about societies that develop in isolation from the main currents of human history. Chapters on the European Reformation (488–503) focus on corruption, beliefs, and reformers, and mention the printing press, but make no connection to the Columbian Exchange, the growth of commercial capitalism, and state formation in Europe. It is also unclear why during the French Revolution, the National Assembly would target church property, an action that supposedly "alarmed millions of French peasants, who were devout Catholics" (656). In the era following the French Revolution, religion receives much less coverage in the text, although it played a major role as a now junior partner in European imperialist penetration of Africa and Asia. The emergence of religion as a political force, particularly in the Islamic world during the second half of the 20th century, is noted but goes unexplained. We learn that "ethnic and religious conflicts have often led to terrible violence" (1083), but not why.

My conclusion is that the history of religion is so problematic, so distressing, that those with the power to decide what gets included in the curriculum would rather distort the historical record than come to terms with the roles religion did play in the past and continues to play in the present.

Historians and Social Scientists Look at Religion

Marvin Harris, in *Our kind: The evolution of human life and culture* (1989), examines over a hundred human biological and cultural mysteries or puzzles. He argues they can best be explained by looking at the nature of human biology and survival needs in frequently hostile environments where individuals, groups, and nations compete for scarce resources. A major topic in the book is the origin of religion as it develops from belief in spirits, which appears to be a universal phenomenon. Harris attributes this universality to a variety of factors that are part of the common human experience including dreaming, drug-induced trances, shadows, reflections, and inexplicable luck. Rituals, taboos, sacred stories and texts, theologies, and moralities, which are particular to different groups, develop later based on the circumstances under which people live in different regions and environments and local histories.

Harris sees one of the great shifts in human history as the changeover from belief in tribal warrior Gods who are affiliated with relatively small groups of people to more universal religions with established hierarchies and elaborate theologies. He credits the shift to the development of states that can regularize food production, normalize trade, enforce laws, and maintain military forces that both control local populations and repel invaders. As states grow into empires, universal religions bond diverse cultural groups and church institutions become vehicles for governing and social control. Harris believes that the shift first takes place in the Assyrian Empire of Persia about 1100 BC with the emergence of Zoroastrianism, is evident in the Ganges river valley of India by 600 BC, and transforms the Roman Empire with the adoption of Christianity as the official religion between 300 and 400 AD.

In another work, *Cows, pigs, wars and witches* (1974), Harris explained the widespread belief in the existence of witches in Christian Europe into the 18th century. He presents two very convincing arguments that show why religion continued to play such an important role in human history. First, according to Harris, there actually were witches, if we understand witches as people who follow, consciously or unconsciously, traditional folk practices, usually covered with a veneer of Christianity. Second, the existence of witches gave weight to the claims of established churches that they had the special role of defending the population from evil spirits that threatened social stability and eternal salvation.

A useful historical study that actually examines the role of religion in Christian society in Europe from the Middle Ages through the Protestant Reformation is *The Pursuit of the millennium: Revolutionary millenarians and mystical anarchists of the Middle Ages* by the British historian, Norman Cohn (1970). Cohn's primary thesis is that during periods of "mass disorientation and anxiety" (17) the poor and displaced expressed dissatisfaction with their conditions and even formulated revolutionary goals through millenarian and messianic beliefs and religious-inspired mass movements that challenged temporal authority.

Starting with the Crusades, the desire of the poor and displaced in European society to improve their lives led them to embrace prophecies about a final struggle between Christ and Antichrist and the end of the world as they knew it. Cohn argued that these beliefs required specific historical factors to emerge. The material conditions that contributed to the transformation of religious belief into political action included demographic pressures caused by increasing population density, rapid economic growth, social changes that undermined traditional support systems, and crises such as prolonged famine and epidemic disease (53–54). Significantly, once these forces were unleashed, they took on a life of their own and assumed power that traditional religious authorities could not control.

Cohn employs what I called in Chapter 1 a "social studies approach to global history" connecting past and present. He believed that part of the appeal of 20th-century autocratic leaders like Hitler and Stalin was their "messianic" ability to connect their vision with the aspirations of the disoriented and anxious poor of the modern epoch. According to Cohn, "stripped of their original supernatural sanction, revolutionary millenarianism and mystical anarchism are with us still" (286).

In *Primitive rebels* (1959), Eric Hobsbawm supported Cohn's position that historians need to focus on the material, as opposed to the spiritual, causes of millenarian uprisings. Hobsbawm described 19th- and 20th-century millenarian movements emerging in traditional societies that were ripped apart by internal or external economic and political forces beyond their control.

As far as I know, neither Cohn nor Hobsbawm analyzed the impact of "mass disorientation and anxiety" on the poor and displaced in the Islamic world today, although in *The age of extremes* (1994), Hobsbawm described Islamic "fundamentalism" as "the most flourishing brand of theocracy, advanced not by the will of Allah, but by the mass mobilization of the common people against unpopular governments" (582). I think the theses advanced by Cohn and Hobsbawm effectively explain the power of Islamic fundamentalism as a political movement and the difficulty local governments and Western powers have had bringing it under control; especially after having previously encouraged it as a weapon against leftwing protest movements. The studies by Cohn and Hobsbawm suggest that instead of responding to Islamic fundamentalism as a religious phenomenon, the world needs to address the material causes of the dissatisfaction, causes that are transforming ideas into violent action.

Closing Note

Starting in the spring 2010 semester, I worked with a female teacher education student born in India, in the northwestern region called Punjab, who is Sikh. I was aware of a Sikh presence in the New York metropolitan area because of the distinctive turbans worn by all Sikh men, but knew little about their religious beliefs or history. My student was well versed in Sikh beliefs and practices, but knew less about their history. For her, it was primarily a religious community.

Although the CIA World Factbook estimates there are approximately 25 million Sikhs today, they are barely mentioned in most global history textbooks (https://www.cia.gov/library/publications/the-world-factbook/geos/in.html, accessed June 16, 2010). McDougal Littell's *World history: Patterns of interaction* (Beck et al., 2005) has three brief references. Sikhs are described as originally a non-violent religious group that blended Buddhist and Hindu beliefs and practices with elements of Islamic mysticism that was severely repressed by Islamic rulers at the beginning of the 17th century (519); as military allies of the British during the colonization of India (794); and as people displaced by the partition of India and Pakistan following independence (998–999).

As I began to learn more about the history of Sikhs, I realized that while its religious traditions began to develop within Hinduism starting in the 9th century, and its first recognized religious leader, Guru Nanak Dev, began teaching in 1496, the Sikh religion as a formal and distinct system of beliefs is really an aspect of Punjabi nationalism and more recent events. Its history starts in 1627 with Punjabi resistance to Islamic Mughal emperors who were trying to maintain their authority by enforcing religious and cultural uniformity in the area under their control (http://www.sikh-history.com, accessed June 16, 2010). From that point on, being Sikh is part of what it meant to be Punjabi and to resist outside rule. One thing that is interesting is that later, in order to maintain their distinctiveness and cultural independence in a region dominated by much larger Hindu and Muslim populations, the Sikhs allied with British colonial forces and enlisted in large numbers in the British army.

Marvin Harris, in *Cows, pigs, wars and witches* (1974), argues that most individuals, because they form part of a group's culture and religion from the inside and accept its fundamental assumptions about life and human relationships, cannot really understand the origin or significance of its practices and beliefs. They are essentially blinded by their commitments. Harris focuses on Jews, Hindus, Muslims, and Christians, and argues that what others see as peculiar cultural practices continue because they help the group survive difficult circumstances. I think Harris's insight is of value here. Sikh religious beliefs are formalized, and Sikh religious beliefs survive, not because of anything inherent in the beliefs themselves, but because of the crucial role the religion played in the struggle of the Punjabis for national survival.

Putting Punjab and the Sikhs into the global history curriculum helps transfer focus away from the Western world while introducing major social studies themes. It makes it possible to look at the material conditions that allow for the growth and survival of religious groups other than Jews and Christians, the impact of geography on history, the history of human resistance, and the development of non-European nationalist movements.

TEACHING IDEAS

When teaching about the role of religion in history I find it is useful to ask a lot of questions and give students time to think and respond. When students feel their personal beliefs are respected, it is easier for them to step back and examine religious ideas and institutions from the perspective of a historian exploring the way societies are organized rather than as threatened believers. Among the questions I ask are: "Why does human belief in religion appear to be nearly universal?"; "Is widespread belief in a supreme being evidence that one exists?"; "What is the relationship between religion, belief in a spirit world and supreme beings, and magic and myth?"; "Why does organized religion as an institution develop as part of the river valley civilization package?"; "Would the history of Western civilization have been significantly different if worship of Yahweh, Mithra, Ra, or Allah had triumphed over Jesus and the Christian Trinity?"; "Was the Roman Catholic Church corrupted by an absence of piety and biblical misinterpretation in the years preceding the Protestant Reformation, or was the problem its interconnection with temporal authority?"; "How do we explain the survival of the Jews and other minority religions in hostile climates dominated by powerful religious institutions that brand them as illegitimate?"; "Why did organized religions tolerate and support injustices such as enslavement (Protestantism, Catholicism, and Islamic beliefs) and class and caste inequality (Hinduism, Buddhism, and Confucianism)?"; "Why are some religious movements identified with struggles for social change and more equitable societies?"; "Why are contemporary political conflicts, as well as conflicts in the past, often presented in religious terms?"

Activity 1 examines why some cultural practices are branded as taboo by religious systems. For me, the key is that the practices, whether sexual, body marking, or dietary, are normal human behaviors. They are generally banned because otherwise people would do them, not because they are outlandish, unclean, or perverted. Most of these taboos are used to define group membership, maintain cohesion, and minimize internal conflict. For example, all the Leviticus bans on seeing the nakedness of others are a way for a semi-nomadic people to avoid sexual tension while living in close quarters. And most of the restrictions on women, in that culture and others, are related to control over reproduction and the inheritance of property. I believe the Hebraic taboo on homosexuality is an effort to distinguish the tribe of Israel from its Greek neighbors, and male circumcision is a form of body marking that reinforces tribal solidarity.

Activities 2–12 are available online at http://people.hofstra.edu/alan_j_singer. Activities 2 and 3 compare text from the Judeo-Christian Old Testament with religious stories from the Nile and Tigris-Euphrates civilizations. Activity 2 provides evidence for cultural diffusion outward from the Egyptian empire to peripheral regions. Activity 3 is especially interesting because it offers an explanation for the origin of the biblical story of Noah and the flood.

Imperial China provides the world with a number of philosophical schools that provide the bases for moral systems. While the teachings of these schools are often religious in nature, students need to discuss whether philosophies that promote reverence for ancestors and offer origin stories but do not focus on "Supreme Beings" are actually religions. I recommend that the global history curriculum concentrate on the philosophies of Imperial China (Activity 4) because the writings of its philosophical schools are well preserved and provide an alternative to Eurocentric approaches that suggest ancient Greece is the source of all modern ideas.

In the contemporary world, there has been much criticism of religious fundamentalists accused of supporting attacks on civilian populations. However, horrendous things have been done in the name of the "true" religion throughout human history. According to the Old Testament First Book of Samuel, David had the victorious Hebrews cut off the foreskins of dead Philistines as a present for King Saul. During the Albigensian Crusade (c. 1200), Roman Catholic forces massacred suspected Christian heretics. A monk assigned to the troops besieging the rebel French city of Béziers, when asked whether to spare the lives of children and loyal Catholics, is reported to have recommended that the Crusaders "kill them all." He would leave it up to God to sort out the guilty from the innocent after they were dead.

Activity 5 explores Islamic religious tolerance towards Christians during the conquest of Spain. Activity 6 examines the treatment of non-Christians during the conquest of Jerusalem during the Crusades. Activity 7 presents students with passages from the Christian New Testament that have been used to justify the enslavement of other human beings. Activity 8, on the other hand, introduces students to the hymn "Amazing Grace" that played a major role in the battle to end the trans-Atlantic slave trade.

Historical explanation has often reflected religious belief. Activity 9 introduces students to a report about war and famine in Mesopotamia during the 6th century. Historians believe it was written by a Christian monk named Joshua about 500 AD. In these edited passages, Joshua describes an alliance between the Roman and Persian empires in an effort to block the westward expansion of the Huns. In an account reminiscent of the stories of Sodom and Gomorrah and the ten plagues of Egypt, both from the biblical Old Testament, Joseph attributes famine in the Tigris-Euphrates River Valley to divine vengeance against people who were sinful.

In 1493, Alexander VI issued a papal bull dividing the non-Christian world between Spain and Portugal. The "New World" was assigned to Spain, and Africa and Asia to the Portuguese. In 1494 the division was confirmed in the Treaty of Tordesillas and a formal nautical boundary was drawn which they later discovered gave Brazil to Portugal. While the papal bull and treaty resolved conflict between Spain and Portugal, they created a reason for other Christian kingdoms to challenge the authority of the Roman Catholic Church. Activity 10 examines statements on temporal and church authority by Martin Luther and by the English Parliament.

Political protest has often been expressed in religious terms. The Judean revolt against Hellenization (discussed in Chapter 5) was proclaimed as a struggle to restore traditional religious practice. A peasant uprising in 16th-century Germany (discussed in Chapter 6) attacked government and church practices "not agreeable to the word of God." In the second half of the 20th century and beginning of the 21st century opposition to what was perceived as Western and Christian incursions into, and domination over, Islamic societies was frequently organized on a religious basis. Activity 11 examines the Constitution of Iran that emerged out of its 1979 Islamic Revolution and asks students to discuss whether a modern government can be based on religious principles and supervised by religious elders.

In the 20th century, the Roman Catholic and Lutheran churches were severely criticized for failure to actively challenge the Nazi regime in Germany and to take risks in an effort to prevent the extermination of European Jews. However, both churches have also produced clergy who were active in struggles against human rights abuses and for expanding human freedom. Lutheran pastor and theologian Dietrich Bonhoeffer was executed in Germany during World War II for participating in an effort to assassinate Adolph Hitler. The Roman Catholic Church was an important part of the movement to overthrow communism in Poland in the 1980s. In Latin America it has produced a series of clerics committed to a "Liberation Theology" based on their interpretation of a passage from Matthew 19:21 where Jesus of Nazareth is reported as saying to his disciples "sell your possessions and give to the poor, and you will have treasure in heaven." Activity 12 introduces students to the writings of Gustavo Gutiérrez Merino, a Peruvian theologian and Dominican priest who is considered a founder of Liberation Theology.

Activity 1. Food Taboos from Leviticus

Instructions: You are a cultural anthropologist studying the origin of traditional Southwest Asian religious beliefs. You accept as true that most religious practices have their origins in local environmental conditions. Your task is to explain the reasons ancient Israelites had so many rules about what foods they could eat and what foods were "unclean" or "abominations." According to the Book of Leviticus in the Judeo-Christian Old Testament (http://www.biblegateway. com/passage/?search=Leviticus+11&version=NIV, accessed June 16, 2010), while the children of Israel could eat cows, goats, and lambs, Yahweh forbade them to eat animals that "chew the cud" but "divideth not the hoof." These animals were described as unclean. They included camels, rabbits (coneys and hares), and pigs (swine). Other "unclean" species were any animals with paws, mice, tortoises, and snails. In addition, Israelites could not eat fish or seafood "that have not fins and scales," or birds such as eagles, owls, and vultures. These were all described as an "abomination unto you." However, the Israelites were permitted to eat chickens, locusts, beetles, and grasshoppers.

11

REVOLUTIONARY MOVEMENTS IN THE 20TH CENTURY

The 19th-century Industrial Revolution in Europe gave European countries a tremendous economic and military advantage over other regions of the world. At the same time, it plunged them into intense competition for resources and markets. The result was capitalist consolidation over economic and political power in Europe and imperialist expansion around the world.

Competition between the nations of Europe for dominance also led to two worldwide conflagrations, World War I (1914–1918) and World War II (1939–1945). These massive military undertakings put enormous strain on the European empires and created the potential for revolutionary uprisings against both capitalism and foreign domination. At the end of World War II, the United States supplanted Europe as the major expansionist military and economic force, which brought it into sharp conflict with revolutionary movements around the world.

In Chapter 6, I discussed Calendar Area VIII Reaction and Revolution (1914–1989). As part of this area of study, I propose an in-depth thematic and comparative unit on revolutionary movements in the 20th century. This unit introduces students to a number of different parts of the world and the focus on revolutionary movements presents the people of these areas as historical actors rather than as pawns dominated by imperialist forces. Much of the material presented in this chapter was originally developed for a theme issue of *Social Science Docket*, 7 (1), Global Revolution, Winter/Spring 2007.

Bob Marley, father of Jamaican Reggae, called on the disposed of the world to stand up for their rights. Bob Dylan heralded times that were changing and demanded that people either join the movement for social change or get out of the way. However, John Lennon and the Beatles cautioned that they would not blindly support calls to overturn society and replace it with something they found equally or even more repressive. Meanwhile Mick Jagger and the Rolling Stones were ambivalent about participating in street actions because they were just poor boys who sang in a rock and roll band. The lyrics to all of these songs, "Get Up, Stand Up," "The Times They Are A-Changin'," Revolution," and "Street Fighting Man," are available at http://www.metrolyrics.com (accessed January 7, 2010).

The 1960s were a time of revolutionary upheaval around the world, especially 1968 when young people, including me, marched in the streets and defiantly challenged governmental authority in Mexico City, Cairo, Warsaw, Buenos Aires, Madrid, Paris, Berlin, Prague, Rome, London, Tokyo, Kingston (Jamaica), New York, and Chicago. We demanded, as did revolutionary movements before and after us, fundamental change in the organization of society and the legal system (justice), opening up the decision-making process to people previously excluded from participation (democracy), the extension of social, political, and economic rights to the dispossessed (liberty), and the elimination of what we considered arbitrary restrictions on personal behavior (freedom). We hoped to achieve these goals through collective struggle and were willing to break laws and put our lives and privileges at risk.

There is still dispute among historians, educators, and government policy makers about why protest exploded around the globe during the 1960s. Explanations include cultural and generational conflicts, sexual liberation and drug use, the changing role of women and the nature of work, extended education and financial dependence, as well as the impact of class and anti-imperialist struggles. Social studies teachers can take advantage of student curiosity about the popular culture of the "Sixties" and identification with the youthfulness of many of the protestors, to generate interest in studying the underlying and immediate causes of revolutionary movements and their short-term and long-term impacts.

A number of important historical themes and essential questions can be examined in a thematic and comparative unit on revolutionary movements in the 20th century. Students will discover that foreign imperialist powers and domestic dictators rarely give up their power without costly and destructive wars and often underestimated the ability and popular appeal of revolutionary leaders such as Patrice Lumumba of the Congo or Ho Chi Minh of Vietnam. Revolutionary wars, whether against foreign occupiers or local oppressors, tend to be violent affairs that employ intimidation and attacks on civilians. Generally, all sides employ terror tactics. This raises the question of whether, or when, ends justify means.

A comparative examination of revolutionary wars shows that they tend to have their own historical logic. Many were initially led by small groups of committed individuals with liberationist goals, developed broad popular support, sometimes suddenly as in Ireland after World War I and in Cuba in 1958, and sometimes over an extended period of time, had difficulty establishing democratic institutions after achieving power, and then deteriorated into dictatorships responsible for human rights abuses. Success in battle by revolutionary leaders did not always translate into success in building a just and democratic society. T-shirts with the image of Ernesto "Ché" Guevara are much more popular than T-shirts celebrating Fidel Castro. In fact, I have never seen one, even when I visited Cuba.

Revolutionary wars, fought to liberate the economic potential of societies, have often left countries impoverished and unable to improve conditions for their citizens. Since the French Revolution of the late 18th century, the return of repressive government following a revolution is termed the Thermidorian Reaction.

The idea of revolution can be romantic, exhilarating, and frightening depending on your social position and individual involvement. Two of history's most famous romantic revolutionaries were the British poet Lord George Gordon Byron (1788–1824) and the Argentine-born doctor Ernesto "Ché" Guevara. Both died while involved in movements to liberate other countries. In 1823, Byron joined insurgents against the Ottoman Turkish occupation of Greece, but he succumbed to fever before seeing any military action. Guevara, an Argentine, joined Fidel Castro and other Cuban revolutionaries and played a major role in overthrowing the Batista dictatorship and building a socialist society in the 1950s and 1960s. He left Cuba to support revolutionary movements in other countries and was assassinated by the U.S. Central Intelligence Agency in Bolivia in 1968. An excellent online source for the life of Ché Guevara in English is http://www.marxists.org/archive/guevara/index.htm (accessed July 2, 2010).

But not all revolutionaries and revolutions are remembered with the fondness of Byron and Guevara. The French Revolution transformed French and European society, but led to periods of "terror," reaction, and dictatorship under Napoleon. Historians have debated whether all revolutions are doomed to follow this pattern. The Haitian Revolution of 1793–1804, the most successful slave rebellion in human history, had a horrendous level of violence against both life and property, and an independent Haiti has been mired in poverty ever since. Similar problems emerged in the struggles for Congolese, Kenyan, and Algerian independence. All of these revolutionary movements confronted savage repression by occupying forces. Students need to consider who are the real terrorists and must societies be cleansed after these conflagrations?

Major works of fiction have glorified and condemned revolutionary upheaval and can be used to help students think about the consequences of human actions. In volume two of *Les misérables*, published in 1862, Victor Hugo (1980) described a revolt as a "whirlwind in the social atmosphere" (883) that "inspires those it lays hold of with extraordinary and mysterious powers" (884). For Hugo, "insurrection is the furious assertion of truth" (887). Other novels that tend to praise revolutionary movements include: Thomas Flanagan (1979), *The year of the French*, which is about the 1798 revolt in Ireland; *Doctor Zhivago* by Boris Pasternak (1958) and Mikhail Sholokhov's *And quiet flows the Don* (1946) about Russia; and Andre Malraux's *Man's hope* (1938) about Spain and *Man's Fate* (1934) about China. *In the time of the butterflies* by Julia Alvarez (1994) is a fictionalized account of the resistance to the U.S.-supported Trujillo dictatorship in the Dominican Republic. The heroes of the resistance and the novel are the Mirabal sisters, known as Las Mariposas or the butterflies, whose assassination by Trujillo's forces led to the overthrow of his regime. This novel is easily accessible to secondary school students.

On the other hand, Charles Dickens' *A tale of two cities* (1967), originally published in 1859, is a classic tale of revolution leading to mob violence and terror. In *Matagari*, Ngũgĩ wa Thiong'o (1989) describes a revolution betrayed in Kenya. One of the most complex portrayals of revolution is the trilogy by Madison Smartt Bell about Haiti from 1793 to 1804. In *All souls' rising* (1995), *Master of the crossroads* (2000), and *The stone that the builder refused* (2004), Bell shows both the dignity of human struggle and the horror of war once social constraints are abandoned. One of the most cautionary comments about revolutionary turmoil is the poem "The Second Coming" written by Irish poet William Butler Yeats in 1919 right after World War I and the Russian Revolution (http://www.potw.org/archive/potw351.html, accessed January 9, 2010). Yeats believed that the "best" were defaulting on their responsibilities, the "worst" were swaying the masses, and that anarchy was in the process of destroying civilization.

Although I would like to, it would be impossible to teach about every revolutionary or reform movement in the 20th century. Teachers must select case studies to represent the rest. The priority should be to examine movements in different parts of the world that illustrate broader historical phenomena.

The Bolshevik Revolution in Russia

The Russian Empire in the 19th and early 20th centuries was both a colonizer in Central Asia and a victim of German and British imperial ambitions. The devastating impact of World War I led first to the collapse of the Czarist monarchy and then to the overthrow of a weak reform government. The Bolshevik or Communist Revolution that overturned this government brought to power a small vanguard party committed to communist ideals, including internationalism and worker control over economic and political decisions. However the decision (or perhaps the need) to consolidate authority during struggles against hostile internal and external enemies led to increasingly autocratic practices and the creation of an authoritarian and bureaucratic state under Josef Stalin by the 1930s.

The Russian Revolution, as the first successful 20th-century revolution, became a model for, and supporter of, revolutionary movements around the world for the next half-century. Essential questions that emerge from a discussion of the Russian Revolution include the nature of human nature and the possibility of a cooperative society, whether revolutionary ends justify violations of human rights, and whether it is possible for a planned economy to provide for the needs of a society comprising hundreds of millions of people. Events leading up to, during, and after the Russian Revolution are well documented and a wide range of primary source materials and competing historical interpretations are available for use in the classroom. I highly recommend http://www.spartacus.schoolnet.co.uk/Russian-Revolution.htm (accessed January 9, 2010) as a source.

Among other topics, it is interesting to compare the success of Lenin, Trotsky, and the Bolsheviks in Russia with the unsuccessful communist revolution in Germany at the end of World War I led by Rosa Luxemburg, Karl Liebknecht, and the Spartacist League. The differences between what happened in Russia and Germany illustrate the contingent nature of history – the impact of unanticipated forces and individual and group decisions – because an industrialized, unionized, defeated, yet cohesive Germany seemed to have had more potential for a communist revolution at that time than an economically backward, equally devastated, and far-flung imperial Russia.

Easter Rising in Ireland

Until the establishment of the Irish Free State in December 1922, Ireland was the world's "oldest" colony. Pope Adrian IV placed it under fealty to the English crown in the 12th century, although a semi-autonomous Irish nobility remained in control over large parts of the country. Starting in the 16th century during the Protestant Reformation the English crown launched military expeditions to secure greater authority and colonized Ireland with Protestant settlers from England and Scotland. From 1600 to 1800 power was concentrated in an Irish Parliament dominated by Protestant landholders from Great Britain. In 1801 the Irish Parliament was abolished and the emerald island officially became part of the United Kingdom, a situation that lasted until the Irish War of Independence (*Cogadh na Saoirse*) at the end of World War I.

The British occupation of Ireland was challenged by periodic insurrections, some with relatively broad popular support such as two civil wars fought in the 17th century. Many were limited uprisings by small groups that hoped to ignite popular opposition and were readily defeated. The rebellions generally took place when the British were otherwise occupied by world events such as conflicts with Napoleonic France. These included the Irish Rebellion of 1798, famine-era revolts during the 1840s led by the Young Ireland Movement, Fenian uprisings in the 1860s, and land wars in the 1880s.

Irish nationalists took advantage of British involvement in World War I to launch an "Easter Rising" in 1916. It drew little support and was quickly put down. However, British authorities made a major miscalculation. The execution of rebels as traitors caused massive public outrage. After a two-year war for independence (1919–1921) twenty-six counties became the Irish Free State while six counties in the northern part of the island remained part of the United Kingdom.

The Irish "Easter Rising" was a disaster that motivated a much broader and successful struggle, which is not an uncommon historical phenomenon. Governments and colonial empires that seem all-powerful and eternal one moment can suddenly become vulnerable and topple. The fall of the *Ancien Régime* in France, the overthrow of the Shah of Iran in 1979, and the collapse of the Soviet

FIGURE 11.1
A monument in
Dublin to labor leader
James Connolly, who
was executed by the
British following the
Easter 1916 Rising.

THE CAUSE OF LABOUR IS THE CAUSE OF I   THE CAUSE OF IRELAND IS THE CAUSE OF LABOUR

JAMES
CONNOLLY
1868-1916

Union in the 1980s are other prominent examples. Students should discuss why historical change seems to happen relatively rapidly after long periods of apparent stability and whether the sacrifices made by Irish revolutionaries were justified by future events.

In addition, I see interesting parallels worth exploring between the Irish Revolution against the United Kingdom after World War I and the Algerian Revolution against France after World War II. In both cases the imperialist power wanted to absorb the colony into its national metropolis and sought to assimilate its people culturally by replacing their home language with the language of the dominant power. The resistance struggles also both emphasized religious differences between the colonies and the colonizers to help promote new national identities.

Non-Violent Civil Disobedience in India

In the 18th century, British involvement in India was largely a commercial venture operated through a quasi-official East India Company that held a British government-granted monopoly on trade with India. The British consolidated colonial power in India during the first half of the 19th century when they used divide-and-conquer tactics to establish control and local "puppet" authorities to govern. After a rebellion in 1857, the British systematized colonial rule and established the "British Raj" which governed India from 1858 to 1947. During this period the economy of India was made completely subservient to the economic needs of the conquering power.

After World War I, a coalition of Indian nationalists led by Mohandas Gandhi, Jawaharlal Nehru, and the Congress Party launched a non-violent campaign of civil disobedience to defy British authority. Military reactions by the British, including troops firing on peaceful demonstrators at Amritsar in 1919, bolstered the resistance. With Britain weakened by World War II, colonialism came to an end on the Indian subcontinent. As independence approached, national unity fostered by the independence movement broke down. Violence erupted and led to the relocation of approximately twelve million people, the deaths of as many as a million, the partition of the Indian subcontinent into separate Hindu and Islamic states, and a half-century of religious conflict and intermittent war.

One of the most dramatic moments in the long struggle for independence, and one that garnered international media attention, was the Salt March in 1930. Britain held a monopoly on the manufacture and sale of salt in India. Gandhi led a group that eventually swelled to over 50,000 people on a 23-day march of 165 miles to a small port on the Arabian Sea where they symbolically made salt from the ocean. Speaking to an enormous crowd, Gandhi declared, "With this, I am shaking the foundations of the British Empire." When leaders of the Congress Party were arrested for defying the Salt Laws, demonstrators attempted to shut down a British-owned salt factory. Police and soldiers savagely attacked and beat unarmed demonstrators.

Students should discuss the extent to which the strategy of non-violent civil disobedience championed by Mohandas Gandhi influenced the African American Civil Rights Movement and Nelson Mandela and the South African anti-apartheid struggle, and whether the Indian model can be effectively adopted by colonized people such as the Palestinians in the occupied territories of Gaza and the West Bank. They should also discuss whether the violence that followed independence could have been prevented, or should be considered an unavoidable and integral part of the history of the independence struggle.

Communist Revolution in China

20th-century revolutionary movements in India and China, the world's two most populous nations, took very different paths. While India struggled for independence using non-violent means, Chinese revolutionaries fought both to end foreign interference and to bring about radical economic and social change. European imperialist forces never directly governed China as the British did in India. However, European powers did succeed in creating extra-territorial "spheres of influence" and forced the Chinese imperial state to accept their economic, political, and military dictates.

The collapse of the imperial government in 1911 brought a divided nationalist party, the Kuomintang, to quasi-power. Civil war between competing factions was avoided until the mid-1920s, when an alliance of non-democratic feudal warlords, the military, and pro-capitalist forces attacked and defeated more radical political parties and workers' groups. The opposition retreated to the interior of the country under the leadership of Mao Zedong and the Chinese Communist Party. There they built model socialist communities and a new army. When China was invaded by Japan in the 1930s, the Communists, rather than the Kuomintang-dominated government, led the resistance.

After the defeat of Japan, the Communists, with broad popular support, seized power. Over the next three decades they tried various strategies to build socialism in an economically backward and vastly overpopulated society. While their measures generally failed, the Communist Party was able to maintain control by generating new social movements in support of its ideals and through a restrictive authoritarian government. In the last two decades, China has remained undemocratic, but has increasingly transformed itself, creating its own version of a controlled capitalist economy.

The Chinese Revolution and the ensuing effort to build a communist society introduces discussion of how revolutionaries mobilize mass movements and how they can present new ideas about social relationships to largely non-literate peasant populations. It also introduces the problems faced by the revolutionaries as they attempt to govern after seizing power. Comparisons of the struggles in India and China and contemporary events in these countries promote discussion of the efficacy of strategies of non-violent civil disobedience versus military campaigns, of social reform versus revolutionary reorganization, and of central planning versus capitalist initiatives.

Southeast Asian Struggles

While India had one independence movement that was not formally divided until the point of independence, and China, which fought a prolonged civil war, remained unified in the end, southeast Asia was never unified, as either an empire or as a colony, and had a number of separate national revolutionary and independence movements in the 20th century. Successful independence movements arose in the Philippines, Indonesia, Vietnam, Cambodia, Laos, Burma, and Malaysia. In the Philippines, Burma, and Malaysia, however, radical forces seeking broader social, economic, and political change were defeated or marginalized. In general these movements were facilitated by the Japanese occupation during World War II which displaced European colonial regimes and stimulated local resistance forces, and the Cold War conflict between the United States and the Soviet Union which made it possible for revolutionaries to secure outside support, especially weapons.

The Vietnamese revolution, although led by nominal communists, was one of the most successful mobilizations of nationalist sentiment against foreign intrusion. Vietnamese nationalists opposed the French after World War I, fought against the Japanese during World War II, and defeated French efforts to reassert colonial control after the war. When the United States replaced the French and established a series of puppet governments in the south, the Vietnamese fought a war of attrition until the U.S. finally withdrew. The years of resistance came with a terrible price tag. The Vietnamese had to survive aerial attacks that were the most intensive reign of destruction by an outside military force in human history. The country was devastated, and although independent, never recovered economically. In Cambodia, which was more on the margins of historical events, a movement for independence and against the "Eurofication" or "Francofication" of Khmer culture degenerated into a brutal dictatorship and genocide.

These movements introduce students to questions about how individuals and societies persevere during revolutionary upheaval and how they can deteriorate and take entirely new directions. Study of Cambodia raises questions about who shares responsibility for the death of up to two million people, roughly 20% of the country's population.

Africa

A problem when discussing the history of Africa is that the continent is too large and too diverse to simply view in umbrella terms. It is not just that the independence movements were different, but they were fought against different European powers, and some, such as Eritrea (from Ethiopia), Biafra (from Nigeria), and Katanga (from Congo), were fought against independent consolidated African states. Because of this complexity I try to pick representative struggles from different regions and focus on similarities and differences during class discussion.

Some of the bloodiest revolutionary struggles in the 20th century took place on the continent of Africa as European colonial powers attempted to expand their empires after World War I and resisted independence movements after World War II. In 1914 there were only two independent African states – Ethiopia, which was targeted for colonization by Italy, and Liberia, which was an American protectorate. Today there are 53 independent countries. I recommend focusing on independence movements in three of them because of their particular histories – the Congo (Democratic Republic of the Congo, previously known as Zaire) in central Africa, Kenya in eastern Africa, and Algeria in North Africa. I also focus on South Africa, where the struggle was for majority rule in a country dominated economically, politically, and socially by a small European minority (approximately 15% of the population).

The Democratic Republic of the Congo is the fourth most populous nation in Africa with an estimated population of 66 million people in 2007. It has been in a constant state of war since it achieved independence from Belgium in 1960. A major reason for this instability is that as a colony of Belgium, and as an independent country, it was an artificial creation of Europe.

At the 1884–1885 Berlin Conference, King Leopold II of Belgium was granted personal control over the land on the southern bank of the Congo River, an area that was considered of limited value because of dense tropical rainforest, rapids and falls that obstructed river traffic, and disease. However, the increasing demand for rubber and the discovery of copper and other minerals made the colony, which was formerly annexed by Belgium in 1908, potentially profitable, and led to the brutal mistreatment of the local people.

A post-World War II nationalist movement led by Patrice Lumumba brought independence, but the West was suspicious of Lumumba because of suspected ties with the Soviet Union and he was assassinated after a military coup. The failure of the independence movement to create a clear national identity and interference by outside political, military, and economic forces produced a half-century of dictatorship, civil war, and atrocities against civilians. The history of the Congo as an independent country helps students explore the questions of whether diverse groups of people placed under the same jurisdiction by outside forces can develop a national identity and whether imperialism ended with independence or continued in other forms.

Kenya, located in the equatorial region of East Africa, was colonized by Britain between 1901 and 1960. During the 1950s, Kenyans rebelled against colonial rule. The British charged that Kenyan rebels were part of a secret and savage society known as the "Mau Mau," whose members were supposedly pledged to slaughter Europeans. The British war against the Kikuyu, the largest tribal group participating in the rebellion, was ruthless and justified by charges that the rebels were terrorists. Eventually, the cost of maintaining the colony forced Britain to accept Kenyan independence. Study of the Kenyan independence movement presents students with the question, "Who are the actual terrorists?"

France conquered the area of North Africa known as Algeria in 1834 and established a colony where French settlers controlled the arable land, access to jobs and education, and local government. At the end of World War II, Algerian Muslims, who made up 90% of the population, organized a National Liberation Front and demanded independence from France. By 1957, over half a million French troops were assigned to suppress the Algerian independence movement. Even after the government of France reversed itself and accepted Algerian demands for "self-determination," French colonists continued to resist, delaying independence until 1962. The struggle for Algerian independence was a major front in the post-World War II struggle to end colonialism and imperialism. Algerian freedom fighters were supported by the Soviet Union, so this conflict also played a role in the Cold War. Battles between Algerians and French colonists often blurred distinctions between civilians and military personnel and raised the question of what constituted legitimate action and what was terrorism. An examination of the Algerian Independence Movement can help students address the question, "When, if ever, is revolutionary violence justified?" As I mentioned earlier, interesting comparisons can be made between the independence struggles in Algeria and Ireland.

The European colonization of South Africa by Dutch (Afrikaner) and British settlers began in the 17th century. Britain secured control over the area as a result of the Anglo–Boer War (1899–1902), but Afrikaner nationalists took over the government in 1948. They instituted a policy of apartheid, or separation, designed to guarantee their continued domination over the country and its resources. Black South Africans were denied citizenship and forced to live in either isolated, impoverished, rural communities or shantytowns surrounding major cities.

The leading organization in the struggle to defeat apartheid and secure majority rule in South Africa was the African National Congress (ANC). At different points in its history the ANC supported both political and military opposition to apartheid. In 1962, Nelson Mandela, a prominent leader of the ANC, was arrested by the South African government. Mandela remained in prison until 1989 when the government, under international pressure, began negotiations with the ANC for majority rule. Democratic elections were held in 1994 and Nelson Mandela was elected president of South Africa. In examining the struggle against apartheid in South Africa, students explore the power of mass social movements to precipitate change and possibilities for peaceful transition in oppressive and divided societies.

The website http://www.angolacoldwar.com (accessed May 19, 2010) focuses on the Angolan anti-colonial struggle and civil war that took place within the context of the Cold War. This site is excellent for teachers to use in creating document-based instructional activities about decolonization movements.

In the Shadow of the United States

Latin American has been dominated by its northern neighbor, the United States, since the Spanish–American War in 1898, although the U.S. justified its special position in the western hemisphere as early as 1823 with the Monroe–Adams Doctrine and in the 1840s absorbed more than half of the territory of its southern neighbor, Mexico. In the 20th century the United States' primary objectives were to defend shipping routes, principally the Panama Canal, against hostile European powers and its economic interests including access to materials and markets. It also sought to suppress potentially destabilizing social movements, to rally international support against the Soviet Union during the Cold War, and to prevent the Soviet Union from acquiring military bases in the region.

Cuba is one of the best examples of a country using the space created by superpower conflicts during the Cold War to break from outside domination. It is also an example of the power of economic imperialism as economic isolation by the United States and its Latin American client states stifled internal development.

Cuban revolutionaries, who were stifled for the first half of the 20th century, were suddenly successful in a bloodless coup when a pro-U.S. dictatorship with criminal ties under Batista lost all popular support and collapsed in 1959. Because of the new government's efforts to socialize the economy, which included the nationalization of U.S.-owned properties, the United States placed Cuba under an international economic embargo that left it isolated from its natural markets and virtually bankrupt. Despite this, the government, while non-democratic, was able to maintain popular support because of campaigns to create mass literacy, end poverty, and provide high levels of health care. Cuba developed close ties with the Soviet Union and supported other revolutionary movements around the world, which antagonized the United States.

Study of the Cuban Revolution introduces the differences between romantic revolutionary ideals epitomized by the mythologized Ernesto "Ché" Guevara and the problem of building and governing a new society faced by Fidel Castro. I recommend comparing events in Cuba with developments in Guatemala, the Dominican Republic, Haiti, and Chile, where elected reformers were overthrown by U.S.-backed forces.

Islamic Revolution in Iran

The Iranian Revolution does not fit easily into the same category as most of the national liberation movements discussed in this unit but I believe it belongs here. After World War II, Iran's elected government was overthrown by the United States and Britain, who feared that the country would nationalize foreign-owned oil assets. They installed an authoritarian monarchy and helped silence all secular opposition groups, but permitted rightwing religious dissent because it was also anti-communist. The Shah and his supporters were finally overthrown by a revolutionary movement in 1979 that established a new government under the overseership of conservative Islamic religious leaders. This government has supported other conservative religious groups in the Middle East in opposition to the United States and its allies. Teachers tend to present revolutions as necessarily progressive forces supportive of broader human freedom. The Iranian Revolution brings this assumption into question.

TEACHING IDEAS

Revolutionary movements have had to find ways to explain ideas and motivate followers who were often non-literate. The poster art of the Russian, Cuban, and Chinese revolutions, especially the Cultural Revolution in China in the 1960s and 1970s, are excellent examples. Working either individually or in groups, students can examine posters, describe what they see, and try to figure out the lesson each poster is designed to teach. As an introduction to the activity, a class can discuss the uses of propaganda. Posters from the Chinese Cultural Revolution are available at http://kaladarshan.arts.ohio-state.edu (accessed January 11, 2010). As a follow-up assignment, students can design and create a poster that teaches a lesson about life in their own community, teaches a lesson about an issue they think is important, or rallies people to either support or challenge a government policy.

Songs are another way revolutionary movements mobilized their supporters. Songs of the Irish revolution are especially effective for teaching because they were written in English. The Clancy Brothers and Tommy Makem have produced an easily available CD called *Irish Revolutionary Songs*. It includes "Kevin Barry," the Irish National Anthem, and "The Rising of the Moon." Other songs, including "The Wearing of the Green" (Activity 1), are available at http://www.ireland-information.com (accessed January 17, 2010).

Activities 2–9 are available online at http://people.hofstra.edu/alan_j_singer. Activity 2 is a 1916 *New York Times* interview with a young woman named Moira Regan who represented Irish rebels in New York City. In the article, Regan was identified as an Irish rebel girl who participated in the Easter Rising. I like to use this interview when teaching about the Easter Rising because of the proximity of her age to the ages of high school students. Regan raises the interesting perspective that although the Irish rebels lost the "Easter Rising" and were executed, they had won because they succeeded in transforming the consciousness and identity of the Irish people from colonized to nation. This is a fundamental step in all revolutionary movements.

Lenin's call for revolution, Activity 3, introduces students to the rational intellectualism of many Marxist movements and raises many questions. Two especially important ones are the possibility of skipping stages of development and whether undemocratic means – dictatorship by a vanguard party in the name of the masses – undermine the possibility of a democratic future.

In an era when people in power and in the media loosely label their opponents as terrorists, the debate over terrorism in Kenya during the 1950s (Activity 4) allows distance for analysis. In the first document, *The New York Times* describes the Mau Mau rebellion as a rebellion against civilization and Christianity. In the second document, an autobiography by Koigi Wa Wamwere, he uses his uncle's experience as a member of the Mau Mau to respond to Western charges that they were terrorists. In a similar way, Activity 5 presents two conflicting views on the Chinese Cultural Revolution of the 1960s.

In December 1960, Patrice Lumumba, a former leader of the struggle for independence in the Congo, its first prime minister, and now a prisoner awaiting execution, wrote a letter (Activity 6) to his wife explaining his views on events that were taking place and his hopes for the future of his country. Activities 7 and 8 are newspaper accounts of events that were part of the revolutionary struggles in India and South Africa. Activity 9 is a passage from a book by Franz Fanon. Fanon was a psychiatrist from the French colony of Martinique in the Caribbean who was working in a mental hospital in Algeria during the Algerian Revolution. Fanon joined the Algerian National Liberation Front and was expelled from the colony by French authorities. In the book *The wretched of the earth* (1961), Fanon discussed the psychological impact of colonialism on colonized people.

Mitchell Bickman (Oceanside, NY), Douglas Cioffi (Uniondale, NY), Charles De Jesus (Queens, NY), Jeffrey Fowler, April Francis (Uniondale, NY), Catherine Graf (Hewlett, NY), John Heitner (Uniondale, NY), Tabora Johnson (San Francisco), Vanessa Marchese (Queens, NY), Danielle Mazzo (Levittown, NY), Tim McEnroe (Brooklyn, NY), Gaurav Passi (Locust Valley, NY), Kerry Schaefer (Levittown, NY), Brad Seidman (Bellmore, NY), Adam Stevens (Brooklyn, NY), and Lisa Torre (Levittown, NY) helped with the development of the teaching ideas in this chapter. Some of this material appeared in *Social Science Docket*, 6 (1), Winter/Spring 2006 and 6 (2), Summer/Fall 2006.

Activity 1. The Wearing of the Green (c. 1798)

Source: http://www.ireland-information.com/irishmusic/thewearingofthegreen.shtml (accessed June 18, 2010)

Background: Songs are important parts of revolutionary social movements. They teach ideas, convey messages, and inspire solidarity. "The Wearing of the Green" was originally an Irish street ballad. Its author is unknown. It was probably composed in 1798 when the United Irishmen, whose official color was green, rebelled against British colonial rule. British authorities declared it illegal for anyone to wear a shamrock in their hat (in Irish it was known as a *caubeen*). The penalty for displaying a revolutionary insignia was death by hanging. Over the years there were many versions of this song. The best-known version is from a play performed in the United States in 1864. Examine the lyrics to the song and answer questions 1–5.

"O Paddy dear, and did ye hear the news that's goin' round?
The shamrock is by law forbid to grow on Irish ground!
No more Saint Patrick's Day we'll keep, his color can't be seen
For there's a cruel law ag'in the Wearin' o' the Green."
I met with Napper Tandy, and he took me by the hand
And he said, "How's poor old Ireland, and how does she stand?"
"She's the most distressful country that ever yet was seen
For they're hanging men and women there for the Wearin' o' the Green."
"So if the color we must wear be England's cruel red
Let it remind us of the blood that Irishmen have shed
And pull the shamrock from your hat, and throw it on the sod
But never fear, 'twill take root there, though underfoot 'tis trod.

When laws can stop the blades of grass from growin' as they grow
And when the leaves in summertime their color dare not show
Then I will change the color too I wear in my caubeen
But till that day, please God, I'll stick to the Wearin' o' the Green."

Questions

1. Why does the song's narrator call Ireland the "most distressful country"?
2. What is the song narrator's response to the British decree?
3. What are the "colors" of the United States?
4. How would you respond if someone tried to make wearing these colors illegal? Why?
5. In your opinion, why were songs important parts of revolutionary struggles?

12

TEACHING ABOUT THE EUROPEAN HOLOCAUST AND GENOCIDE

The European Holocaust of the World War II era occurred nearly three-quarters of a century before the publication of this book and few survivors are still alive, yet discussion of the events and their historical significance remains heated. One of the reasons is that what happened to European Jews during World War II became the justification for the foundation of the state of Israel as a Jewish homeland in Southwest Asia in 1948 and for subsequent actions taken by Israeli governments. These include the seizure of land owned by indigenous Arab communities, pre-emptive invasions of Israel's neighbors in the name of self-defense, and the occupation of Palestinian territories in the "West Bank" and Gaza for over 40 years. As a result, the European Holocaust is both history and current events.

Even the name I chose as a heading for this chapter, "Teaching about the European Holocaust and Genocide," introduces controversy into any discussion of the Holocaust because by calling it the European Holocaust I am taking sides in a number of debates. The modifier European leaves room for labeling other catastrophes or genocides as holocausts, such as the trans-Atlantic slave trade or the depopulation of the Americas. The modifier also identifies it as a European phenomenon, as a part of Western Civilization. I am not restricting it to just something that happened to Jews or that was done by the Nazi Party in Germany.

The term "holocaust," which is Greek in origin, originally meant a burnt offering to the Gods. In the 12th century it was used to describe massacres of European Jews by Christians. For most of the millennium, however, it referred to any slaughter or massacre. Winston Churchill described the Turkish slaughter of the Armenians during World War I as a holocaust (Churchill, 1929: 158).

During World War II, the term holocaust was used to describe the mass murder of civilian populations by the Nazis, not just their assault on the Jews. It was probably not until the 1960s that the argument gained traction that the Nazi effort to exterminate European Jews was a singular event in world history and that the term "the Holocaust" should be restricted to describing this event. A major proponent of this view was Elie Wiesel, a European Holocaust survivor, who wrote the book *Night* (Hill and Wang, 2006) about his experience in Auschwitz and Buchenwald. Wiesel was awarded a Nobel Peace Prize in 1986.

The United States Holocaust Memorial Museum website currently defines the Holocaust as "the systematic, bureaucratic, state-sponsored persecution and murder of approximately six million Jews by the Nazi regime and its collaborators" (http://www.ushmm.org, accessed December 29, 2009). Wikipedia has a well-researched entry on the debate over the use of the term holocaust at http://en.wikipedia.org/wiki/The_Holocaust (accessed December 29, 2009).

Earlier versions of this chapter appeared as "Multiple Perspectives on the Holocaust?" in *Social Science Docket*, *3* (1), Winter/Spring 2003, 2–10 and as a presentation "Living and Teaching in the Shadow of the Holocaust and Genocide" at the Museum of Jewish Heritage in New York City in January 2005.

Elie Wiesel, a European Holocaust survivor who has written widely about his experience in German death camps during World War II, challenges teachers to consider, "How do you teach events that defy knowledge, experiences that go beyond imagination? How do you tell children, big and small, that society could lose its mind and start murdering its own soul and its own father? How do you unveil horrors without offering at the same time some measure of hope?" (Totten and Feinberg, 1995: 323).

One way that social studies teachers have traditionally engaged students in examining and evaluating complex and sensitive issues is to present, and have them explore, multiple perspectives or points of view about a topic. But is it meaningful to present multiple perspectives on the Nazi effort to exterminate European Jews and other people labeled as undesirables during World War II?

While writing the New York State Great Irish Famine curriculum, Maureen Murphy and I grappled with a similar problem. Our solution was to use an essential question approach to studying about the Great Irish Famine and other controversial historical topics. For the Great Irish Famine curriculum, these questions include: What forces were shaping Ireland and the world before the Great Irish Famine (e.g., the Colombian Exchange, the Reformation in Europe, and colonialism)?; Was the Great Irish Famine an act of nature or an act of man?; How did the Great Irish Famine change Ireland and the world?; What is the legacy of the Great Irish Famine?

We never pretended that the famine did not take place or tried to minimize its impact on Ireland and the world. Neither did we condemn Britain for acts of genocide. Instead of presenting British action or inaction in Ireland during the famine as an example of genocide, we provided documentary evidence that makes it possible for students to examine the question from different perspectives and to arrive at different conclusions.

I believe a similar "essential questions" approach lends itself to studying about and understanding the European Holocaust. The United States Holocaust Memorial Museum (1993) in Washington, DC identifies questions frequently asked by visitors that can be the starting point for a study of the European Holocaust. They include: What was the Holocaust?; Who were the Nazis?; Why did the Nazis want to kill large numbers of innocent people?; How did the Nazis carry out their policy of genocide?; and How did the world respond to the Holocaust?

In my high school social studies and teacher education global history classes, over the years we have explored a series of pointed, controversial, and I believe historically important questions that can be answered from different perspectives. These questions differ from the questions posed at the United States Holocaust Memorial Museum in that they place the European Holocaust within a much broader historical context. A discussion of these questions, listed below, forms the basis for much of this chapter.

Essential questions that I propose for discussing the European Holocaust include: What is Fascism?; What is the relationship between Fascism and Nationalism?; Why did Fascism come to power in certain countries and not others?; Is there a relationship between Fascism, industrial capitalism, and imperialism or between Fascism and Communism?; What is the relationship between Fascism and Nazism?; Does one cause or do multiple causes explain the Nazi rise to power in Germany?; Can one person, Adolph Hitler, be held solely or primarily responsible for Nazism, the European Holocaust, and World War II?; Why did Nazi Germany target the Jews?; What was the responsibility of other nations for creating the conditions for Fascism and Nazism and for permitting Hitler to gain and exploit power?; Was acquiescence to Fascism and Nazism by individuals, groups, and nations a form of complicity?; What was the responsibility of individuals living in that era?; Are all people capable of complicity?; Can we generalize from the experience of a handful of European Holocaust survivors, resisters, recorders, and rescuers?; Is the European Holocaust a "singularity," something so unique and horrible that it cannot be compared with any other historical event?; How is the European Holocaust similar to or different from other genocides?; Do we live in a world where the forces of good are aligned against the forces of evil (such as in the *Star Wars* epic) and the opposing sides are clearly defined?; and In today's world, does either terrorism or repression equal genocide?

Multiple Perspectives on Fascism

The first group of essential questions on my list are related to the problem of defining Fascism. I start with Fascism rather than Nazism for two reasons. Fascism developed in other countries besides Germany. If Nazism is a subset of Fascism, it helps us to understand its origins. Defining Fascism also challenges historians to explain why a particularly virulent anti-Semitic variety emerged and seized power in Germany in the intra-war years. The Nazis "dehumanized" Jews and other people including the Romani, homosexuals, people with handicapping conditions, Socialists, Anarchists, and Communists to justify their extermination. I think it is a serious historical and philosophical mistake to "dehumanize" Nazis or Germans in order to separate ourselves from complicity with them or the possibility of similar behavior on our part.

Unfortunately, the perpetrators of the European Holocaust were all too human. The novel *Suite Française* by Irène Némirovsky (2006), while fictional, is an important primary source. Némirovsky was an expatriate Russian Jew living in France who wrote the novel during the early years of the German occupation as she and her family tried to avoid being sent to a concentration camp. Némirovsky was deported and died in Auschwitz in 1942 and the manuscript remained unpublished for decades. In the novel she depicts the French as petty and willing collaborators with the occupying force, and the Germans, while capable of brutality when their authority was challenged, as essentially ordinary young men who were separated from their homes and families and longed to be accepted by their captives. At the end of the novel, these young men were preparing to be sent to the Eastern Front, where many would become involved in mass extermination campaigns, including the slaughter of my family members in Rohatyn, a small town southeast of Lviv near the Polish/Ukrainian border.

In *Ordinary men: Reserve police battalion 101 and the final solution in Poland*, Christopher Browning (1994) argues that circumstances make it possible for any group of people to engage in murderous atrocities. Using judicial interrogations from the 1960s, he examined a group of ordinary middle-aged German men assigned to cleanse the ghettos of Poland and assist in the deportation of Jews to concentration camps where they would be exterminated. Although there is evidence that many of these men initially had nightmares and drank heavily to anesthetize their consciences, few tried to avoid their bloody assignments and most were eventually transformed into cold-blooded killers.

Browning's research supported studies done by Stanley Milgram (1963), a Yale University psychologist, who found that when ordered to by authority figures, "ordinary" people would willingly administer what they believed to be massive electrical shocks to other people.

Another problem with attributing the European Holocaust to the inhumanity of the Germans or a possible cultural flaw is that non-Germans in occupied countries often assisted with the deportation of Jewish citizens and even in their mass murder. Among the most notorious were the Ukrainian "auxiliary police" who forced Jews into the ghettos where they enforced Nazi policies and later assisted in transporting Jews to death camps (Garrard and Garrard, 1996). In the concentration camps, Jewish *Sonderkommando* assisted in mass executions in order to save their own lives (Graf, 2005).

A number of historians, activists, and political thinkers have explored the emergence of Fascism in Europe during the first half of the 20th century and they have reached very different conclusions about its fundamental nature. In 1935, the Communist International called Fascism "the open terrorist dictatorship of the most reactionary, most chauvinistic and most imperialist elements of finance capital" (Kellner, 1984: 408). It accused the "ruling bourgeoisie" of using Fascist movements to enforce "predatory measures against the working people," to rally support "for an "imperialist war of plunder," and as a means for "attacking the Soviet Union."

While the Soviet and German leaders viewed their respective systems as fundamental opposites, Hannah Arendt, in *The origins of totalitarianism* (1951), argued that Fascism and Communism are actually kindred totalitarian responses to the collapse of the nation-state system in Europe. Arendt believed that in the absence of traditional institutions in the era after World War I, an unfortunate, unprincipled, and unrestrained alliance emerged in certain countries between elites and a mass movement of rootless people with no stake in society. She calls them "atomized, isolated, individuals" (323). According to Arendt, this alliance was the basis of both Fascist and Communist movements. In post-war Germany, anti-Semitism represented an effort to resurrect a battered German nationalism and was central to the conditions that produced Fascism, transformed it into Nazism, and led to World War II (165). During the Cold War era of the 1950s and 1960s, Arendt's ideas about the connections between Fascism and Communism became the dominant view in the United States (Schlesinger, 1962).

The Age of Extremes

Eric Hobsbawm, author of *The age of extremes: A history of the world, 1914–1991* (1994), shares Arendt's view that Fascism emerged from a "collapse of the old regimes" (126). However, in his interpretation, anti-Semitism, Fascism, and "totalitarianism" played only minor roles in events leading up to World War II. Hobsbawm argues that World War II was neither fought over the fate of European Jewry nor to spread or stop totalitarianism. Instead, it was a continuation of the imperialist conflagration of World War I following a brief respite to rebuild, rearm, and repopulate. According to Hobsbawm, the second round of war started when Germany was attacked by England and France because of Hitler's attempt to create a pan-German nation including territories that had been stripped away from the Germanic central powers at the Versailles peace conference in 1919 (Austria, the Sudetenland in Czechoslovakia, Alsace-Lorraine in France, and western Prussia in Poland). In this interpretation, the war would have taken place as soon as Germany had sufficiently recovered from World War I, regardless of the emergence of Hitler or Fascism.

That said, Hobsbawm believes that Fascism was successful in Germany because of very specific circumstances: there was "a mass of disenchanted, disoriented, and discontented citizens who no longer knew where their loyalties lay" (127); an oppositional socialist movement that appeared to threaten social revolution; and, nationalist resentment against the post-war treaties. He notes that

Fascism made no progress in Britain, despite that country's endemic anti-Semitism, because its traditional conservative rightwing was able to maintain control after World War I.

Hobsbawm rejects (127–129) both the traditional liberal claim that Fascism was a social revolution from the right and the orthodox Marxist argument endorsed by the Communist International that Fascism represents the ultimate expression of "monopoly capitalism." Hobsbawm claims that Hitler quickly eliminated party factions that took the "revolutionary" rhetoric of National Socialism seriously and that German industrialists and bankers would have preferred more traditional conservative forces, even though they were able to come to terms with Fascism once Hitler had achieved power. He concludes that Fascism was no more inherent in monopoly capital than the American New Deal or British labor governments, and as a result, disappeared with the end of the world crisis in 1945.

Mein kampf

One of the most surprising things I have read in recent years is a 1933 *New York Times* book review of Adolph Hitler's *Mein kampf* (My Battle). Essentially, James Gerard of *The New York Times* gave it a positive review. He argued that:

> Those who would solve the riddle of Hitlerism and the present extraordinary attitude of the German people must search the history of Germany . . . Hitler could not have attained such power unless he represented the thoughts and aspirations of a majority of the population.
>
> (*The New York Times*, October 15, 1933: V1)

The most startling section is toward the end of the review. According to Gerard,

> Hitler is doing much for Germany; his unification of the Germans, his destruction of communism, his training of the young, his creation of a Spartan State animated by patriotism, his curbing of parliamentary government so unsuited to the German character; his protection of the right of private property are all good; and, after all, what the Germans do in their own territory is their own business, except for one thing – *the persecution and practical expulsion of the Jews.*"
>
> (*The New York Times*, October 15, 1933: V1, italics added)

In other words, Fascism is not that bad, except for Hitler's unfortunate willingness "in his rise to power" to take "advantage of this prejudice."

I was raised as a Jew in the years after World War II and was taught that there was something unique and twisted about the German "national character" that brought Hitler to power and produced Nazism and the Holocaust. My father, who had close relatives exterminated by the Nazis, would not allow my younger brother or me to purchase "flower power" Volkswagens because of their origins in Germany during the Nazi era. The idea that Nazism was caused by a flaw in the German national character was supported by the work of Louis Snyder, an historian at my alma mater, the City College of New York. In *Hitler and Nazism* (1961), Snyder cites A. J. P. Taylor, who argued that "The history of the Germans is a history of extremes. It contains everything except moderation" (39). In addition, Snyder claims that there are four "basic facts" where "historians do not differ." "The Germans were politically weak even before Hitler. Hitler exploited the beliefs and fears of a frustrated people. His clear purpose was to destroy European civilization and replace it with a barbarian empire. The Germans accepted him as the Messiah for whom they were awaiting. This political monster brought disaster and ruin both to Germany and the world" (40–41).

Today, as an historian and a social studies teacher, I have come to largely agree with Hobsbawm's assessment that Fascism, Nazism, and the Holocaust grew out of specific historical circumstances after World War I and are not tied to anything that is specifically German. I think this view is supported by a telling quotation from a 1938 statement by Winston Churchill where he said,

> I have always said that if Great Britain were defeated in war I hoped we should find a Hitler to lead us back to our rightful position among the nations . . . He [Hitler] embodied the revolt of Germany against the hard fortunes of war . . . Adolph Hitler is Fuehrer because he exemplifies and enshrines the will of Germany . . . I will not pretend that if I had to choose between Communism and Nazism, I would choose Communism.
> (http://en.wikiquote.org/wiki/Winston_Churchill, accessed December 31, 2009)

As a social studies teacher, I found a useful document for teaching about the "climate" of the inter-war years in Europe was William Butler Yeats' poem, "The Second Coming" (http://www.online-literature.com/yeats/780/, accessed December 31, 2009). Yeats believed that World War I had unleashed the worst of humanity, signaling the arrival of the anti-Christ and the approach of Armageddon. Curiously, in the late 1920s and the 1930s, Yeats, who was a staunchly anti-British Irish nationalist, became sympathetic with the Fascist cause in Ireland.

The idea that social change can be experienced as a profound, unsettling disaster, and unleash destructive forces, is also a major theme in Chinua Achebe's 1958 novel about European colonialism in Nigeria, *Things fall apart* (1994) and in much of the current discussion of the impact of globalization on non-Western countries. Students can discuss what they think would happen to political, economic, and social institutions in the United States if our way of life suddenly seemed to be falling apart.

Why Germany Targeted the Jews

If Fascism, even its Nazi variety, is not an inherently German evil, we have to find another explanation for the direction it took in Germany. Many people look at the 19th-century music and ideology espoused by Richard Wagner and others as prophetic of what was to develop. In 1881, Wagner wrote, "I regard the Jewish race as the born enemy of pure humanity and everything that is noble in it . . . perhaps I am the last German who knows how to stand up . . . against the Judaism that is already getting control of everything" (Johnson, 1987: 394). In *Mein Kampf*, Hitler described Jews as "a parasite in the body of other nations" (http://www.hitler.org/writings/Mein_Kampf/mkv1ch11.html, accessed December 31, 2009). Lucy Dawidowicz, author of *The War Against the Jews, 1933–1945* (New York: Bantam, 1986), argues that "the idea of the mass annihilation of the Jews" had already been foreshadowed by "apocalyptic-minded anti-Semites during the nineteenth century" (3) and claims that "a line of anti-Semitic descent from Martin Luther to Adolph Hitler is easy to draw" (23). Paul Johnson, in *A history of the Jews* (1987), describes Luther's 1543 pamphlet *Von den Juden und ihren Lügen* (On the Jews and their Lies) as "the first work of modern anti-Semitism, and a giant step forward on the road to the Holocaust" (242). In the pamphlet, Luther urged that Jewish "synagogues should be set on fire, and whatever is left should be buried in dirt so that no one may ever be able to see a stone or cinder of it." Luther was not content with a verbal assault on Germany's Jews. He was instrumental in having them expelled from Saxony in 1537 and his followers sacked the Berlin synagogue in 1572.

However, I do not think charges of traditional German anti-Semitism offer a sufficient explanation of what took place. The Germanic world also produced a series of world-class Jewish intellectuals who were highly respected and largely assimilated. These included people as diverse in achievement as Heinrich Heine, Felix Mendelssohn, Karl Marx, Gustav Mahler, Sigmund Freud, and Albert Einstein. At the same time, other European countries had histories of anti-Semitism and they did not try to systematically exterminate their Jewish citizens. Jews were expelled and executed by the Inquisition in Spain at the end of the 15th century. In the 1880s, there were violent anti-Jewish pogroms (riots) across western Russia. In the 1890s, the French military framed, convicted, and imprisoned Captain Alfred Dreyfus, a Jewish officer, blaming him for France's defeat in the Franco-Prussian War. Few literary works by prominent authors are as overtly anti-Semitic as England's William Shakespeare in *The Merchant of Venice*, where he describes the hardness of Shylock's "Jewish heart" or Charles Dickens in *Oliver Twist* (published as a serial 1837 through 1839) where the miserly Fagan is continually referred to as "the Jew." I think a number of developments had to come together to make Jews particularly vulnerable in Nazi Germany rather than in these other countries.

First and foremost was the impact of Germany's defeat in World War I, the one-sided Treaty of Versailles that forced Germany to pay war reparations, and the hyper-inflation, unemployment, and depression that wracked the economy in the post-war years. As early as 1916, as the German military and government sought an explanation for impending defeat, Jews were targeted. Later, the Nazi Party accused Jews of betraying Germany during the war and causing its defeat, promoting leftist revolutionary movements, and mismanaging the German economy.

As conditions grew more desperate, many Germans (Dawidowicz argues the vast number) were willing to blame a vulnerable scapegoat for their misery. Much of what we know about Nazi ideas comes from *Mein Kampf*, written by Adolph Hitler while he was imprisoned in 1923 and 1924 for leading a failed coup. In this book, Hitler excoriates Jews for all of Germany's troubles. For me, the key question is not what Hitler wrote or why, but "What conditions made it possible for his ideas to receive such a high measure of acceptance?" In November 1933, the National Socialist (Nazi) Party received 33% of the vote in parliamentary elections, and in January 1933, Hitler, as the representative of the government's largest party, took office as Chancellor. Students also need to consider whether the countries that foisted the post-war treaty on Germany and ignored its plight in the 1920s share responsibility for what happened.

The Jewish population of Germany was both large enough and small enough to be targeted and scapegoated in a time of crisis and dislocation. It was large enough that most Germans had some familiarity with Jews. It was small enough that it could be "removed" without major social dislocations. In 1933, Jews made up roughly 1% of the total population of Germany. Approximately 300,000 Jews fled Germany by 1939, while an estimated 200,000 German and Austrian Jews died in the "final solution." Students need to learn that other groups, especially socialists, communists, intellectual and religious dissenters, "Gypsies" or Romani, Poles, the handicapped, and homosexuals, were stereotyped and victimized as well (www.ushmm.org/wlc/en/article.php?ModuleID=10005276, accessed February 19, 2011).

A significant number of Jews were socially and economically prominent and some, especially Polish-Jewish immigrants, were distinctive because of their clothing and cultural practices. Small size, occasional prominence, and distinctiveness made it possible to identify and scapegoat Jews for Germany's troubles. If the Jewish population had been significantly larger or less easy to identify, Fascism would still have triumphed in Germany, but Jews might not have been targeted in the same way.

One of the paradoxes of European anti-Semitism was that Jews could be attacked at the same time as monopoly capitalists and international communists. Hitler charged that Marxism was "Jewish doctrine." Some people identifiable as Jews were prominent in each group. In the popular mind, Jews represented the alien other, the outsider, and the non-Christian. In a society experiencing sharp dislocation, Jews symbolized the forces (greedy capitalists, traitorous, atheistic socialists, modernization) threatening the traditional way of life and were easy to blame. A similar strand of anti-Semitism has been identified in populist rhetoric in the United States in the 1890s.

There was no Jewish nation-state to intervene in defense of Jews and respond to anti-Semitism, similar to Slavic Russia's support for Slavic Serbia at the start of World War I. It is important to remember that the "final solution," the plan to exterminate European Jewry, was not implemented until 1941, 8 years after the Nazis came to power in Germany. Only 2.5% of the Jews who were exterminated by the Nazis were German. The rest were people, like my father's family, who were caught on the battlefields of Eastern Europe or trapped in occupied countries.

Individual and Collective Responses

As a child growing up in the 1950s learning about the history of my own people, and later as a teenager, I was angered and also devastated by the knowledge that Eastern European Jews, including my relatives, had been murdered by Nazi Germany. Knowledge of oppression did not satisfy me. I felt humiliated and I wanted to scream out, "Why didn't we fight back?" What finally helped me come to terms with the Holocaust was reading about Jewish resistance in Leon Uris's books about the Warsaw Ghetto (1961) and the creation and defense of the State of Israel (1960). I realize that the key for my coming to terms with the 20th-century history of Jews was recognition of human resistance. Even as an adult, I laughed uncontrollably during the movie *Genghis Cohn* (1995), when a Jewish comedian, moments before his execution by a firing squad, tells his Nazi murders to "kush mir in tokhes" (kiss my ass). Sometimes "chutzpah" is the only defiance that is possible.

The book *Anne Frank: The diary of a young girl* (1995) touches readers partly because of her innocence and normalcy, but also partly because of her decision, just before her family was captured, to publish a book called *The secret annex*, based on her diary, that would help document wartime suffering in the Netherlands. The idea of keeping a diary and using it as a way to maintain our dignity and fight back against our oppressors is the only way most of us are able to confront such enormous horror.

Yet as a historian, I recognize that most Jewish resistance to Nazi oppression was symbolic and usually it was futile. We learn much about the human spirit from Anne Frank, the Warsaw ghetto fighters, the actions of German pastor Dietrich Bonhoeffer who was executed for participating in a plot to assassinate Hitler, the efforts of diplomats such as Rauol Wallenburg (Sweden) and Hirokio Sugihara (Japan) to help Jews escape, acts of decency (and self-interest) by people like Oskar Schindler, and the collective courage of the people of Le Chambon in France. However, how much should it be the focal point in a history-based social studies curriculum? We often have students read and discuss the statement on individual choices by Pastor Martin Niemöller:

> First they came for the communists, and I did not speak out – because I was not a communist; then they came for the trade unionists, and I did not speak out – because I was not a trade unionist; then they came for the Jews, and I did not speak out – because I was not a Jew; then they came for me – and there was no one left to speak out for me.
>
> (http://en.wikiquote.org/wiki/Martin_Niemöller, accessed December 31, 2009)

But what does it explain about the causes of Nazism? Was the European Holocaust simply the result of the failure of individuals to act while there was still time?

Meanwhile, other acts of organized resistance that had a much greater impact on the war and made significant contributions to the defeat of Nazi Germany and its allies are largely ignored in the curriculum because these freedom fighters believed in communism. In France, Italy, Greece, and

Yugoslavia, communists battled against great odds long after official government forces had surrendered and began to collaborate in the extermination of Jewish citizens. In Asia, Mao Zedong and Ho Chi Minh led communist revolutionary armies (supported by Western aid, weapons, and advisors) against the Japanese. *Facing History and Ourselves* (http://www.facinghistory.org), an organization that I greatly respect, has produced *Holocaust and human behavior* (1994), a 576-page resource guide on the Holocaust (downloadable at their website) that includes over fifty pages on "Bystanders and Rescuers." Communist involvement in the resistance is never mentioned.

The politics of the Cold War and its influence on the social studies curriculum have meant a series of errors of omission or emphasis as textbooks try to distinguish between the "good guys" (U.S.) and the "bad guys" (Soviet Union and communists). Prentice Hall's *World history: Patterns of civilization* (Beers, 1991) had a sub-section on "The Holocaust revealed" which explained that while "the Allies had received reports about Hitler's attacks on Jews," it was not until "Allied troops marched into Germany" that "they learned the full horror of his campaign of genocide" (708).

While on some level this statement is true, it is misleading. Anne Frank's diary says that the family learned of the mass execution of Jews from British radio broadcasts in October 1942. As early as July 1942, the United States State Department began inquiring into the massacre of Jews in Eastern Europe (Wyman, 1984: 24). Throughout the war, *The New York Times* reported on Nazi Germany's attacks on Jews, though most reports were consigned to small pieces on the inside pages. In October 1941, it published a story on the murder of over 10,000 Jews in Galicia (Poland) based on reports from Hungarian army officers. In May 1942, it reported that German troops had executed more than 100,000 Jews in the Baltic states (Wyman, 1984: 20–21). Also in May 1942, the Jewish Labor Bund in Poland delivered an extensive report on the mass murder of Polish Jews to the Polish government-in-exile in London. Information from the report, including the estimate of 700,000 casualties, was broadcast by the BBC on June 2, 1942. It was also the basis for a United Press release sent to the United States and the story appeared in different forms in the *Seattle Times*, *Boston Globe* and *The New York Times* (Wyman, 1984: 21–22).

In 1944, the United States refused to bomb the rail lines being used to transport Jews to their death in Auschwitz. The military dismissed the idea as "impractical," yet the United States bombed the area around Auschwitz on a number of occasions, including an attack on August 20, 1944 that released over one thousand bombs in the vicinity (Facing History, 1994: 407).

Prentice Hall also credits the United States, Britain, and France with helping Germany rebuild after the war, while the Soviet Union is accused of wanting to punish them, but the willingness of the West to rehabilitate and use former Nazis during the Cold War was not mentioned (715). Werner Von Braun, a scientist in charge of the German wartime rocketry program was later given a similar position in the United States. In another post-war action that bears scrutiny, the United States negotiated an agreement with the head of Germany's Russian espionage unit and paid former Nazi agents millions of dollars a year to spy on its war-time ally. In the 1950s, this group was assigned to create West Germany's espionage agency (Martin, 2002: A13).

Even claims of victimization can be problematic. While Greek resistance fighters battled the Nazis even when villages were threatened with massacre and the Soviet Union withdrew its forces and factories eastward in order to continue the fight, France and the Netherlands quickly surrendered rather than risk destruction, and most of their citizens passively collaborated with Nazi occupiers. One French town, Oradour-sur-Glane near Limoges, has a particularly interesting history. On Saturday, June 10, 1944, four days after the allied invasion at Normandy, a German SS Division entered the town without warning, rounded up its population, and slaughtered 642 people, including 205 children (*The New York Times*, 1944: 1: 4; Hébras, 1994).

No one is quite sure of the reason. Town residents had no known ties with resistance forces. Some chroniclers suspect the Germans simply made a mistake and attacked the wrong village.

FIGURE 12.1 Derelict cars and abandoned homes at Oradour-sur-Glane, 1997.

Another possibility is that the German occupying army wanted to make a statement to the French people that despite D-Day, the war and occupation were not over.

When local people rebuilt Oradour-sur-Glane after World War II, they decided to use a neighboring site, and keep the ruins of the original town as a tribute to the people who died there and as a memorial to the horror of Nazi occupation. However, the memorial presents only one portion of the town's involvement in World War II. The residents of Oradour-sur-Glane were living peacefully on that Saturday in the middle of the bloodiest war in human history. They had sought safety and temporarily succeeded in withdrawing from the war by cooperating with the occupying forces, a point that Irène Némirovsky (2006) made in *Suite Française*.

Lessons of the European Holocaust

The theme of the October 1995 issue of *Social Education* (v. 59, n. 6) was "Teaching About the Holocaust." In an introduction to the issue, Michael Simpson of the National Council for the Social Studies wrote: "Effective teaching about genocide must offer students more than the sensational facts and dates of atrocities. They need to understand the processes that can result in genocide, as well as the human forces that can prevent or resist it" (Simpson, 1995: 321). The key point here is that students and citizens need to understand the lessons of the European Holocaust in order to "prevent or resist" genocide in the future. However, understanding the European Holocaust, or even defining genocide, have not been simple tasks.

Raphael Lemkin coined the word "genocide" in 1944 in his book *Axis rule in occupied Europe*. Lemkin combined the Greek word for tribe, *genos*, with a Latin suffix designating a killer or destroyer, *cide*. In 1951, the United Nations approved (with the agreement of the United States) a "Convention on Prevention and Punishment of the Crime of Genocide." The Convention broadly defined genocide as:

> any of the following acts committed with intent to destroy, in whole or in part, a national, ethnic, racial or religious group, such as: a) killing members of the group; b) causing serious

bodily or mental harm to members of the group; c) deliberately inflicting on the group conditions of life calculated to bring about its physical destruction in whole or in part; d) imposing measures intended to prevent births within the group; e) forcibly transferring children of the group to another group.

(http://www.un.org/millennium/law/iv-1.htm, accessed June 19, 2010)

This definition has stirred up continuing debate because of the difficulty of proving *intent*, and because it expands the notion of genocide to include other kinds of victimization. For example, under this definition, Britain's decision to limit food aid during the Great Irish Famine, European involvement in the trans-Atlantic slave trade, and the decimation of the native population of the Americas by old world diseases during the Colombian Exchange probably would not qualify as genocidal actions despite the magnitude of the devastation and the clear benefit some groups received from what happened.

In 1979, the President's Commission on the Holocaust, appointed by United States President Jimmy Carter, described the European Holocaust as "a crime unique in the annals of human history, different not only in the quantity of violence – the sheer numbers killed – but in its manner and purpose as a mass criminal enterprise organized by the state against defenseless civilian populations" (http://www.ushmm.org/research/library/faq/languages/en/06/01/commission/# letter, accessed July 6, 2010). Many groups which promote Holocaust education programs and memorialize its victims share this view. A problem, however, is if the Holocaust is a "unique" occurrence, a historical "singularity," it limits the broader lessons that can be drawn from understanding Nazi efforts to exterminate European Jewry.

Ali Mazuri of SUNY-Binghamton offered a very different view of the European Holocaust during debate over the New York State Curriculum of Inclusion in 1990–1991. Mazuri argued that

> What was distinctive about Nazi Germany was that it was an extreme case of something much more widespread in the Western world – racism and a sense of cultural superiority. Hitler was the worst case of something which – in milder forms – is still rampant in the Western world. Racial and cultural arrogance.
>
> (Cornbeth and Waugh, 1995: 113–118)

Mazuri also argued that the Greek-derived word "holocaust" should remain a generic metaphor applicable to the experience of other people who were victims of atrocities. These positions were widely and sharply attacked by state political leaders, at public meetings and in the press.

Connecting with the Present

A major theme in this book is that a social studies approach to global history means constantly connecting the present with the past as we try to understand them both. It is connections with the present that are the most difficult part of teaching about the European Holocaust and I believe the most vital. Study of the European Holocaust forces us to address at least two fundamental questions: When are nations obligated to intervene when other countries pursue genocidal policies? What is the responsibility of individuals to respond to government policies that threaten civilization populations at home and abroad? Sometimes answers to these questions appear to point in contradictory directions and they can be very difficult to resolve, such as when a government claims its actions are justified by a greater good.

There has been general international agreement that certain events during the past 100 years rose to the level of genocide, including the massacre of Armenians in Turkey during World War I (although the Turkish government continues to dispute this), Khmer Rouge actions in Cambodia between 1975 and 1979, Serbian ethnic cleansing campaigns in the former Yugoslavia between 1992 and 1995, and Hutu attacks on Tutsis in Rwanda in 1994. In other cases, the international community was or is divided. These include Soviet actions that lead to the starvation of Ukrainian peasants in the 1930s, China's treatment of its own rural areas during the 1950s, ethnic conflicts in Indonesia during the 1960s that targeted the overseas Chinese community, the mass execution of indigenous peoples in Guatemala during a long civil war from 1978 to 1996, and the dislocation and murder of ethnic minorities in southern Sudan and Darfur between 2003 and 2009. Study of the European Holocaust should lead students into discussions of other documented or potential genocides and whether international action is desirable, or even possible, to prevent similar events in the future.

When I spoke about "Living and Teaching in the Shadow of the Holocaust and Genocide" at the Museum of Jewish Heritage in January 2005, I warned the audience at the beginning that my views were different from those of most Holocaust speakers and that some of them would be upset by what I had to say. I invited them to discuss these issues with me, with each other, and with their families and friends.

It is easy to condemn Hitler, the Nazi Party, and Germany in the 1930s, but I asked the audience, what kind of country had the United States become in the first decade of the 21st century? Just as we demand to know why people did not resist Hitler and his teachings, I believe future generations will demand to know what Americans did when the Bush administration ordered the United States military to launch preemptive strikes that killed thousands of innocent people, destabilized entire regions of the world, and fed into terrorist impulses. Did we speak up against injustice, as Reverend Niemöller called on us to do (http://en.wikipedia.org/wiki/First_they_came... , accessed July 6, 2010), or did we quietly go along out of a sense of vengeance for the events of September 11, 2001 and out of the belief that what happened to the people of Southwest and Central Asia did not really affect us?

Americans need to remember the cynical words of Hermann Goering, one of the founders of the Gestapo, who during the post-World War II Nuremberg trials told an interviewer:

> Why of course the people don't want war. Why should some poor slob on a farm want to risk his life in a war when the best he can get out of it is to come back to his farm in one piece? Naturally the common people don't want war; neither in Russia, nor in England, nor for that matter in Germany. That is understood. But, after all, it is the leaders of the country who determine the policy and it is always a simple matter to drag the people along, whether it is a democracy, or a fascist dictatorship, or a parliament, or a communist dictatorship. Voice or no voice, the people can always be brought to the bidding of the leaders. That is easy. All you have to do is tell them they are being attacked, and denounce the peacemakers for lack of patriotism and exposing the country to danger. It works the same in any country.
>
> (http://www.websters-online-dictionary.org/Go/Goering.html,
> accessed December 31, 2009)

It happened in Germany, and unless we learn the lessons of the European Holocaust, it will happen over again, and it can happen here.

In his book *The rebel*, French philosopher Albert Camus argued that ends can never be known in advance, so suspension of judgment on means is never justified. According to this view of history and morality, neither the extermination of people viewed as sub-human, nor tactics such as "Shock and Awe" and the use of weapons of mass destruction on civilian targets, no matter how leaders attempt to justify them, are ever warranted. In fact, pursuing these actions turns us into our own worst nightmare.

Holocaust survivors and educators have adopted the slogan, "Never Forget." While collective memory is vital, I believe it is an insufficient goal. In *Survival at Auschwitz*, Holocaust survivor Primo Levi (1996) writes that in order to stay alive, an inmate must quickly accept that "heir ist kein warum" (there is no why here) (29). As social studies students and teachers and historians grapple with understanding the causes and implications of the European Holocaust, our objectives must always be to ask and demand an answer to the question "Why?" and then to act, based on our understanding.

TEACHING IDEAS

There are a number of websites and curriculum packages that provide excellent material for teaching about the European Holocaust. Although I have significant differences and disagreements with positions taken by the United States Holocaust Memorial Museum, their *Teaching about the Holocaust: A resource book for educators* (Washington DC: 2001) is a very good place to begin. Their *Guidelines for Teaching about the Holocaust* are available online at http://www.ushmm.org/education/foreducators/guideline/ (accessed December 31, 2009). The museum website has extensive materials that include a Holocaust Encyclopedia, online exhibits, artifacts, documents, photographs, and a wonderful collection of animated maps. The museum itself is a very worthwhile trip for secondary school students. For me, the two most powerful parts of the tour were the room of shoes (http://www.vanderbilt.edu/News/register/Nov5_01/images/holocaust.jpg, accessed December 31, 2009) and the cattle car. As visitors approach the cattle car the corridor gradually narrows and darkens until you are unexpectedly crowded together in a dark confined space.

Brown University's *Choices for the 21st Century Education Project* has an excellent curriculum package "Crisis, Conscience and Choices: Weimar Germany and the Rise of Hitler." Printed and downloadable versions can be purchased online (http://www.choices.edu/, accessed December 31, 2009). Some free material is also available at the site. This package helps establish the reasons why the Nazi Party came to power in Germany.

In my view, the best material on the European Holocaust is the curriculum package developed by *Facing History and Ourselves* (http://www.facinghistory.org, accessed December 31, 2009). It is extensive, its documents are readily accessible to secondary school students, and it is designed so that study of the events of the European Holocaust is used to challenge students to think about the contemporary world. There are excellent materials examining the roles of bystanders, resisters, rescuers, and survivors. Its goal is to "inspire young people to take responsibility for their world" and its approach to teaching about the European Holocaust is "based on the premise that we need to – and can – teach civic responsibility, tolerance, and social action to young people, as a way of fostering moral adulthood."

There are also some very ill-conceived curriculum projects. In 2002 a group of my teacher education students reviewed websites that focused on the European Holocaust and uncovered a webquest designed for secondary school students that asked them to decide "Holocaust: Fact Or Fiction?"

According to this site, "there are people who believe that 'The Holocaust' never happened." Students were challenged, based on the readings, pictures, movies, and discussion they engaged in during the webquest to decide "if 'The Holocaust' is fact or fiction and report your findings to your ethics, social studies, and English classes." As part of the project, students were directed to examine what were identified as "Holocaust Denial Sites." They included www.nizkor.org/faqs/leuchter, www.ihr.org/leaflets/denial.html, and www.Holocaust-history.org/denial-hoax.

We contacted the creator of the webquest who wrote back that, "the idea behind this quest, besides tolerance and respect, is to teach students that there are other views to an issue." She insisted that, "in all my years teaching, no student has come away thinking that the Holocaust did not happen. If you click on the denial links, and the students have learned how to evaluate a website, they can see through the hollow and erroneous thinking of Holocaust deniers."

I disagree with the way this website, which is no longer online, legitimized claims that the Holocaust did not happen or had been exaggerated. Why introduce students to unsubstantiated claims that can never be established or frame a supposedly open research question in such a way that no student ever arrives at one of the possible answers? The issue is not whether the Holocaust happened, but why it happened and its historical and philosophical significance. Nothing can ever be "proven" beyond any doubt, especially to people who are committed to conspiracy theories and simply dismiss as phony any evidence that runs counter to their beliefs.

Jay Kreutzberger, Calhoun High School (Merrick, NY), Michelle Sarro, Great Neck North Middle School, Jaime Kahn Samuelson of Farmingdale High School, and Lisa Torre Nessler, MacArthur High School (Levittown, NY) helped with the development of the teaching ideas in this chapter. Some of this material appeared in *Social Science Docket, 3* (1), Winter/Spring 2003 and *4* (1), Winter/Spring 2004.

All activities in this chapter are available online at http://people.hofstra.edu/alan_j_singer. Activity 1 is an excerpt from a memoir written by a survivor of the Armenian genocide during World War I. A lesson plan on the Armenian genocide and a complete activity sheet are included in Chapter 19. For more information on the Armenian genocide visit http://www.armenian-genocide.org (accessed May 19, 2010).

Activity 2 asks students to evaluate the decision by *Time* magazine to select Adolph Hitler as "Man of the Year for 1938." Activities 3 and 4 involve students in defining fascism and genocide. In Activity 5 students map and graph Jewish casualties in selected countries during the European Holocaust. Activity 6 is a call to resistance from the Warsaw Ghetto in Nazi-occupied Poland. In Activity 7 students compare eyewitness and survivor accounts from different 20th-century genocides. Activity 8 is an excerpt from an article about genocide in Cambodia. Activity 9 looks at debate in the Clinton administration over whether to define events in Rwanda as genocide and focuses on the political nature of the decision. Activity 10 is from a first-person account of the Rwandan genocide. It is the story of Jacqueline Murekatete. Students can learn more about her, the Rwandan genocide, and genocide prevention campaigns from the website Miracle Corners of the World at http://www.miraclecorners.org (accessed January 2, 2010).

Online Resources for Teaching about Genocide

Armenian Genocide Resource Library for Teachers (http://www.teachgenocide.org, accessed May 19, 2010). This site is part of the Genocide Education Project. Although the group focuses primarily on the Armenian genocide, there are also material and survivor stories from the Rape of Nanking, Rwandan genocide, Bosnian genocide, and the European Holocaust.

Cambodian Genocide Project (Yale University) (http://www.yale.edu/cgp/index.html, accessed May 19, 2010). This site reports on the origin, development, and conclusion of the 1970s genocide in Cambodia. It includes primary sources (pictures, original United States and Cambodian government documents and maps) and reports on war crimes trials. It is an excellent site for teachers to use for developing document-based instruction and assessments.

Echoes and Reflections (http://www.echoesandreflections.org, accessed May 19, 2010). This site promotes a multimedia curriculum on the European Holocaust developed by the Anti-Defamation League, the USC Shoah Foundation Institute, and Yad Vashem. The curriculum includes personal testimony and a wealth of primary sources. Some material from the curriculum is available online.

Facing History and Ourselves (http://www.facinghistory.org, accessed May 19, 2010). This organization uses study of the European Holocaust as a starting point for addressing responsibility and injustice in the contemporary world. The site contains educational resources including units and individual lesson plans and a downloadable version of their curriculum, "Facing History and Ourselves: Holocaust and Human Behavior."

Genocide Intervention Group (http://www.genocideintervention.net, accessed May 19, 2010). The Genocide Intervention Group is an internationally recognized NGO (non-governmental organization). This site has material on Sudan, Burma, Afghanistan, Pakistan, Iraq, and Somalia, and on the civil war in the Congo that has left millions of people dead and displaced. For the Congo, it provides Congolese news reports on the crises, United Nations statistics, and United States Department of State briefings.

Nanking Massacre (http://www.nanking-massacre.com, accessed May 19, 2010). There continues to be debate over whether the Japanese massacre of Chinese civilians in Nanking in 1937 constituted genocide. Primary sources include pictures, Japanese inventories of looted goods, and military documents. It is an excellent site to use for document-based instruction and assessments that engage students in defining and recognizing genocide.

Nations Borders Identities Conflict (http://nbiconflict.web.unc.edu, accessed May 19, 2010). This site sponsored by the University of North Carolina examines conflict situations in a number of localities including the Rwandan genocide.

Prevent Genocide International (http://www.preventgenocide.org, accessed May 21, 2010). Provides research material and promotes activism to prevent genocide and other crimes against humanity.

Through My Eyes (http://www.throughmyeyes.org.uk, accessed May 19, 2010). Eyewitness accounts of conflict in the 20th century. Conflicts include India's struggle for independence and refugees' first-hand accounts of the Rwandan genocide. The site is maintained by the Imperial War Museum of London. An excellent resource for teachers and students.

United States Holocaust Memorial Museum (http://www.ushmm.org, accessed May 19, 2010). This site reflects themes and materials from the United States Holocaust Memorial Museum in Washington DC. It includes eyewitness accounts and primary sources from the European Holocaust. There are different sections designated for students and teachers.

PART III

Waves of Global Integration

13

THREE WAVES OF GLOBAL INTEGRATION

This brief chapter serves as an introduction to Part III and the chapters on teaching about the Columbian Exchange, imperialism, and globalization in the contemporary world.

Over roughly the past 500 years, human civilization has been transformed by three separate, but overlapping, waves of global integration. Prior to the 15th century the world was divided into geographical and cultural regions that had little contact with and knowledge of each other. The eastern and western hemispheres were completely separated and within the western hemisphere there was minimal exchange between the north and south and little, if any, awareness of the existence of the other region. In China, Western Europe, and Sub-Saharan Africa there was some consciousness of the other areas because of long-distance trade, but much of what passed for information about other civilizations was fabrication and myth.

Global history began gradually, with Portuguese exploratory voyages along the west coast of Africa in the first half of the 15th century. While China had sponsored much more elaborate voyages of trade and discovery in the Indian Ocean, by the middle of the 15th century these had been suspended and China had withdrawn into itself. Other societies, including the Norse, Polynesians, and possibly West Africans, may have produced trans-oceanic voyagers, but if they did, they failed to leave significant historical footprints.

The first global wave, which I call the Columbian Exchange and Age of Colonialism, established water routes between Western Europe, Sub-Saharan Africa, and the Americas, and between Western Europe and South and East Asia. It is defined by a variant of commercial capitalism known as mercantilism, the development of increasingly effective central governments in a number of European states, European colonial empires in the western hemisphere or New World, and the enslavement of millions of Africans who were shipped to the Americas as unfree labor.

It took approximately 350 years until a European-dominated global network built on trade, conquest, settlement, voluntary and forced human migration, and cultural domination was in place, but by that point it was in the process of being superseded by a second wave of global integration stimulated by an imperialism "package" combining industrial capitalism, nationalism, urbanization, and imperialism. During the second wave of global integration, roughly between 1750 and 1989,

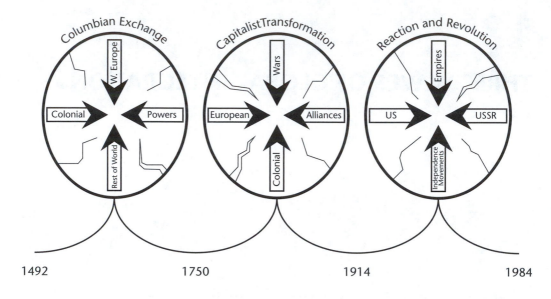

DYNAMIC GLOBAL SYSTEMS

FIGURE 13.1 Tension within historical systems led to new developments.

capitalist transformation, mass production, technological change, the emergence of powerful states with engaged citizenries, competition for resources and markets around the world, resistance, and war reorganized the world. This wave starts with the Industrial Revolution in Britain. It includes the domination of Africa, Asia, and Latin America by Europe and the United States, produces two devastating world wars with tens of millions of casualties, and ends when the Soviet Union – along with a worldwide communist challenge to capitalism – collapses.

During the last decades of this era, increasing financial and industrial integration, supported by intensive utilization of fossil fuels, computerization, and a mature transportation network, set the stage for a third wave of global integration which is generally identified as globalization. One reason to focus on three waves of global integration is to show that globalization in the contemporary era is the product of long-term historical trends.

While the three waves of global integration and global history began with Portuguese exploration of the West African coast and the Columbian Exchange, it is unclear where or whether this historical epoch will end. In the second half of the 19th century and for much of the 20th century, Marxists argued that a form of socialism marked by centralized state economic planning and collective ownership of the means to produce and distribute goods would eventually replace capitalism. Their ideas, however, were discredited by a commitment in many cases to economic determinism and inevitability and the identification of their ideas with Soviet-style authoritarianism. Meanwhile, the third wave of global integration, which started at some point in the second half of the 20th century, is still taking shape.

One concern is that in the contemporary era, trans-national capitalism has grown bigger and more powerful than the imperialism "package" from whence it emerged and it may be impossible for that system to either regulate it or to ameliorate potentially destructive forces. Economic tremors in one region, caused by excessive office construction in Asian cities, the deflation of a housing bubble in the United States, debit financing in the Mediterranean basin of the European Union, or the undervaluing of China's currency, have the potential to shake, and even shatter, the global economic system. In addition, trans-national capitalism, unleashed from national loyalties and regulatory restraints, supported by computerization and instantaneous communication, and utilizing mature financial and distribution networks, has taken on a dynamic of its own with the potential to undermine the national state system built up during the preceding 500 years, a system that still organizes, governs, taxes, represents, and provides services for, most of the people of the world.

New York Times columnist Thomas Friedman (2005) popularized the idea that globalization in the modern era has produced a world that is flat, without the disruptive forces that impeded economic development in the past. But it may be more useful to describe it as seismically unbalanced, with capitalist economic forces producing goods for non-existing markets, promoting change without plan, and maximizing short-term profit without concern for long-term social and environmental consequences. It is as if Shiva, the Hindu God of creation and destruction, walks the Earth and is out of control.

14

THE COLUMBIAN EXCHANGE AND THE AGE OF COLONIALISM (1420–1763)

> The first wave of global integration begins with European exploration of the coast of West Africa in the 15th century and leads to the exploration, conquest, and resettlement of the Americas. It is the Columbian Exchange that transforms local and regional history into global history. It sets off waves of massive human migration, establishes chattel slavery, provides the resources for capitalist industrialization, and sets the stage for Western Europe's domination of the world.

Columbus was certainly not the first Old World mariner to reach the western hemisphere. We know that in about 1000 AD Norsemen or Vikings from pre-Christian Scandinavia established settlements in the North Atlantic, including one for a brief time in what is now Newfoundland, Canada. Plausible claims have been made based on ocean currents, botanical evidence, and cryptic textual references for other trans-oceanic voyagers, including Andalusian Arabs from Spain, West Africans, and Polynesians. Legends from a variety of cultures have been used to make the case for trans-oceanic travelers to the New World from China, India, Japan, and an Irish monk known as Saint Brendan who supposedly crossed the Atlantic in the 6th century.

Some of these voyages may actually have happened. I especially like the possibility that West African fishermen, blown out to sea by a storm, could have been caught in South Atlantic currents that carried them to South America. A similar thing happened to a fleet of thirteen Portuguese ships under the command of Pedro Cabral in 1500. But this does not change the historic significance of the Columbian voyages at the end of the 15th and start of the 16th centuries. Earlier "legendary explorers," if they did make the voyages, left behind so few footprints that historians cannot reliably establish the validity of the claims. Even the documented Norse settlements were abandoned and forgotten without leaving a mark on the local sites, Scandinavia, Europe, or the broader world.

The Columbian voyages, on the other hand, led to a series of exchanges between the eastern and western hemispheres that transformed the world. They included foods, cultures, diseases, technologies, and massive amounts of transplanted people. They mark the shift from regional to global history. I identify the Columbian Exchange including the European colonization of the Americas as the first wave of global integration.

Significant characteristics distinguish this wave from subsequent waves of global integration that intensified some of the developments first witnessed here. The Colombian Exchange precipitated European colonization in the western hemisphere in ways that were unheard of either before or after in human history. In previous historical eras conquerors replaced local elites as ruling groups but local populations and their cultures continued a relatively uninterrupted existence. Examples are China under the Mongols, Spain and Italy under the Moors, England following the Norman Conquest, and India under a series of invaders. In Ireland, in the 17th century, British invaders attempted to displace the indigenous Irish with English and Scottish settlers, but this happened post-Columbian Exchange during the era I have identified as the Age of Colonization.

European colonization of the Americas followed four distinct patterns, though there were shifts from one to another once infrastructures were established or when one colonial power seized territory from another. Settler colonies were established in relatively temperate climate zones, where native population density was low, such as in what would become British North America and the southern cone region of South America (present-day Argentina, Chile, and Uruguay). In these regions, land-hungry European settlers either exterminated local people (intentionally through warfare or unintentionally via disease) or drove them into less hospitable areas in the interior.

Plantation colonies were established in semi-tropical areas where captive and enslaved Africans provided the labor power to produce cash crops such as sugar, tobacco, indigo, rice, and later, cotton, for export to European markets. In some areas such as in central Mexico and the Andes where large native populations survived the initial onslaught, they became bonded labor on agricultural plantations and in mines, or serfs tied to the land in the fashion of European feudalism.

Religion, especially Roman Catholicism, was used as an agent of colonialism, although local church officials often did intercede in an effort to protect converts from abuse. In the Spanish colonies, missionaries often followed directly after gold-seeking explorers. The missions or missionary colonies they established among the indigenous people, in the Mexican northwest (currently the U.S. Southwest) and in the Amazonas, later became trading posts, and still later, settlements. In some areas, especially in what would become French Canada, indigenous people became partners in trade, particularly the fur trade, and in these trade colonies their societies were left relatively intact. New York City, which was originally Dutch New Amsterdam, was founded primarily with this purpose, although it became a settler colony by the time the British absorbed it in 1664.

Impact of the Colombian Exchange

To understand the full impact of the Colombian Exchange, I would start by revisiting societies on both sides of the Atlantic Ocean that were most directly affected, first in the Americas, then in Africa, and finally in Europe. When the Spanish conquistadores arrived in the Americas in search of "God, Gold, and Glory," the Aztecs dominated the Valley of Mexico in North America and the Andean region of South America was dominated by the Inca.

One thing I found striking when I read Bernal Díaz del Castillo's *The conquest of New Spain* (1973) is that the Spanish soldiers were overwhelmingly impressed by the glories of the Aztec civilization they were in the process of looting. Diaz and Jared Diamond (1997) describe how Old World diseases, especially smallpox, European iron-based weapons including swords, armor, and muskets, and the Spanish use of war horses and dogs, led to the defeat of the Aztecs. Over the course of 100 years, the population of the Valley of Mexico declined by 90%.

The Colombian Exchange had a different, though also devastating, impact on the people of West Africa. The devastation of the indigenous population of the Americas meant a new labor force had to be introduced to develop the land and resources. In some areas, particularly in the more mountainous and outlying regions, enough of the native population survived to be exploited. In others, poor and displaced Europeans were either voluntarily or involuntarily used as bonded labor. However, during the course of about 150 years, first on agricultural plantations in the Caribbean and Brazil and then more generally, enslaved Africans became the primary un-free workforce.

Africans were captured and brought to the New World for a number of reasons. West-coast Africans had some immunity to both the Old World viral diseases wiping out the native population of the Americas and tropical bacterial and parasitic diseases debilitating the newly arrived Europeans. They already lived in agricultural societies so captives could adapt to do the required work. Slavery, albeit in a form far different from the one that developed in the Americas, already existed in these areas and competition between tribes could be exploited to ensure a steady supply of new captives. At the time, there were no effective centralized states or empires in the coastal regions that could stop the onslaught.

An estimated 13 million Africans were shipped to the New World from coastal slave ports. Millions of others died in tribal warfare stimulated by the demand for slaves, during raids, while being transported to the coast, or when left behind in decimated communities. According to *The Slave Trade* by Hugh Thomas (1997), this included approximately three million people from Congo and Angola, and two million each from Senegal/Gambia, Sierra Leone, the region around Dahomey and the region near Benin, who made the trans-Atlantic voyage bound in chains beneath the decks of European slave ships. The largest group, four million people, were shipped to Brazil.

An excellent primary source describing African village life destroyed by European enslavement and the horrors of the "Middle Passage" is *The interesting narrative of the life of Olaudah Equiano, or Gustavus Vassa the African* (Gates, 1987). Equiano eventually became educated and free and wrote his memoir as part of the campaign in England to outlaw the trans-Atlantic slave trade (http://doc south.unc.edu/neh/equiano1/menu.htm, accessed June 20, 2010). The destruction of African communities and societies left Africa vulnerable to 19th-century European imperialism and colonization, and, I would argue, contributed to the wars, poverty, and hardship we see in Africa today.

Europe Profits

Perhaps the most profound impact of the Columbian Exchange was on the nations of Western Europe, who went from the periphery of wealth, power, and civilization in what was a regionalized world to the commanding center of a global world in the course of about 250 years. As they competed for trade and colonies, Western European nations used the labor of enslaved Africans, the indigenous population of the western hemisphere, and indentured Europeans, the resources and land of the Americas, and trade with East Asia, to amass a level and concentration of wealth previously unknown in the world. The investment of this wealth in building the physical infra-structure of European nations, in military might, in New World plantations, in creating commercial and banking networks, and later in new technologies and industries, was an essential element in the nascent Industrial Revolution in Britain and eventually led to European global domination.

European nations profited from the trans-Atlantic slave trade in a number of ways. Between 1761 and 1807, British ships made 5,693 slave-trading voyages and delivered over 1.4 million enslaved Africans at an average profit of 9.5% per person. Between 1673 and 1800, the enslaved African population of Jamaica, a British colony, grew from 40,000 people to 337,000. By 1800, they operated 800 sugar mills producing 70,000 tons of sugar that was valued in the millions. At the same time, British manufacturing exports to the Americas and Africa increased in value over 750% between 1699 and 1774. In 1770, indirect profits from the Triangular Trade between Britain, Africa and the Americas, which included the sale of goods to the plantation colonies, insurance and banking industry earnings, and income derived by the shipping industry, were roughly equal in value to the combined profits from the trans–Atlantic slave trade and plantation production.

This new wealth fundamentally transformed European society. Population nearly doubled between 1700 and 1800. Internal European trade flourished, financing was available for scores of new projects and capital formation skyrocketed. One of the most striking changes was in the Netherlands where slave-trade profits supported population growth and paid for the construction of canals and dikes and the reclaiming of previously flooded land that doubled the size of the country. An essential question that can be examined with students is "Would the industrial development of Europe and the United States have proceeded in the same way without the profits from the trans–Atlantic slave trade and the products produced by the labor of enslaved Africans?"

Slavery and the Slave Trade Web Resources

Abolition Project (http://abolition.e2bn.org/index.php, accessed May 19, 2010). This site examines the British Abolitionist movement and slave resistance in British Colonies. The primary sources include Abolitionist literature and posters and maps of British colonial plantations. The illustrations provide an in-depth look at life on a sugar plantation for a slave. The site was created by the United Kingdom's Museum Archives and Libraries (MLA) Humanities Project.

Africans In America (http://www.pbs.org/wgbh/aia/part1/1narr4.html, accessed May 19, 2010). The first section of this PBS website based on the documentary series *Africans in America* focuses on the trans–Atlantic slave trade. It includes eyewitness accounts of life on a slave ship, illustrations of the slaves on the slave ships, and shipping maps. An excellent resource for students.

Cape Coast Castle Museum (http://ghana-net.com/cape_coast_castle_museum.aspx, accessed May 19, 2010). This is a well-illustrated site with limited text. The museum, located in Ghana, is housed in a building that served as a fortress and base of operations for European slave traders.

International Slavery Museum (http://www.liverpoolmuseums.org.uk/maritime/collections/slavery, accessed May 19, 2010). The International Slavery Museum is part of the Merseyside Maritime Museum in Liverpool, UK. The site provides a detailed outline of England's role in the slave trade, audio interviews of lectures about the slave trade, and a reading list of related books on the trans–Atlantic slave trade.

New York and Slavery: Complicity and Resistance (http://nyscss.org/resources/publications/new-york-and-slavery.aspx, accessed May 23, 2010). Lessons and edited documents on the impact of slavery and the trans–Atlantic slave trade on global history are included in the first chapter of the curriculum that was awarded a National Council for the Social Studies program of excellence award in 2005.

Spartacus Educational (http://www.spartacus.schoolnet.co.uk, accessed May 19, 2010) is a British online encyclopedia geared to secondary school students but is especially useful for global history teachers. It includes an in-depth examination of slavery and the trans–Atlantic slave trade from 1750 to 1870.

Trans–Atlantic Slave Trade Database (http://www.slavevoyages.org/tast/index.faces, accessed May 19, 2010). This site, created by Emory University, documents slave ship routes and cargoes and includes the names of enslaved Africans as listed on ship inventories. An excellent reference site for teachers which provides links to other online sources.

TEACHING IDEAS

All activities in this chapter are available online at http://people.hofstra.edu/alan_j_singer. European explorers and conquerors and Arab merchants wrote most of the accounts we have of pre-Columbian and early post-Columbian western hemisphere and Sub-Saharan African societies. These must be read carefully as outsiders bring biases to their writing, often as they attempt to justify their actions. However, some of the reports are useful because the narrator brings a sense of awe or at least of respect to the world they are describing. Activity 2 in Chapter 6 presents excerpts from Bartholomé de Las Casas' report on the treatment of Native people by the Spanish conquistadores. Activity 6 in Chapter 5 is a report by an Islamic merchant on his visit to the West African Kingdom of Mali.

In this chapter, Activity 1 is a report by a Spanish conquistador on governance and road building in the Inca Empire in Andean Peru. Activity 2 has students examine photographs of surviving pre-Columbian Meso-American structures at Machu Picchu in Peru and at Chichen Itza on the Yucatan Peninsula of Mexico. These pictures are from my trips. *National Geographic* magazine offers an online lesson comparing both sites (http://www.nationalgeographic.com/xpeditions/lessons/04/g912/twocitiesinca.html, accessed February 22, 2010). The Peabody Museum at Yale University has an excellent online unit package for teaching about Machu Picchu at http://www.peabody.yale.edu/education/pages/curric_mpss.html (accessed February 22, 2010).

Activities 3 and 4 allow students to view Native Americans and Africans through their own eyes, but there are reliability problems with both documents. Activity 3 purports to be a Native American view of an early encounter with Europeans. However, it takes place in the early 17th century and Europeans wrote down the story much later. The document in Activity 4 was written by Olaudah Equiano, an African who was enslaved as a youth, secured freedom in Britain, and became an abolitionist. It was first published in 1789 so we are reading about a society that had already adjusted to contact with Europeans and the trans-Atlantic slave trade. In addition, Equiano brings his own set of biases. He is writing about a society he left decades earlier and portrays Africa in a way that supports the crusade to end slavery and the slave trade. The International Slavery Museum (Liverpool, UK) online exhibit has supporting material on life in West Africa before the arrival of Europeans, including a reconstruction of an Igbo compound that might be similar to the one where Olaudah Equiano spent his childhood (http://www.liverpoolmuseums.org.uk/ism/collections/africa/, accessed February 22, 2010).

The charts and graphs in Activities 5 and 6 examine the impact of the grossly unequal Columbian Exchange on the peoples of the Americas, Africa, and Europe. Activity 5 explores the extent of the trans-Atlantic slave trade. Activity 6 looks at how the wealth generated by the trans-Atlantic slave trade and trade in slave-produced commodities fundamentally transformed European society.

Before the Industrial Revolution at the end of the 18th and beginning of the 19th centuries, other than agricultural production, profit from trade was the most important economic activity. It took centuries to build local, regional, and inter-continental trade networks that moved prized goods such as silks and spices across Eurasia and Africa to new markets. The economic system based on profiting from trade is now known as commercial capitalism.

The Columbian Exchange flooded this system with gold and silver from the Americas and new desirable agricultural products such as cane sugar, coffee, and tobacco. It also generated profit from the trans-Atlantic slave trade. To manage this economic system, colonial powers developed a number of economic innovations including joint stock companies, banking and insurance institutions, and stock and commodities markets.

Colonial powers wanted to ensure that profits from overseas enterprises flowed into their treasuries. In the 17th and 18th centuries, they developed a form of commercial capitalism known as mercantilism, or managed trade. Under this system, colonies could only trade with their "Mother Country." Even goods destined for other markets had to pass through its ports. Activity 7 provides students with three documents explaining the increasing importance of trade in this period and the emerging mercantilist system. The technical tone of these documents is important because the economic system they are describing is rooted in the horrors faced by native people in the Americas and Africans because of the trans-Atlantic slave trade.

15

IMPERIALISM: THE EAGLE'S TALONS

In 1900, while the United States was engaged in establishing a colonial empire in East Asia and the Caribbean, Mark Twain (1900) declared "I am opposed to having the eagle put its talons on any other land." The closer you get to the present, the more likely personal views on events in the past and present will influence the way a social studies teacher designs the curriculum, selects documents, organizes lessons, and asks questions. While the major imperialist powers during the second wave of global integration were European countries, how students and teachers view events in this period is very much shaped by how they view what is taking place today. For example, when United States President George W. Bush (2001) made the following statement in the wake of the events of September 11, 2001, was he promoting the spread of democratic institutions or defending an imperialist agenda?

> Every nation has a choice to make. In this conflict there is no neutral ground. If any government sponsors the outlaws and killers of innocents, they have become outlaws and murderers themselves . . . We defend not only our precious freedoms but also the freedom of people everywhere to live and raise their children free from fear.
> (http://middleeast.about.com/od/afghanistan/qt/me081007b.htm, accessed July 7, 2010)

Samuel Clemens, best known by his pen-name Mark Twain, is remembered for his novels about American life and his humorous short stories, but there was also a serious and political dimension to his career. He frequently wrote and spoke out against United States imperialist expansion and was a vice-president of the Anti-Imperialist League from 1901 until his death in 1910.

Some of Twain's sharpest barbs were aimed at Belgium's exploitation of the Congo in equatorial Africa. The "Congo Free State" had been designated the personal fiefdom of the King of Belgium by the European powers at an 1884–1885 conference on the division of Africa, held in Berlin. In the pamphlet *King Leopold's soliloquy* (1905), Twain images King Leopold delivering an incoherent defense of imperialism as the agent of religion, civilization, and modernization. In a 1905 interview published in the Boston *Herald*, Twain charged,

The condition of things in the Congo is atrocious, as shown by the photographs of children whose hands have been cut off. Leopold thinks this can go on because the Congo is a distant out-of-the-way country. But once we can get England and America to investigate, and take this matter up, something will be done. We Americans are especially interested, because it was our recognition of the flag there that led to recognition by other powers.

(http://www.historywiz.com/soliloquy.htm, accessed February 11, 2010)

Unfortunately for the people of the Congo, little improved before independence in 1960, and the country continues to be plagued by bloody civil wars and rogue armies that have targeted civilians and been responsible for deaths in the millions.

The brutality of European imperialism in the Congo drew the attention of the world. This was partly because of the efforts of people like Twain, Irish-British diplomat Roger Casement, who was decorated for humanitarian work in the Congo and the Amazon, and E. D. Morel, a Franco-English journalist and founder of the international Congo Reform Association, whose articles and books exposed the magnitude of the horrors taking place there.

Morel published *The black man's burden* (1920) as a response to the poem, "The White Man's Burden" (http://www.wsu.edu/~wldciv/world_civ_reader/world_civ_reader_2/kipling.html, accessed February 15, 2010), where English poet Rudyard Kipling called on the United States to join Britain in the daunting task of bringing civilization to a savage non-White world populated by peoples he considered "half devil and half child." In the book, part documentation and part polemic, Morel described Africa's struggle to resist "the material gods of the white man, as embodied in the trinity of imperialism, capitalistic exploitation, and militarism" (http://www.archive.org/stream/ blackmansburden00moreuoft#page/8/mode/2up/search/trinity, accessed February 15, 2010).

While there is little debate that in the Congo imperialism produced human tragedy that bordered on genocide, the real question for students of global history is whether these practices were excesses and exceptions or whether they represent the actual dynamic of unfettered imperialism. To explore this question, students and teachers need to examine what I call the "imperialism package" that defines this historical era: the interrelationship between industrial capitalism, European nationalism, and imperialism. It is a package that, once developed, eventually – perhaps inevitably – led Europe and much of the rest of the planet down the path into global war from 1914 to 1945.

When Morel wrote *The black man's burden* immediately after the end of World War I, he believed the world stood on "the threshold of a new era" and that Britain would take a lead role in ending the "atrocious wrongs which the white peoples have inflicted upon the black" and in bringing "humane" government to Africa (vii). Morel was soon disappointed. Even before the book's publication, Britain instituted mercantilist economic policies in its West African colonies that required 90% of their principal exports be shipped directly to British ports.

Roger Casement, who was knighted in 1911 by the British crown for his opposition to the excesses of imperialism (and was hanged by the same British crown in 1916 for supporting the Irish "Easter Rising" and independence movement) discovered that imperialist behavior in the Congo was not unique. In 1906, Casement was assigned by the British foreign service to Brazil were he learned that a Peruvian-headed, British-registered company had enslaved thousands of local Indians in the Peruvian Amazon and was using torture, rape, and murder to force them to work on its rubber plantations (Grandin, 2010: BR11). In this case local entrepreneurs, rather than European or United States companies, were integrated into the exploitative imperialist system that provided industrialized countries with raw materials.

Imperialism is distinguished from colonialism, the first wave of global integration discussed in the previous chapter, in three important ways. The acquisition of territory in the Americas for settlement, either by transplanted Europeans or enslaved Africans, was a primary goal in the Age of Colonialism. During the Age of Imperialism, however, when Europe's attention turned towards Africa and Asia, actual settlement was a minor concern. In territories that were conquered and colonized in this era, such as India by the British, and Southeast Asia by the French, local populations remained in place. Land and people were exploited for raw materials and as markets to support the expansion of industrial capitalism, a dynamic economic force that did not exist in the previous era. Competition between imperialist powers also tended to be sharper, fueled by nationalism and the mobilization of citizens to support national interests.

In the late 19th century, support for imperialism was deeply imbedded in the culture of Western nations, including the United States where westward and overseas expansion were justified as Manifest Destiny. John Stuart Mill, a noted British philosopher and economist, justified British imperial control over Third World people because of its importance for England's economic development. According to Mill,

> These outlying possessions of ours are hardly to be looked upon as countries, carrying on an exchange of commodities with other countries, but more properly as outlying agricultural or manufacturing estates belonging to a larger community. Our West Indian colonies, for example, cannot be regarded as countries with a productive capital of their own . . . [but are rather] the place where England finds it convenient to carry on the production of sugar, coffee and a few other tropical commodities.
>
> (Mill, 1848: 17)

John Ruskin, another well-known English writer and thinker of that era, also justified imperialist expansion around the world. In an 1870 lecture at Oxford University titled "Imperial Duty," Ruskin argued that imperialism spread civilization. Britain's "destiny," according to Ruskin, was to be a "source of light, a centre of peace" and the "mistress of Learning and of the Arts" for the entire world. To promote this destiny, Ruskin believed Britain   .

> must found colonies as fast and as far as she is able, formed of her most energetic and worthiest men, seizing every piece of fruitful waste ground she can set her foot on, and there teaching these her colonists that their chief virtue is to be fidelity to their country, and that their first aim is to be to advance the power of England by land and sea, and that, though they live off a distant plot of ground, they are no more to consider themselves therefore disfranchised from their native land, than the sailors of her fleets do, because they float on distant waves.
> (http://www.wwnorton.com/college/english/nael/20century/topic_1/jnruskin.htm, accessed February 16, 2010)

According to *Churchill's empire: The world that made him and the world he made* by Richard Toye (2010), British Prime Minister and World War II hero Winston Churchill was one of Europe's leading advocates for imperialism and one of its most callous practitioners. As a young man, Churchill was a journalist who avidly joined in Britain's "jolly little wars against barbarous peoples" (Toye, 2010: 35). In 1897, he sent dispatches to the *Daily Telegraph* from the Swat Valley of Pakistan, where he reported on, and celebrated, how British forces systematically destroyed villages, tore down houses, filled wells with debris, cut down shade trees, burned crops, and broke down reservoir dams (Churchill, 1898). In South Africa, Churchill defended placing Blacks he derisively called "kaffirs" in internment camps where 14,000 people died. He argued that the camps minimized suffering and boasted of the great fun he had galloping about the countryside (Toye, 2010: 61, 68). In the post-World War II era Churchill pursued similar policies in British-occupied

Kenya in order to clear the fertile interior highlands of the native Kikuyu people (Toye, 2010: 294). One of the 150,000 internees was U.S. President Barack Obama's paternal grandfather, who was imprisoned for 2 years and tortured by the British (Hari, 2010: 11).

In the 1920s, while a member of Parliament, war secretary, and colonial secretary, Churchill directed the "Black and Tan" British occupying force to burn down the homes of rebelling Irish Catholics and to beat civilians. He also advocated using poisonous gas against Kurdish rebels in Iraq to "spread a lively terror" (Simons, 1994: 179–181). Churchill derided Indians as "a beastly people with a beastly religion" (Toye, 2010: 227) and during a 1943 famine in Bengal he blocked aid for months, blaming the colonized Indians for their own problems.

By the first half of the 20th century, prominent intellectuals, in both the West and in conquered nations, started to become much more critical of imperialism and its impact. They also began to systematically explore the relationship between imperialism, nationalism, and capitalism. J. A. Hobson, an English economist, defined imperialism as "the endeavor of the great controllers of industry to broaden the channel for the flow of their surplus wealth by seeking foreign markets and foreign investments to take off the goods and capital they cannot use at home" (Seldes, 1966: 324). Hobson considered imperialism to be the natural expansion of nationality.

During the Russian Revolution, Lenin described imperialism as "capitalism dying, not dead" (Lenin, 1929: 340). Earlier he had argued that "imperialist wars are absolutely inevitable" under the economic conditions generated by monopoly capitalism (http://www.marxists.org/archive/lenin/works/1916/imp-hsc/pref02.htm, accessed February 15, 2010). In a 1919 speech after the conclusion of World War I, French novelist Anatole France declared: "Let us create rational human beings, capable of . . . resisting those blooded ambitions of nationalism and imperialism which have crushed their brothers" (Seldes, 1966: 254).

India, one of the main victims of British imperial ambition, produced some of imperialism's most bitter critics. Mohandas Gandhi, when asked by an interviewer what he thought of Western Civilization, sarcastically declared it would be a good idea (http://www.democracynow.org/blog/2008/1/30/western_civilization_an_idea_whose_time_has_come, accessed July 7, 2010). In 1958, Indian Prime Minister Jawaharal Nehru argued that "Imperialism, or colonialism, suppressed, and suppresses, the progressive social forces. Inevitably, it aligns itself with certain privileged groups or classes because it is interested in preserving the social and economic status quo" (Sheean, 1960: 311).

While I argue that imperialism and capitalism are integrally related, students should also question this idea. Western capitalism continued to thrive after European empires were dismantled following World War II and Western-type economies successfully developed in many Asian countries. During the Cold War the Soviet Union presented itself as an anti-imperialist and anti-capitalist champion and defender of national self-determination in the Third World. The United States and its allies countered that the Soviet Union pursued imperial policies in the Eastern European countries that were members of the communist bloc. After the collapse of communism and the breakup of the Soviet Union into fifteen independent states, it became clear that many of these new states considered themselves captives of what was essentially a continuation of the old Czarist Empire. In the 21st century, Russia continues to be plagued by separatist ethnic movements and civil unrest among nationalities that believe themselves to still be the victims of Russian imperialism.

TEACHING IDEAS

In a period when the global military and economic policies of the United States and its Western allies have contributed to wars in Afghanistan and Iraq, increasing concerns about the impact of globalization on the national and international economy and workforce, and constant apprehension over the possibility of "terrorist" attacks, the nature of imperialism needs to be continually addressed in global history classes. I recommend beginning comparisons of past and present while examining the expansion of ancient world empires and continuing to explore them whenever looking at clashes between stronger and weaker forces.

Students should debate whether foreign expansion by militarily and economically powerful countries can be a force for positive global change (e.g., the transformation of the role of women in traditional societies), must always be condemned as a cause of exploitation, chaos, and war (e.g., the upsurge in religious fundamentalism in the Islamic world), or somehow can be justified on occasion because of specific local circumstances (e.g., intervention to prevent genocide). They should also discuss the economic and cultural impacts of imperialism on both the dominated people and the imperializing powers.

All activities in this chapter are available online at http://people.hofstra.edu/alan_j_singer. The first three activities focus on Britain during the second half of the 19th and beginning of the 20th centuries. Activity 1 is a timeline of British overseas military engagements during the middle of the 19th century. It includes campaigns in South Africa, New Zealand, the Punjab (Pakistan), Ireland, the Black Sea region, Burma, China, Persia (Iran), India, Ethiopia, West Africa, and Egypt. Activities 2 and 3 are statements in defense of British imperialism by John Stuart Mill and John Ruskin. Activity 4 defends the morality of French imperialism in Southeast Asia. The document illustrates the connection between imperialism and racism.

Activities 5 and 6 are critiques of European imperialism. English economist John Hobson discusses the relationship between imperialism, capitalism, and war. E. D. Morel denounces European imperialism in Africa. Activities 7 and 8 explore the impact of imperialism on the Congo region in Africa and the Amazon region of South America. There are photographs online of Africans mutilated by European overseers at http://academic.brooklyn.cuny.edu/english/melani/english2/images/congo_photos.html (accessed May 19, 2010).

Activity 9 examines resistance to Dutch imperialism in Indonesia. It spotlights an Islamic woman who led resistance forces. Activities 10 and 11 are mid-20th-century critiques of imperialism by Jawaharal Nehru, Prime Minister of India, and Ernesto "Ché" Guevara, an Argentine-born leader of the 1959 Cuban Revolution.

16

GLOBALIZATION: THE FIFTH HORSEMAN OF THE APOCALYPSE

While a social studies approach to global history is constantly drawing comparisons between past and present, it remains important that students systematically examine political, economic, and social developments in the contemporary era. This chapter discusses globalization in the late 20th and early 21st centuries, what I identify as the third Wave of Global Integration since the start of a truly global history with the Columbian Exchange. When looking at the contemporary era, I suggest focusing on recurring themes and essential questions developed during the course of the curriculum, while building lessons around current events. An essential question that I focus on in this area of study is "Who pays the price for change?"

The Burcad Badeed, the notorious Somali sea bandits, do not get a very good press anywhere in the world. They are characterized as cutthroat pirates, similar to those who plagued the seas in past centuries, to be feared by civilized people comfortably living thousands of miles from their bases on the Horn of Africa.

The Burcad Badeed are responsible for hijacking ocean-going freighters traveling one of the world's busiest shipping routes, the Gulf of Aden that connects Asian producers of industrial goods and Persian gulf oil countries with European markets via the Suez Canal. Over 20,000 ships a year travel this route and they carry a significant portion of the world's oil supply.

According to the International Maritime Bureau (http://www.icc-ccs.org, accessed March 1, 2010) in 2009, the Burcad Badeed received an estimated $60 million in payments from major global shippers after holding ships, cargo, and crews for ransom. In recent years, piracy has also been a major problem for shipping off the coasts of Nigeria and Bangladesh and in the straits between the islands of Indonesia and between Indonesia and the Southeast Asian mainland.

Most social studies teachers know very little about Somalia other than what they learn from sensationalized media reports. This is not the first time Somalia has been in the news in recent decades. During the Cold War, the United States and the Soviet Union armed and financed competing militarized gangs and gang leaders, euphemistically called warlords, in this region of East Africa. Sometimes the gangs were anointed as governments, but they were rarely more than armed thugs. With the end of the Cold War, funding for the gangs was cut off and the situation in Somalia rapidly deteriorated into a chaotic civil war. These events provided the backdrop for the book (Bowden, 1999) and movie (2001) *Black Hawk down*.

Somalia has not had a functioning government or national economy in two decades and is in effect no longer a country; gangs, factions, strongmen, and warlords control different regions. Without a government, navy, or police force, it was impossible to stop either local piracy or the dumping of toxic wastes and illegal fishing by European and Asian vessels along the 1,880-mile Somali coastline, which was in effect a much more lucrative form of globalized capitalist piracy.

I found a front-page article in *The New York Times* in May 2009 (Gettleman, 2009) that was particularly informative about how these economic and political conditions produced the Burcad Badeed. The author interviewed Abshir Boyah, a leader of one of the pirate bands. Boyah, aged 43, became a fisherman when he dropped out of school as a child. He became a pirate when foreign trawlers using high-tech equipment destroyed the local fishing industry in the mid-1990s. The United Nations estimates that between $300 and $500 million worth of seafood is taken by European and Asian vessels from East African waters every year.

In order to survive, Boyah and other local fisherman organized a volunteer coastguard to frighten away the foreign vessels or force them to pay fees for fishing in Somali territorial waters. Gradually the volunteer coastguard invested in bigger boats and more effective weapons and started to seize foreign vessels fishing or traveling in the Gulf of Aden; fees and taxes soon became demands for ransom (http://insidesomalia.org; http://www.illegal-fishing.info, accessed March 1, 2010).

Somalia, victimized by both the Cold War and unregulated globalization, remains drastically poor. Three-quarters of its population of over nine million people live below the poverty line. Life expectancy at birth is 48 years, one of the lowest in the world. About two-thirds of the adult population is illiterate. According to the CIA World Factbook, it ranks 224th in the world in per capita income, above only Liberia, Burundi, the Congo, and Zimbabwe (http://stats.uis.unesco.org/unesco/; https://www.cia.gov/library/publications/the-world-factbook/, accessed March 3, 2010).

Historically, economic change has often produced massive social dislocation that has driven the displaced to desperate measures. In "The moral economy of the English crowd in the eighteenth century" (1971: 76–136), Edward Thompson examined the causes of food riots in preindustrial England, a period and locale where they occurred frequently. Thompson argued that food riots were the product of societies undergoing basic economic and political reorganization. In preindustrial society, peasants in England and other parts of Europe became accustomed to food, especially bread, being sold at "just prices." In the shift to a capitalist market economy, a communal moral imperative that had held down prices was replaced by production and sale for profit and the price of food soared. Thompson concluded that while people rioted because they were hungry, they were also protesting against what they perceived of as a fundamental injustice.

George Rudé (1964: 198–204) studied rioting and mob violence in revolutionary France and industrializing England during the 18th and early 19th centuries and concluded that most participants had previously been law-abiding citizens. While they were poor and displaced, they were not members of a criminal underclass as authorities claimed. My own research on Irish participants in the 1863 New York City Draft Riots reached a similar conclusion (Singer, 2004: 259–263).

Eric Hobsbawm (1959: 13) argues that banditry was also frequently a "primitive form of organized social protest," which explains why legendary European bandits such as Robin Hood in England, Janosik in Poland, and Diego Corrientes in Andalusia (southern Spain) were folk heroes protected by local populations. Peter Linebaugh and Marcus Rediker, authors of *The many-headed hydra* (2000), claim that many of the people accused of piracy during the era of the trans-Atlantic slave trade and European colonization of the Americas were actually engaged in an epic struggle to assert control over their own lives in a period of intense victimization of people displaced by warfare and economic development. Many English "pirates" originally went to sea after being impressed into service in the British navy and merchant fleet. Some had been kidnapped; others were debtors who had migrated into the cities from rural villages after the privatization of land that was originally set aside for common use.

Essential questions about globalization that students should explore in the global history curriculum include: "Is prosperity in Europe, East Asia, and North America at the expense of Third World people like the Somalis?" and "Are the Burcad Badeed criminals who must be stopped and punished or are they victims of globalization who need to have their lives rebuilt?" Students should also consider, "Who are the real criminals?" Is it people who steal to live, or the nations, oligarchs, corporations, and financial institutions that conspire to eliminate traditional prerogatives in the name of profit and drive these people into banditry? A broader question is "Who pays the price for change?"

New York Times columnist Thomas Friedman (2005) popularized the idea that globalization in the modern era has produced a world that is flat, with fewer of the disruptive forces that impeded economic development in the past. He reached this conclusion while filming a television interview with Nandan Nikelani, the Chief Executive Officer of Infosys Technologies. At the time, Friedman and Nikelani were in a conference room near Bangalore in south-central India, the city known as that country's Silicon Valley. At the Infosys campus employees were writing software programs for American and European companies, running the "back rooms" of major multinational corporations, providing computer maintenance for research projects, and answering customer phone calls routed to India from all over the world (5). During the interview Nikelani bragged that from the company's conference room he could coordinate a virtual meeting involving key players from across the globe including American designers, Indian software writers, and Asian manufacturers, with participants from New York, London, Boston, San Francisco, and Singapore.

The outsourcing on which Bangalore and the Indian Silicon Valley depends was made possible by massive investments in technology in the 1990s. Computers became cheaper, more powerful, and dispersed around the world. They are connected by a vast and invisible network of satellite, broadband, and undersea cables and supported by new software, more efficient email programs, the Internet, and search engines like Google. This newly networked technology made it possible for "intellectual work, intellectual capital," to be delivered from anywhere to anywhere. "That's globalization," Nikelani proclaimed.

The changes resulting from globalization are both subtle and grand. The shops in my neighborhood now regularly sell off-season flowers, fruits, and vegetables flown in from the southern hemisphere. Immigrants have opened new ethnic restaurants. In New York families go out for Thai or Chinese food, in London for Pakistani dishes, and in Paris for couscous. While Friedman and Nikelani see these developments as a "new milestone in human progress," everyone on earth does not experience the current changes this way; there are too many road bumps and potholes. Millions of undocumented immigrants from Mexico and Central America have crossed the border into the United States; millions more from North and West Africa take risky sea voyages on leaky boats in an effort to get into European Union countries. Many were subsistence farmers in their own countries, bankrupted by subsidized industrial farms in the U.S. and European Union.

The populations of Third World cities, if you can call these extended shanty towns "cities," have grown astronomically as people flee the countryside hoping for work and better lives. The official population of Mexico City is about nine million people, but the unofficial population in the greater metropolitan area is over twenty million, as are the unofficial metropolitan populations of Mumbai, India (official population 14 million), Karachi, Pakistan (official population 13 million), and São Paulo, Brazil (official population 11 million). In Lagos, Nigeria (official population approximately 8 million) and Cairo, Egypt (official population approximately 7 million), the two most populous cities in Africa, the unofficial metropolitan populations are probably about 18 million. During the eras of colonial settlement and the industrial revolution, international borders were relatively open, and displaced people could move to cities and countries where there was work. In the contemporary era of globalization, capital or money is free to move across international borders, but people are much more restricted.

As a parent, teacher, citizen, and human being, I worry about the impact of unrestrained, capitalism-fueled and directed globalization on the future. I worry for my children, grandchildren, and students, for the national economy, democratic government in the United States, conditions for people living in the misdeveloped and exploited "Third World" and for the environment of planet Earth. I think there is a lot to be concerned about – record-breaking human migration, frightening new weather patterns, imperialist war, and the fact that nothing is manufactured in the United States any more. Samir Amin (1990), former director of the United Nations African Institute for Economic Development and Planning, calls the combination of factors impacting on the Third World "maldevelopment."

Three books that I find especially useful for understanding the current wave of global integration are Naomi Klein, *The shock doctrine* (2008), Joseph Stiglitz, *Freefall: America, free markets, and the sinking of the world economy* (2010), and Eric Hobsbawm, *On empire: America, war, and global supremacy* (2008). While the authors focus on different aspects of globalization, one of the things they share in common in their analyses is that they hold the United States, the world's largest military and economic power, largely responsible for problems confronting the contemporary world.

Klein's main thesis is that the official story – that the seeming triumph of deregulated capitalism in the contemporary world is a product of freedom – is false. According to Klein, this "triumph" is actually identified with brutal coercion and its history is written in economic, political, and psychological shocks to the people of the world (19). Since World War II American psychologists and economists, with the support of the CIA and rightwing politicians, have promoted systemic shock therapy as a cure for everything from misguided "Keynesian" governmental policies to leftwing political movements pledged to economic redistribution. She believes the political and corporate wings of this movement are simply greedy, self-serving, and short-sighted. The movement's mantra is privatization, government deregulation, and deep cuts in social spending no matter what the resulting cost. Klein accuses its practitioners of capitalizing on human misery or even promoting it in order to extend their political influence across the globe and maximize unfettered corporate profits.

At the core of Klein's narrative is her discussion of the impact on Latin America of disaster capitalism and free market ideologues backed by American military and economic muscle. Throughout the region, but especially in the "southern cone," countries had flirted with "developmentalism," a relatively flexible economic philosophy that accepted government intervention in the economy to actively promote the broader social good. Developmentalists tended to be nationalists unwilling to accept that local interests should be subservient to economic formulas and to the designs of global corporations and imperialist nations.

When developmentalists came to power in Guatemala and Iran in the 1950s, Brazil and Argentina in the 1960s, and Chile in the late 1960s, they threatened to nationalize key industries and operate them for the benefit of the nation as a whole. In each case, elected governments were overthrown by U.S.-sponsored coup d'états that were supported with money from major international corporations.

The Chilean military, with the support of the United States, administered three distinct "shocks" to its country: it overthrew the civilian government, imprisoned, tortured, murdered or drove into exile any potential opposition, and rapidly revamped the economy based on free market principles – it privatized five hundred government-owned corporations, cut back on social services, eliminated the regulation of companies, and ended trade barriers. Within 3 years, annual inflation in Chile reached 375%, the highest rate in the world at the time, the country was flooded with cheap foreign imports, and financial privateers were making fortunes. By 1982, over 170,000 industrial jobs had disappeared and the economy had crashed. While it has since recovered and the country is once again a democracy, Chile remains one of the most unequal societies in the world, ranked 116 out of 123 countries on an equality scale used by the United Nations.

Joseph Stiglitz is a Nobel Prize-winning economist, a professor at Columbia University, a former member of President Bill Clinton's Council of Economic Advisors, a former vice-president and chief economic advisor to the World Bank, and a strong advocate for capitalism as an economic system. Stiglitz, however, has been sharply critical of globalization dominated by free market ideologies and unregulated corporations. He challenges the assertion by free market economists that unregulated markets are self-correcting and that government regulation impedes economic innovation.

Stiglitz argues that the global economic crisis that began in 2007 was not an accident, but the result of both failed U.S. economic policies and deep-seated global structural imbalances. According to Stiglitz, the crisis was precipitated by irresponsible practices by U.S. banks, brokerages, and insurance companies and the failure of the federal government and private regulatory agencies to rein in the "Frankenstein laboratories of Wall Street" (14). As with the Asian financial crisis of 1997, once it began, the financial collapse spread from company to company, from market to market, and from country to country like a contagious virus.

The underlying cause of the current economic crisis is inadequate and unbalanced global demand for products. The world's industrial capacity is much greater than the ability or willingness of people to purchase goods, either because they do not need them or because they need them and cannot afford them. The U.S. housing bubble both temporarily postponed the economic downturn and made it worse. It made possible sustained borrowing and consumer purchasing which helped to subsidize global production and caused it to expand, but when the bubble burst no other countries could absorb enough of the production to bail out the global economy. Asian economies, including China and Japan, have too little aggregate domestic demand and rely heavily on the U.S. to purchase their exports. As the U.S. economy slipped, tens of millions of people lost their jobs worldwide, including 20 million in China alone. The United Nations Secretariat estimated that approximately 100 million people would fall into poverty or remain in poverty as a result of the Great Recession. The situation is exacerbated by technological innovation during the last few decades that made it possible for a small fraction of the global workforce to produce all the goods that people need.

Stiglitz accepts, as do most, if not all, capitalist economists, that the U.S. economy is cyclical and that the current recession will eventually end. However, he is concerned that the flaws in the global economy will not be corrected and the system will become increasingly vulnerable. Economic crises in Third World countries have occurred on a regular basis during the past 40 years. A working paper developed for the International Monetary Fund argued that between 1970 and 2007 there were 124 economic upheavals including 42 systemic banking crises or banking and currency crises in 37 separate countries, including the 1997–1998 Asian Tiger crisis that threatened a global collapse until bailed out by U.S. government borrowing and the housing bubble. But the world can no longer count on U.S. consumer demand as its economic growth engine.

In *On empire: America, war, and global supremacy* (2008), Eric Hobsbawm identified the military power of the United States as the greatest threat to global peace in the contemporary era. According to Hobsbawm, "To give America the best chance of learning to return from megalomania to rational foreign policy is the most immediate and urgent task of international politics" (59). Other countries can destabilize regions, but unchecked, the U.S. demonstrated the potential to plunge the entire world into war. It would be interesting for American students, examining events from a global perspective, to debate whether the U.S. is the world's best hope for peace and freedom or the greatest threat.

Many people hoped for a reduction in global tension after the collapse of the Soviet bloc and the end of the Cold War. However, according to a database maintained by Uppsala University in Sweden (http://www.pcr.uu.se/research/UCDP/index.htm, accessed November 30, 2009), the number of armed conflicts in the second half of the 20th century actually peaked in the 1990s. Hobsbawm attributed this to the absence of a system based on competing superpowers, a system he traces back to the Treaty of Westphalia in Europe in 1648, that keeps allies, clients, colonies, and internal dissidents under control (64).

Two related essential questions, for government officials as well as for social studies students and teachers, which were widely debated during the last decade of the 20th century and the first decade of the 21st, are: "Is it possible to export democracy to other countries?" and "Do national security concerns justify human rights violations?" Both questions became prominent in the public consciousness when the United States invaded Afghanistan and Iraq following the events of September 11, 2001. President George W. Bush claimed that the goal of American foreign policy was to "defend not only our precious freedoms but also the freedom of people everywhere" and he committed the U.S. to building stable democratic regimes in both countries (http://middleeast.about.com/od/afghanistan/qt/me081007b.htm, accessed July 7, 2010). After more than 9 years of war and occupation, as of this writing, Bush and his successor, President Barak Obama, were unsuccessful at bringing either country into the fold as a democracy.

Advocates for the latest wave of global integration tend to recognize the short-term dislocations but to argue in favor of the long-term benefits. However, evaluating long-term benefits is tricky. The Columbian Exchange and capitalist industrialization provided long-term benefits to Western Europe and North America as regions, but not to everyone who lived there, and certainly not to the indigenous peoples of Africa, the Americas, and most of Asia. 20th-century British economist John Maynard Keynes argued: "The long run is a misleading guide to current affairs. In the long run we are all dead. Economists set themselves too easy, too useless a task if in tempestuous seasons they can only tell us that when the storm is past the ocean is flat again" (1923: 80).

The *Book of Revelations*, the last book of the Christian New Testament, tells the story of the Four Horsemen of the Apocalypse (http://en.wikisource.org/wiki/Bible_(King_James)/Revelation #Chapter_6, accessed June 20, 2010). They are supposedly brought to life by Jesus of Nazareth to wreck havoc upon the Earth as part of the last judgment prior to the resurrection of the saved. The horsemen represent conquest, war, famine, and death. According to the story, there are at least three other potential pairs of beasts and riders set to plague humankind. It may well be that in globalization we have discovered a fifth horseman of the apocalypse.

Recommended Websites

Kenneth Leman (Singer, 2008: 342–344), a member of the Hofstra New Teachers Network, uses a package of websites to help high school students participate in the debate over globalization. While many of these sites require a high level of academic skill to understand, Ken encourages students to use as many of them as possible. Students can use multiple sites to write extended research reports or be responsible for reporting to class on a specific site. These sites were last accessed on May 23, 2010.

Center for Economic Policy and Research (http://www.cepr.net). This private think tank site offers a balanced and critical view of economic globalization, discussing many of the relative advantages and disadvantages to countries around the world. *Globalization: A primer* is an excellent overview of the interrelated factors affecting the world economy. The vocabulary may challenge students with lower reading abilities.

International Monetary Fund (http://www.imf.org). Posted by one of the two supranational organizations that controls international capital, this site offers its own primer on economic globalization. It makes good use of graphs and requires prior understanding of key economic terms. The bias of this site is clearly in favor of globalization as an evolving process of expanding the market economy to all countries. While it freely acknowledges bad consequences of globalization, it takes the approach that such consequences are the by-product of change rather than systemic inequality.

World Bank (http://www.worldbank.org). An excellent site for the better reader. It contains a wealth of information on World Bank policies and practices and explains how money moves around the world and why.

Youth for International Socialism (http://www.newyouth.com/). This is a key site in the anti-globalization movement. It offers a fairly balanced but critical view of global inequalities and explanations of protests at WTO, G8, and IMF meetings.

Worldwatch Institute (http://www.worldwatch.org). This site provides a wide variety of alternative analyses of globalization's downside. Its focus is on environmental degradation.

Mother Jones (http://www.motherjones.com) and AFL-CIO (http://www.aflcio.org). Mother Jones contains easy-to-read reports on globalization's ill-effects. The AFL-CIO site provides organized labor's view of issues.

The Fair Trade Federation (http://www.fairtradefederation.org). This site focuses on the FTF's activities to promote fair wages for overseas workers engaged in global production. The FTF's eight "Practices and Principles" challenge students to think about fair wages and employment practices and whether these can be promoted within the global economy.

Human Rights for Workers (http://www.senser.com). This site addresses globalization and human rights issues such as child labor.

TEACHING IDEAS

Whether you think globalization is a positive or negative force in recent world affairs, and that is certainly an issue for students to debate, there is little question that it has been intensifying. The Swiss Institute for Business Cycle Research publishes an annual KOF Index of Globalization that measures economic, social, and political dimensions of globalization in 158 countries. Students can visit the KOF website (http://globalization.kof.ethz.ch, accessed June 20, 2010) and discuss the criteria the organization uses to measure globalization (Activity 1).

I like to joke with high school students that when I took New York State standardized science and mathematics assessments in the 1960s, they would not let us use pocket calculators –

because they had not invented them yet. I still remember the first time I saw a color television set (we watched *The Lone Ranger* in a neighbor's apartment) and my first portable radio (I was sitting on the beach in 1962 when Mickey Mantle, just back from a major injury, hit a pitch-hit home run off of Baltimore ace Steve Barber). Most students have their own "technology memories" that we can use to highlight how changes in technology have changed the way we live. If you are lucky enough to have students who grew up in other countries or who have visited their families there, you can engage them in discussions of how differences in levels of technology reflect differences in standards of living. An essential question for this topic is whether technological change is always beneficial or does it come with human and environmental costs (Activity 2).

Activities 3–7 are available online at http://people.hofstra.edu/alan_j_singer/. In September 2000, the United Nations adopted eight Millennium Development Goals to be achieved by 2015. They included halving the rate of extreme poverty around the world, gender equity, halting the spread of HIV/AIDS, and providing universal primary education for all children. One way to measure the "success" of a society is the quality of human life of its members, including the health of its people, the state of their housing, the availability of education for their children, and work conditions. Students can use online statistics and reports available from UNESCO (http://stats.uis.unesco.org/unesco/TableViewer/document.aspx?ReportId=143&IF_Language =eng, accessed November 30, 2009) and the United States C.I.A. World Factbook (http://www.cia.gov/library/publications/the-world-factbook, accessed November 30, 2009) to evaluate whether the Millennium Development Goals are being achieved and the relative "success" of contemporary societies to meet the needs of their people (Activity 3).

The "World Economic Situation and Prospects" report (http://www.un.org/esa/policy/wess/wesp.html, accessed June 20, 2010) is prepared by a group of United Nations committees including the Department of Economic and Social Affairs, the United Nations Conference on Trade and Development, and regional commissions. It provides a summary of global economic performance and projections for short-term changes in the world economy (Activity 4). Students examine three charts, create graphs, and try to identify trends. Economist Joseph Stiglitz argues that underlying causes of the current economic decline are economic imbalance and inadequate global demand. These problems are illustrated in the chart in Activity 5.

Activity 6 is based on an excerpt from the book *The world is flat* (2005) by Thomas Friedman. Students are asked to evaluate Friedman's hypothesis. Activity 7 is designed as a concluding project for a global history curriculum. Students are asked to imagine it is 100 years in the future and they are writing a magazine article describing changes that took place during the previous century.

Activity 1. Index of Globalization

Source: http://globalization.kof.ethz.ch, accessed June 20, 2010.

Background: The Swiss Institute for Business Cycle Research publishes an annual Index of Globalization that measures economic, social, and political dimensions of globalization in 158 countries. Small countries active in global financial markets are considered the most globalized. They include Belgium, Ireland, Switzerland, and Singapore. On the other extreme are countries such as Myanmar (Burma), the Democratic Republic of the Congo (formerly known as Zaire), and Burundi that remain virtually outside the global system. In 2010, Germany ranked highest on the globalization index among the industrialized nations (18th) while the United States ranked 27th overall.

Instructions: Examine the Index of Globalization chart below. It is a composite score based on three criteria. "Economic globalization" measures imports, exports, and foreign investments either in the country or by the country around the world. "Social mobilization" measures things such as international phone calls and emails, international tourists, and immigrants. "Political globalization" is measured by the number of embassies a country has in other countries and its memberships in international organizations. More populated countries with larger domestic markets and more internal communication tend to score lower on the index. In your opinion, is this an accurate or useful measure of globalization? What criteria would you use to measure global interaction? Why?

Index of Globalization (selected countries)

Rank	Country	Index
1	Belgium	92.95
2	Austria	92.51
3	Netherlands	91.90
4	Switzerland	90.55
5	Sweden	89.75
18	Germany	84.16
24	United Kingdom	80.18
27	United States	78.80
45	Japan	68.16
63	China	62.68

Activity 2. Technological Memories

Instructions: Between 1981 and 2010 changes in technology radically changed our world. Some of these inventions are listed below. Select three of the inventions and for each one, describe your first encounter with the invention and how it has shaped your life.

1981 – IBM PC
1984 – CD-ROM and Apple Macintosh computer
1985 – Microsoft Windows operating system
1986 – Fuji disposable camera
1987 – Disposable contact lenses
1988 – Digital cell phone
1989 – High-definition television
1990 – The World Wide Web, Internet protocol (HTTP), and WWW language (HTML)
1991 – Digital answering machine
1993 – Pentium processor for computers
1996 – Web TV
2001 – iPod
2002 – Birth control patch
2003 – Hybrid car
2005 – YouTube

PART IV

Resources

17

ONLINE RESOURCES FOR TEACHERS AND STUDENTS

Christopher Verga and Claire Lamothe, while completing the Master of Arts program for certified teachers at Hofstra University, led a group of social studies teachers who assisted in assembling this annotated list of global history websites. They also recommended websites that are included in other parts of this book. Claire is a middle school teacher in Hempstead, New York. Chris teaches students in need of supervision at a Suffolk County, New York facility.

My two favorites websites for researching global history are Spartacus Educational and Internet History Source Books Project – sites I used extensively in preparing this book. I also used Wikipedia. Concerns have been raised about the reliability of Wikipedia as a source, although studies since 2005 have compared Wikipedia favorably with other online ency- clopedias and reference sites (http://en.wikipedia.org/wiki/Reliability_of_Wikipedia, accessed May 26, 2010). I often use Wikipedia as a first stop in online research, but never as the only stop. The Internet History Source Book Project is an excellent source for locating and learning about primary source documents. However, in my teaching and for the purposes of this book I often use a different section from a longer work than the one offered on the website. Original texts of hard-to-find books are often available at Google Books (http://books.google.com, accessed May 26, 2010) or Project Gutenberg (http://www. gutenberg.org, accessed May 26, 2010).

New York State requires that students pass a global history assessment to receive an academic diploma. It is usually taken at the end of the tenth grade following 2 years of study. Past tests are available online at http://www.nysedregents.org/GlobalHistory Geography, accessed July 7, 2010. A number of sites offer assistance for preparing for the test. One of the most useful is supported by the Oswego school district (http://www.regents prep.org/Regents/global/global.cfm, accessed July 7, 2010).

BBC – A History of the World (http://www.bbc.co.uk/history, accessed May 19, 2010). Includes a timeline of British history, links to documentaries, *This Day in History*, *Ancient History In-Depth*, *Archaeology In-Depth*, and an encyclopedia of famous people. *Ancient history in-depth* looks at Egyptians, Greeks, Romans, Vikings, Anglo-Saxons, Ancient Indians, and the pre-historic British. The site also provides material on the ancient Americas, Asia, Africa, and the Middle East. An excellent resource for students.

Best of History (http://besthistorysites.net, accessed May 19, 2010). Contains annotated links to over 1,200 history websites as well as links to hundreds of lesson plans, history teacher guides, history activities, and history games. Students will especially enjoy the games.

British Museum (http://www.britishmuseum.org, accessed May 19, 2010). The museum offers a number of useful resources including a history of the world in 100 objects (in conjunction with the BBC) and Ancient Civilizations (http://www.ancientcivilizations.co.uk, accessed May 19, 2010), which explores cities, religion, buildings, writings, technology, and trade in different ancient societies.

Documenting the American South (http://docsouth.unc.edu, accessed May 18, 2010). While this is primarily a collection of slave narratives from the United States, it also includes primary source material on people such as Olaudah Equiano and Toussaint L'Ouverture.

E-Museum: University of Minnesota at Mankato (http://www.mnsu.edu/emuseum, accessed May 18, 2010). This site offers an eclectic mixture of materials from across the ages and around the world. It includes sections on anthropology, archeology, culture, history, and pre-history. Its culture section has especially good material on world religions and Native Americans. A very useful site for students.

History Learning Site (http://historylearningsite.co.uk, accessed May 21, 2010). An excellent resource from Britain that is easily navigated by students. Primary focus is Western Civilization and British history.

History Wiz (http://www.historywiz.com, accessed May 20, 2010). An interesting resource on many topics with edited primary sources, great images, and maps easily accessible by students.

Interactives (http://www.learner.org/interactives, accessed May 18, 2010). Annenberg Media provides interactive units on the collapse of civilizations and the European Middle Ages and Renaissance. The collapse unit has students compare conditions in the Mayan Yucatan, Mesopotamia, the Mesa Verde region of the United States, and Mali and Songhai in the Sahel region of West Africa.

International World History Project (http://history-world.org/mainmenu.htm, accessed May 18, 2010). This site contains material easily accessible by students from the pre-Sumerian period up to the present era, including reference material, maps, and famous speeches.

Internet History Source Books Project (http://www.fordham.edu/halsall, accessed May 19, 2010). This website was created by Dr. Paul Halsall while at Fordham University and is still housed there. It provides an extensive collection of primary source documents throughout the span of human history. It includes sourcebooks for ancient, medieval, and modern history and a number of different areas of the world. The excerpts are geared for a college classroom so documents must be edited for secondary school use.

Kidipede – History for Kids (http://historyforkids.org, accessed May 21, 2010). A well-illustrated, easy-to-read website organized chronologically and by region. Intended for middle school students.

Map Collection (David Rumsey) (http://www.davidrumsey.com and http://rumsey.geo garage.com, accessed May 18, 2010). This site contains over 22,000 maps and images. They include historic maps of the world, Europe, Asia, and Africa and rare maps of 18th- and 19th-century North and South America.

Marxists Internet Archive (http://www.marxists.org, accessed May 21, 2010). Features primary source documents and encyclopedia references on revolutionary working-class struggles, primarily from the 20th century. One of its best features is its coverage of the Russian Revolution. The site includes eyewitness reports, contemporary accounts of the Revolution, political parties, the Soviet government, and influential people. Educators can use the site to create activity sheets that include firsthand accounts of people who lived through the Revolution.

Metropolitan Museum of Art (http://www.metmuseum.org/toah, accessed May 18, 2010). The website of the Metropolitan Museum of Art in New York City provides students with a timeline of art around the world with images, essays, and maps.

National Archives (United Kingdom) (http://www.nationalarchives.gov.uk, accessed May 19, 2010). Includes images from the archives and lesson material on medieval and early modern Europe, the British Empire, and the 20th century. The section on Empire and Industry, 1750–1850 has extensive material easily accessible to students on slavery, the slave trade, and abolitionist campaigns.

New York Times Historical (http://www.nytimes.com). Searchable database for articles since 1851. Uploading of articles requires a modest fee.

Mr. Dowling (http://mrdowling.com, accessed May 21, 2010). Mike Dowling is a geography teacher from Florida. This is probably the most extensive teacher-created and maintained website in the world and includes edited readings (a little on the simple side), lessons, and assessments. Topics cover the entire range of human history.

Paleomap Project (http://www.scotese.com/earth.htm, accessed May 19, 2010). The Paleomap Project explores the physical and climate history of the earth. It is a great resource for educators trying to make connections between climate and location and the development of civilization in certain areas.

PBS – Empires: People and Passions That Changed the World (http://www.pbs.org/ empires, accessed May 21, 2010). One of many PBS-maintained websites based on a television series. According to the website, "Within the long history of civilization are great eras of struggle, triumph, and loss. These periods are reflective of the best and worst of humanity: explosive creativity, ultimate depravity, the use and abuse of power, and war." Topics for this series include Egypt, Greece, Rome, Islam, The Medici, Napoleon, Japan, and 19th-century Britain. Each topic offers a timeline, lessons, and illustrations. The unit on Greece has an outline of the origins of the Greek empire, video clips, a 3D build-your-own Parthenon, material on life as an Athenian, and an outline of the Greek alphabet and a list of basic words. All PBS sites are excellent resources for teachers and valuable sources for students. A complete list is available at PBS Teachers (http://www.pbs.org/teachers/socialstudies, accessed May 21, 2010).

Primary Source (http://www.primarysource.org, accessed May 20, 2010). According to its mission statement, the goal of this site is to promote "history and humanities education by connecting educators to people and cultures throughout the world." It provides teachers with lists of material on selected topics, but few resources are actually available here.

Spartacus Educational (http://www.spartacus.schoolnet.co.uk, accessed May 19, 2010). Spartacus Educational is a British online encyclopedia geared to secondary school students but is especially useful for global history teachers. Featured entries and documents include Industrial Revolution, Slavery 1750–1870, Emancipation of Women, Roman World, Medieval World, Military History, World War II and Cold War, English Civil War, Germany 1900–1945, Nazi Germany, Monarchy, Religion and Society, the British Trade Union Movement, Child Labor 1750–1900, Cartoonists 1700–1980, and History Timelines.

United Nations (http://www.un.org/en, accessed May 19, 2010). Students learn about the United Nations as well as development issues, human rights campaigns, and international law. An excellent source for teachers of maps and documents. Material for students is at http://www.un.org//Pubs/CyberSchoolBus (accessed May 19, 2010). Current events and advocacy projects are discussed at United Nations International Children's Emergency Fund (http://www.unicef.org, accessed May 19, 2010).

Visualizing Cultures (http://ocw.mit.edu/ans7870/21f/21f.027/home/index.html, accessed May 19, 2010). This site created at MIT uses visual images from the past to explore history. The first two packages on the site focus on Japan in the modern world and early-modern China.

Women in World History (http://www.womeninworldhistory.com, accessed May 19, 2010). This site writes women into the global history curriculum. Includes lessons, biographies, and documents.

World Factbook (https://www.cia.gov/library/publications/the-world-factbook, accessed May 19, 2010). Maps, flags, world leaders, country data, and comparisons prepared by the American Central Intelligence agency.

World History Archives (http://www.hartford-hwp.com/archives, accessed May 20, 2010). The goal of this website is to provide documents to support the study of world history from a working-class and non-Eurocentric perspective. It offers an incredible array of primary and secondary sources from a left perspective. An excellent resource for teachers.

World History for Us All (http://worldhistoryforusall.sdsu.edu, accessed May 19, 2010). This site is sponsored by San Diego State University and the National Center for History in the Schools. It offers a nine-unit curriculum geared to state and national standards with themes, essential questions, and lesson plans for teaching world history in middle and high schools. Includes content and conceptual summaries with useful primary source documents, charts, and graphs. This site is primarily for teachers.

World History Matters (http://worldhistorymatters.org, accessed May 21, 2010). Developed by the Center for History and New Media, it offers lessons and documents on global history in general and a special focus on women in history. Very useful for teachers and accessible to students with higher academic skills.

18

AUTOBIOGRAPHIES, HISTORICAL FICTION, AND MOVIES

> The autobiographies and historical fiction I recommend here can be used for supplemental reading assignments in social studies classes. They can be used more effectively if a school allows coordination and joint planning between social studies and English teachers.
>
> I do not show entire movies in class, but a brief segment can be very useful for illustrating an idea, a region, or an event. As a rule of thumb, two to five minutes is ideal, ten minutes is maximum. I use movies as "documents" to promote class discussion. As with any document, I give students specific questions to consider or write about.

A. Autobiographies

Autobiographies give students a unique look at events from the inside. However, people who tell their life stories can have an axe to grind, an ideological bias, or a political agenda. They can also be so narrowly focused that the authors are unable to effectively provide historical context. The stories in many of the recommended books center on war and oppression, rather than on ordinary life, which is probably why they first came to public attention.

The historical reliability of some of the accounts discussed here has been disputed, but I believe the broader story remains useful. Students have to read these autobiographies critically as historians examining questionable evidence.

I like to assign books that have teenage characters. In recent years a number of books have appeared by and about child soldiers and "lost boys" in Sudan, but at this point there is none that I am comfortable recommending.

Here are my recommendations, listed alphabetically by author.

Olaudah Equiano (2006) *The interesting narrative of the life of Olaudah Equiano* (New York: Bedford/St. Martin's). First published in London in 1789, this first hand account of slavery and the trans-Atlantic slave trade by a formerly enslaved African played a major role in the campaign to abolish the slave trade. Equiano was born along the Niger River in West Africa in about 1745. He was kidnapped by slave traders as a boy, survived the middle passage, and eventually became literate and secured his freedom. This is a long, difficult, and emotionally draining book. I recommend assigning sections rather than the entire text.

Zlata Filipovic (1995) *Zlata's diary* (New York: Penguin). Zlata Filipovic's family lived in Sarajevo and struggled to survive during the civil war that followed the collapse of Yugoslavia in the early 1990s. The book is self-consciously modeled on *Anne Frank: The diary of a young girl* and is simply written by an eleven-year-old girl. My principal misgiving is that it was written with an eye toward publication, which can distort the feelings it is intended to portray. It is a very easy read for middle-level readers.

Anne Frank, Otto Frank and Mirjam Pressler, eds (1993) *Anne Frank: The diary of a young girl* (New York: Bantam). The book reprints the secret diary of a teenage Jewish girl in the Netherlands written during World War II. After years of hiding in an attic, Anne and her family are captured by the Nazis and sent to a concentration camp, where she dies. While the account is very narrowly focused, the family receives limited news from the outside world, and it is an understated, yet powerful personalization of the extermination of six million people because of their ethnicity and religious beliefs. It is an easy read for middle-level readers.

Ji-Li Jiang (2001) *Red scarf girl* (New York: Harper Trophy). When she was a twelve-year-old, Ji-Li was an enthusiastic member of the youth division of the Red Guard at her school. The story takes place during the Chinese Cultural Revolution in the 1960s. The book was written after Jiang emigrated to the United States and, writing retrospectively, she is critical of the events she describes and the treatment of her family. It is intended for middle-level readers.

Gerald Keegan (1991) *Famine diary* (Dublin: Wolfhound Press). The authenticity of this book is disputed. The manuscript, which purports to be an autobiographical account of the Great Irish Famine and the Irish Diaspora, first surfaced in the 1890s. Whether it is genuine or not, it is a very accurate historical account told from the perspective of a young schoolteacher. It is an easy read for middle-level readers.

Mark Mathabane (1998) *Kaffir boy* (New York: Free Press). This is a first-person account of life under apartheid in South Africa. Mathabane and his family lived an impoverished life in the shantytowns surrounding Johannesburg in South Africa. This book is accessible to high school-level readers.

Rigoberta Menchú and Elisabeth Burgos-Debray (1984) *I, Rigoberta Menchú* (Verso). This is an edited first-person account of the life of Nobel Peace Prize-winning indigenous activist Rigoberta Menchú. The details of this book have been disputed. Menchú admits that not all of the events described here actually happened to her, but claims the book is an accurate description of the life and struggles of indigenous people in Guatemala. This book is accessible to high school-level readers.

Shlomo Perel and Margot Bettauer Dembo (1999) *Europa, Europa* (Somerset, NJ: Wiley). Perel was a Jewish teenager with blond hair and blue eyes whose family fled Germany and the Nazi regime just before the outbreak of World War II. Perel was captured, first by the Russians and then by the Germans, but survived the fate of other Jews because the Nazis mistook him for German and enlisted him in the Hitler Youth. This book is accessible to high school-level readers.

Doris Pilkington, also known as Nugi Garimara (2002) *Rabbit-proof fence* (New York: Hyperion). The author tells the story of her grandmother who was born from a transient relationship between an Australian Aboriginal woman and a European father. British policy was to take mixed-race children away from their maternal families and forcefully acculturate them in residential schools. Three girls resisted and trekked over 1,000 miles across open desert to be reunited with their own people. It is an easy read for middle-level readers

Loung Ung (2001) *First they came for my father* (New York: HarperCollins). This is a first-hand account of the Cambodian genocide. The author's father was a military policeman in the pre-revolutionary government and the family was forced to flee the Khmer Rouge and go into hiding. After her father was captured and killed and the children were separated from their mother, Loung was sent to a camp for orphans were she was trained as a child soldier. This book is accessible to high school–level readers.

B. Historical Fiction

One of the few books I remember actually reading in high school was a fictionalized biography of Napoleon written by the novelist Emil Ludwig (New York: Boni & Liveright, 1926). As a result, Napoleon remained my favorite historical character for decades and I longed to travel to France.

Since then I have read a number of works of historical fiction that are accurate portrayals of time periods, locations, and events. They help me enter the past and experience the lives of the people I am studying. I especially look for work by indigenous authors who are writing about their own cultures and societies. The books are listed alphabetically by author, with one title per author.

Chinua Achebe (1994) *Things fall apart* (New York: Anchor). Achebe is an award–winning novelist from Nigeria. *Things fall apart*, first published in 1958, is a classic work about the impact of European imperialism on African society in the late 19th century. This book is often assigned in high school English classes.

Monica Ali (2008) *Brick Lane* (New York: Scribner). This is the story of a Bangladeshi girl who is sent to live in London in an arranged marriage. It provides a vivid portrayal of Europe's growing Islamic immigrant community. It is easily accessible to high school readers.

Tariq Ali (1998) *The Book of Saladin* (New York: Verso). The author is a prominent leftwing British political commentator who is originally from Pakistan. This novelized version of the life of Saladin, the Islamic general who led the resistance to the European Crusades and liberated Jerusalem from Christian rule in 1187, is one of a five–part series that explores different periods and locales in Islamic history. It is easily accessible to high school readers.

Julia Alvarez (1995) *In the time of the butterflies* (New York: Pume). This novel tells the story of the four Mirabal sisters, known as Las Mariposas. Three of the sisters were assassinated in 1960 for defying the Trujillo dictatorship in the Dominican Republic. Their struggle and martyrdom helped to overthrow the dictatorship. This is one of the more easily readable of the recommended titles.

Russell Banks (2004) *The darling* (New York: HarperCollins). This very disturbing novel explores events in a West Africa country, Liberia, during one of the recent bloody civil wars over the control of resources, especially diamonds. The narrator of the book is an American woman who had been married to a Liberian government official. After the murder of her husband she flees and her two sons become child soldiers for one of the competing armies. It is a difficult read for advanced students, but it is definitely worth the effort.

Madison Smartt Bell (1995) *All souls' rising* (New York: Pantheon). This book is part one of a three–part fictionalized account of the Haitian Revolution led by Toussaint L'Ouverture and is perhaps the best historical novel I have ever read. Many of the scenes portray graphic violence and brutality, which is an accurate depiction of what took place. It is a difficult read for advanced students, but it is definitely worth the effort.

Andre Brink (1980) *A dry white season* (New York: Penguin). I first learned of this book when I saw the movie. The movie was great. The novel is even better. Brink dissects apartheid through the eyes of an Afrikaner teacher who slowly uncovers injustices he had always ignored. In the background is the 1976 student rebellion in Soweto. It is easily accessible to high school readers.

Patrick Chamoiseau (1997) *School days* (Lincoln, NE: University of Nebraska Press). This book looks at education as forced acculturation on the French Caribbean island of Martinique. This is one of the more easily readable of the recommended titles.

Edwidge Danticat (1999) *The farming of bones* (New York: Penguin). The setting of this novel is the Dominican Republic in the late 1930s. Dictator Rafael Trujillo wants to build support for his autocratic rule by stimulating nationalism and through a campaign to "whiten" the country by expelling or killing Black Haitians who live in the border region between the two countries. It is easily accessible to high school readers.

Charles Dickens (2007) *Hard times* (New York: Simon & Schuster). First published in 1854, the book is set in a fictitious factory town in England during the Industrial Revolution. It explores class tensions and includes a classic portrayal of a school using the factory model. It is easily accessible to high school readers.

Denise Giardina (1998) *Saints and villains* (New York: Ballantine). A fictional account based on the actual participation of a German theologian in an unsuccessful plan to assassinate Hitler and overthrow the Nazi regime. The author raises many questions about the obligation of moral and religious individuals to put their lives at risk to resist the immoral actions of others. It is easily accessible to high school readers.

Khaled Hosseini (2004) *The kite runner* (New York: Riverhead). This novel uses the story of two boys to explore the turmoil in Afghanistan in the second half of the 20th century. I did not like the book or movie as much as most critics because it tells its story from the perspective of a privileged family and is very unsympathetic to the people who side with the Islamic rebels. It is easily accessible to high school readers.

Yu Hua (2004) *Chronicle of a blood merchant* (New York: Anchor). This book examines life in rural China after the communist revolution is supposed to have transformed society. It is easily accessible to high school readers.

Duong Thu Huong (2002) *Paradise of the blind* (New York: Harper Perennial). This book focuses on daily life and family conflicts in Hanoi, Vietnam under communist rule with the Vietnamese war in the background. It is easily accessible to high school readers.

Witi Ihimaera (2003) *The whale rider* (New York: Harcourt). An important question for discussion, one that is explored in this book, is "What does it mean to be part of an indigenous culture, in this case the Maori, in the modern world?" This is one of the more easily readable of the recommended titles.

Ghassan Kanifari (1998) *Men in the sun and other Palestinian stories* (Boulder, CO: Lynne Rienner). Kanifari was a Palestinian activist and novelist whose family was displaced by the Arab–Israeli wars. This novel tells the story of three Palestinian refugees who leave refugee camps in Lebanon to seek work in Kuwait. It was banned in some Middle Eastern countries because it was critical of local governments. It is easily accessible to high school readers.

Bette Bao Lord (1997) *The middle heart* (New York: Ballantine). In the forefront are traditional friendships and love stories. In the background are World War II and the mid-20th century Chinese Revolution. It is easily accessible to high school readers.

Walter Macken (1968) *The silent people* (New York: Macmillan). The second book in a trilogy on Irish history is set in 1826 and looks at the tensions between Ireland and Britain that culminate in the Great Irish Famine. It is easily accessible to high school readers.

Frank McCourt (1996) *Angela's ashes* (New York: Scribbner). This combination memoir and story is based on the author's life growing up in poverty in Limerick, Ireland. This is a very popular novel that is easily accessible to high school readers.

Rohinton Mistry (2001) *A fine balance* (New York: Vintage). By the 1970s India had supposedly outlawed the caste system, but this powerful book shows that it remained deeply imbedded in the culture and continued to dictate what happened in people's lives. It also examines the government corruption, poverty, and local tyranny that infest what is supposed to be the world's most populous democracy. It is a difficult read for advanced students, but it is definitely worth the effort.

V. S. Naipaul (1979) *A bend in the river* (New York: Knopf). Naipaul is a Nobel Prize-winning author, born in Trinidad, of South Asian ancestry. While I find Naipaul out-Britishes the British in his allegiances, he offers a critical view on events in the Third World. *A bend in the river* explores the impact of corruption in an unnamed newly independent country, possibly the Congo. The Nobel committee called Naipaul the heir to Joseph Conrad "as the annalist of the destinies of empires in the moral sense: what they do to human beings." It is a difficult read for advanced students, but it is definitely worth the effort.

Irène Némirovsky (2006) *Suite Française* (New York: Vintage). This is an amazing book about everyday life and accommodation to defeat in occupied France during World War II. The French are surprisingly petty and the Germans surprisingly human, especially given that the author was born Jewish and wrote the novel while resisting being sent to a concentration camp where she died. It is easily accessible to high school readers.

Arundhati Roy (2008) *God of small things* (New York: Random House). The book explores the complexities of religion and caste in India in the 1960s through the eyes of "mixed-caste" children who are marginalized by their families. It is easily accessible to high school readers.

Mongane Wally Serote (1981) *To every birth its blood* (Portsmouth, NH: Heinemann). The book explores the lives of Black Africans living under apartheid in South Africa. Serote was an anti-apartheid activist and a leader of the African National Congress. He later became South Africa's Minister for Arts and Culture. The language in this book is risqué, and students, supervisors, and parents should be alerted, but it is worth reading.

Ngugi wa Thiong'o, also known as James Ngugi (1989) *Matigari* (Portsmouth, NH: Heinemann). Thiong'o is a Kenyan political activist who champions writing in indigenous African languages and has criticized the legacy of imperialism and authoritarian and corrupt governments on the continent. Matagari is a former guerrilla who finds he must challenge the new rulers of an independent Kenya to achieve the goals they had fought for in the war for independence. It is easily accessible to high school readers.

Barry Unsworth (1992) *Sacred hunger* (New York: Norton). This novel, which was awarded a British Booker Prize, explores the impact of the trans-Atlantic slave trade on enslaved Africans, slave traders, sailors, and European merchants. It is a difficult read for advanced students, but it is definitely worth the effort.

Emile Zola (2004) *Germinal* (New York: Pengiun). In the mid-19th century, Zola set out to document the impact of industrialization and modernization on French society in what became a twenty-volume series. *Germinal*, which was first published in 1885, focuses on a coal-miners' strike. While this novel is a work of fiction, it is also a sociological and historical study. It is a difficult read for advanced students, but it is definitely worth the effort.

C. Movies

Even the most interesting documentaries and historical movies have problems that social studies teachers need to consider. Documentaries often have limited interest, fictional accounts frequently sacrifice accuracy for dramatic considerations, and television, especially *The History Channel*, promotes violence, disasters, and sensationalism to attract an audience. Students love Mel Gibson's *Braveheart* (1995), but little in it is historically verifiable and I do not know which part I would show to a class. Selecting a piece to show to a class is a problem even with the best movies.

Even when accuracy is not an issue, there can be other problems. For example, storylines in a number of movies center on a European character, rather than on a member of the culturally marginalized social group it is supposed to portray. In *Cry Freedom* (1987) and *Gandhi* (1982), the narrators are White newspaper reporters. In *Schindler's List* (1993), a European Holocaust drama, the central character is a Nazi industrialist. *The Last Samurai* (2003) stars Tom Cruise as an American military advisor who embraces traditional Japanese culture.

We also have to be aware that what students "see" in the film clip may not be what we intend to present. I doubt if any global history teacher would show a segment from a classic Tarzan movie from the 1930s to represent Africa or Africans because the depictions are caricatures and arguably racist. Yet teachers in a workshop I conducted on using movies to teach global history selected movie segments about events in contemporary Africa that under closer examination left viewers with a sense that Black Africans are savage and dependent on White Europeans to ensure humane behavior. These segments, from *Blood Diamond* (2006), *Hotel Rwanda* (2004), *Tears of the Sun* (2003), *Sometimes in April* (2005), *The Last King of Scotland* (2006), and *Black Hawk Down* (2001), also ignored the impact of imperialism, globalization, the remnants of colonization, and capitalist exploitation on the situations portrayed in the movies. No one selected *The Constant Gardener* (2006), which offers a much more critical account of the West and Western corporations in creating the conditions that exist in Africa today.

The following are movies recommended as supplements to the global history curriculum. Many are based on novels mentioned earlier. They are organized by regions of the world and are listed in roughly chronological order in each region.

Australia, New Zealand, and Oceana

Rabbit-proof Fence (2002) is about European efforts to forcibly assimilate Australian Aborigines in the first half of the 20th century. It tells the story of three young mixed-race girls who escape from a boarding school and attempt to rejoin their extended matriarchal families. Scenes depict Aboriginal life on reservations and the treatment of the children in the boarding school. *Whale Rider* (2002) is about efforts to preserve Maori culture in New Zealand and asks: What does it mean to be part of a traditional cultural community in contemporary society? Scenes show a tribal elder trying to convince young boys to practice the traditional culture.

Latin America and the Caribbean

I recommend four movies about the colonial period. *The Mission* (1986) is about Spanish settlement in South America and the debate over whether indigenous people should be converted or enslaved. *The Last Supper* (1976) is about slavery in 18th-century Cuba, and *Burn!* (1970) is about British colonialism in the Caribbean. *Sugar Cane Alley* (1984; French with English subtitles) examines life on a plantation in the French-speaking Caribbean.

Latin America and the Caribbean have long histories of leftwing struggles against imperialists and their local allies and these stories have been presented in movie form. *The Motorcycle Diaries* (2004) is based on a journal kept by a youthful Ché Guevara in the 1950s. The scenes depicting life and mining in the Andes are particularly powerful. *In the Time of the Butterflies* (2001) tells the story of four sisters known as Los Mariposas (the butterflies) who helped to topple the dictatorial Trujillo regime in the Dominican Republic. *Missing* (1982) is about the overthrow of the democratically elected Allende government by U.S.-backed forces in Chile and the systematic murder of people allied with the left and the student and labor union movements.

There are a number of good movies about recent civil wars in Central America. The opening scenes in *El Norte* (1984; Spanish with English subtitles) are about political and economic oppression in Guatemala. They effectively illustrate the world described by Rigoberta Menchú in her autobiography. *Salvador* (1986) is an American-made movie that is sympathetic towards the leftwing peasant revolutionaries and highly critical of the U.S.-backed military and death squads. In *Romero* (1989), Archbishop Romero speaks up against the rightwing pro-government death squads that are victimizing the poor of El Salvador and he is assassinated. *Hombres Armados (Men With Guns)* (1997) takes place in an unnamed Central American country where "campesinos" (peasant farmers) are murdered by private mercenaries and police working for the landowners.

Environmental issues are addressed in *The Emerald Forest* (1985) and *The Burning Season – The Chico Mendes Story* (1994). These films examine the impact of development on traditional forest people and exploited workers in the Amazon rainforest.

Brazil has a developing movie industry which has produced a number of excellent movies. *Kiss of the Spiderwoman* (1985) looks at the repression of the political opposition. *Central Station* (1998) explores the relationship between a retired teacher and an orphan. *City of God* (2002) is a painful examination of poverty and youth gangs in the notorious shantytowns near Rio de Janeiro.

Asia

Ran (1985; Japanese with English subtitles) is about conflict in the royal family in 15th-century Japan. *Shogun* (1980) is a made-for-television mini-series about European merchants in Japan. *The Last Samurai* (2003) is not a particularly good movie that celebrates feudal arrangements over modernization. However, it does have very good scenes depicting 19th-century Japan.

Scenes from *The Last Emperor* (1987) illustrate the opulence of the Forbidden City during the last Chinese dynasty, whereas scenes from *The Empire of the Sun* (1987) show the privileged European community and the extreme poverty of ordinary people living in Shanghai. *Little Buddha* (1994) offers both a look at life in the Himalayas and insights into Buddhist religious beliefs.

A number of movies look at anti-imperialist struggles and challenges to local elites and military governors. *Gandhi* (1982) has many dramatic scenes about Indian life, the struggle for independence, and conflicts between Hindus and Muslims. Especially useful is the depiction of the Salt March. *The Year of Living Dangerously* (1983) is about revolutionary uprisings in Indonesia. *Beyond Rangoon* (1995) and *Indochine* (1992) are about revolutionary times in South East Asia. *The Killing Fields* (1984) examines the Khmer Rouge in Cambodia.

Interesting movies to recently come out of China include *Raise the Red Lantern* (1991), about an educated woman who becomes the fourth wife of a feudal nobleman in the 1920s, *The King of Masks* (1999), about an itinerant performer who adopts a homeless boy as an apprentice, only to discover that the boy is a girl, and *Not One Less* (1999), about education in rural China.

Sub-Saharan Africa

Sankofa (1993) examines the Atlantic slave trade at its point of origins, as do the opening scenes in the epic *Roots* (1977). *Shaka Zulu* (1986) has some useful scenes on the Zulu effort to resist British rule.

The anti-apartheid struggle in South Africa is covered in *Cry the Beloved Country* (1951/1995), *Cry Freedom* (1987), *A World Apart* (1988), *A Dry White Season* (1989), and *Sarafina!* (1992). *A Dry White Season* includes scenes where the police attack student protesters in Soweto in 1976. *In My Country* (2004) and *Inviticus* (2009) examine attempts to build national unity after majority rule is implemented.

A number of movies have focused on recent conflicts in Africa, which are often rooted in the European colonial past. *Lumumba* (2001) looks at the continuing impact of colonialism on the Congo. *Hotel Rwanda* (2004) and *Sometimes in April* (2005) are both about the Rwandan genocide. *Blood Diamond* (2006) is about the impact of the illegal diamond trade on West African societies. *The Last King of Scotland* (2006), which stars Academy Award–winner Forest Whitaker as Idi Amin, is about his brutal reign in Uganda. *The Constant Gardener* (2006) looks at the exploitation of vulnerable African communities by European pharmaceutical companies.

North Africa and the Middle East

The Battle of Algiers (1966; French with English subtitles) is about the Algerian uprising against French colonialism. It raises the question, "Who are the terrorists?" Terrorism is also addressed in the movie *Paradise Now* (2005), about two Palestinian young men plotting a suicide bomb attack in Tel Aviv. *Babel* (2006) is about the inability of people to connect with each other in a global age. It includes stark scenes of life in rural Morocco. Movies have explored the Israeli–Palestinian conflict from different perspectives. They include *Munich* (2005), about the Israeli retaliation for a Palestinian attack on Israeli athletes at the 1972 Olympics, and the documentary *Blood and Tears* (2007).

Ancient and Pre-Industrial Europe

Spartacus (1960) is about a slave rebellion during the Roman Republic and is much better than *Gladiator* (2000). *The Return of Martin Guerre* (1981; French with English subtitles) is about French peasant life during the Crusades. *Beckett* (1964) and *A Man for All Seasons* (1966) are about conflicts between Church and King in England. *Amazing Grace* (2007) was produced in commemoration of the 200th anniversary of the abolition of the trans–Atlantic slave trade. It tells the story of English abolitionists at the turn of the 19th century.

Modern Europe

Movies about the early industrial era include *David Copperfield* (1999), and *Germinal* (1993; French with English subtitles), which examines the impact of industrialization on French coal-miners. There are excellent scenes of work, a strike, and women organizing against local merchants. *The Organizer* (1963; Italian with English subtitles) examines similar scenes of industrial unrest. *The Wind that Shakes the Barley* (2006) and *Michael Collins* (1996) are about the post–World War I Irish independence movement and civil war.

All Quiet on the Western Front* (1930 and 1979) portrays trench warfare during World War I. Similar scenes are depicted in *Legends of the Fall* (1994). *Paths of Glory* (1949) is about the way French troops are treated by their officers. In *Gallipoli* (1981), young Australians enlist in the British army to see the world and are used as cannon fodder on the Turkish Front. *Enemies at the Gate* (1991) is about the Battle of Stalingrad, perhaps the major turning point of World War II. *The Guns of Navarone* (1961), about the Greek resistance, remains my favorite movie about World War II.

Good-Bye Lenin* (2003) is a humorous look at the end of communism in Eastern Europe, while *Welcome to Sarajevo* (1997) and *No Man's Land* (2001) look at civil war in the Balkans after the collapse of Yugoslavia. *Strike* (2006) tells the story of Polish dockworkers and the Solidarity campaign that helped overthrow a pro–Soviet communist regime.

European Holocaust

The Garden of the Finzi-Continis (1971; Italian with English subtitles*), The Diary of Anne Frank* (1959), *Judgment at Nuremburg* (1961; with scenes from the concentration camps), *Playing for Time* (1980), *Schindler's List* (1993), and *The Truce* (1996) examine Nazi efforts to exterminate European Jews. *Defiance* (2008) and *Uprising* (2001) are very good movies about Jewish resistance. *Sophie Scholl: The Final Days* (2005) is about German students who oppose Hitler. *Night and Fog* (1955; French with English subtitles) and *Weapons of the Spirit* (1990) are important documentaries. *Weapons of the Spirit* focuses on French Huguenots who help Jews escape the Nazis.

19
LESSON PLANNING

In *Social Studies for Secondary Schools 3rd edition* (New York: Routledge, 2008) I discussed four different lesson plan formats (Chapter 8, pp. 218–243) and examined in depth the component parts of an activity-based lesson (Chapter 9, pp. 254–274), which is the format that I prefer. For this book I am reproducing here the ingredients of an activity-based lesson. This is followed by a sample lesson plan on the Armenian genocide using the format and an activity sheet. In this format, state standards would be listed in the Goals objectives and Main ideas/understandings sections.

A. Ingredients of an Activity-based Lesson

Unit: This locates the lesson in the overall conceptual sequence of what is being taught.

Aim: A question that a particular lesson is designed to answer or a statement or phrase introducing the topic of a lesson. Usually it is written on the board at the start of the lesson. Sometimes it is elicited from students during the early stages of a lesson.

Goals/objectives: The skills, concepts, and content that students will learn about during the lesson. Can also include social/behavioral/classroom community goals. Goals are broad and achieved during a long period of time. Objectives are specific short-term goals that are achievable during a particular lesson.

Main ideas/understandings: The underlying or most important ideas about a topic that inform a teacher's understanding and influence the way lessons and units are organized. These are the ideas that teachers want students to consider. They can be formulated as statements or as broad questions that become the basis for ongoing discussion.

Materials: The maps, documents, records, and equipment needed by teachers and students during the lesson to create the learning activities.

Activities/lesson development: This is the substance of the lesson. In this section a teacher explains how students will learn the goals and objectives. It includes discussions, document analysis, mapping, cartooning, singing, performing drama, researching, cooperative learning, and teacher presentations.

Do now activity: An introductory activity that immediately involves students as they enter the room. It almost always involves providing students with material to read or analyze and questions to answer.

Motivation(al) activity: A question, statement, or activity that establishes a learning context and captures student interest in the topic that will be examined. Motivations connect the subject of the lesson to things that students are thinking about or are interested in. They often relate the main ideas and historical content that will be explored with contemporary events.

Questions: Prepared questions that attempt to anticipate classroom dialogue. They are designed to aid examination of materials, generate class discussions, and promote deeper probing. Medial summary questions make it possible for the class to integrate ideas at the end of an activity.

Transitions: These are key questions that make it possible for students to draw connections between the information, concepts, or understandings developed during a particular activity with other parts of the lesson and to a broader conceptual understanding.

Summary: A concluding question or group of questions that make it possible for the class to integrate or utilize the learning from this lesson and prior lessons.

Application: Extra optional questions or activities planned for this lesson that draw on and broaden what students are learning in the unit. These can be used to review prior lessons or as transitions to future lessons.

Homework assignment: This is a reading, writing, research, or thinking assignment that students complete after the lesson. It can be a review of the lesson, an introduction to a future lesson, background material that enriches student understanding, an exercise that improves student skills, or part of a long-term project.

B. Sample Lesson Plan

Unit: Genocide in the 20th century (this is the second lesson in the unit following an introductory lesson defining genocide).

Aim question: Why should the world remember the Armenian Golgotha?

Goals/objectives: Students will examine maps to locate the Ottoman Turkish Empire and to evaluate evidence of genocide.

Working in teams and individually, students, acting as historians, will evaluate evidence presented by photographs, newspaper articles, and personal testimony.

Based on the evaluation of evidence, students will draw historical conclusions about the treatment of the Armenians in Turkey during World War I.

Main ideas/understandings: Between 1915 and 1918 over one million ethnic Armenians living in modern-day Turkey were murdered or marched into the desert to die of exposure, thirst, or starvation by the Turkish military, police, and militias.

Although the government of Turkey continues to deny that genocide took place, primary sources including photographs, newspaper reports, and the memoirs of survivors document these events.

The failure of the world to defend the Armenians or even remember what happened to them was taken into account by Adolph Hitler when he planned Germany's attack on Poland in 1939 and the extermination of European Jews and other people.

Materials: Quote from Adolph Hitler; PowerPoint with maps and photographs from http://www.firstgenocide.com/; http://iconicphotos.wordpress.com/2009/06/30/armenian-genocide/; http://www.armenian-genocide.org; and http://april24timessquare.com/, accessed March 27, 2010; edited passages from the memoir, *Armenian Golgotha* (NY: Vintage, 2010) written by Grigoris Balakian.

Activities/Lesson Development

Do now: Read this statement by German *Fuehrer* (leader) Adolph Hitler to commanding generals just prior to the invasion of Poland in 1939 and answer questions 1–3.

> What the weak western European civilization thinks about me does not matter . . . I have sent to the East only my 'Death Head units' with the orders to kill without pity or mercy all men, women and children of the Polish race or language. Only in such a way will we win the vital space we need. Who still talks nowadays of the extermination of the Armenians?
> (*The New York Times*, "Partial text of talks on Poland," November 24, 1945, p. 7)

Questions

1. What order did Adolph Hitler give to German generals attacking Poland?
2. Why did Hitler believe the attack on Poland was justified?
3. In your opinion, why did Hitler refer to the extermination of Armenians by Turks during World War I?

Motivation: "Golgotha" is the biblical name for the hill in Jerusalem where Jesus of Nazareth is supposed to have been crucified. The name has come to mean a place or occasion of great suffering. In the 20th century it was used to describe events that would later be called genocide. Between 1915 and 1918 over one million ethnic Armenians living in modern-day Turkey were murdered or marched into the desert to die of exposure, thirst, or starvation by the Turkish military, police, and militias. **In your opinion, why did Adolph Hitler refer to the annihilation of Armenians in this statement just before the start of World War II?**

Transition: We will be examining photographs, maps, newspaper accounts, and a personal memoir of a survivor that document what happened to Armenians in Turkey during World War I. The question we need to consider is: Why should the world remember the Armenian Golgotha?

Activity. PowerPoint Slides Showing Photographs, Maps, and Newspaper Headlines

Questions (about map and photographs)

1. In what area of the world was the Ottoman Turkish Empire located?
2. This map shows the Ottoman Turkish Empire at the outbreak of World War I. What contemporary countries were parts of this empire?
3. What do we learn from the key for the map on extermination sites?
4. What do we learn from the map on extermination sites?
5. These photographs of Armenian deportees were taken by Armin Wegner, a second lieutenant in the German army. Wegner was stationed in the Ottoman Empire in 1915. Describe what you see in each picture.

6. As a historian, would you consider these photographs strong evidence that the Armenian genocide took place?
7. How might Turkish officials interpret these photographs differently?

Transition: What other evidence would you want to see before you definitively concluded that genocide took place in Turkey?

Questions (about newspaper articles)

1. What evidence is provided in these *New York Times* headlines and excerpts?
2. Lord Bryce was a British official who also charged that German troops committed atrocities in Belgium. In your opinion, is he a trustworthy witness? Explain.

Activity. Memoir of Father Grigoris Balakian (students will read the memoir and answer the questions working in teams)

Questions (about survivor memoir)

1. Who was the author of this memoir?
2. According to the Turkish officer, how many Armenians were killed in this district?
3. How were the people murdered?
4. In your opinion, based on this evidence should the treatment of Armenians in Turkey be considered genocide? Why?

Summary: Are you convinced by the evidence that actions taken against the Armenians during World War 1 were genocide? Why?

Application: In March 2010 a committee of the United States House of Representatives approved a resolution that the Armenian Golgotha was genocide. However, the Turkish government, a military ally of the United States, continues to lobby against the resolution. It does not want it approved by the House and Senate and signed by the U.S. President. In your opinion, do you think the U.S. government should formally endorse the view that what happened to the Armenians was genocide? Explain.

C. Sample Activity Sheet

Aim: Why should the world remember the Armenian Golgotha?

Do now: Read the statement by German *Fuehrer* (leader) Adolph Hitler to commanding generals just prior to the invasion of Poland in 1939 and answer questions 1–3.

> What the weak western European civilization thinks about me does not matter . . . I have sent to the East only my 'Death Head units' with the orders to kill without pity or mercy all men, women and children of the Polish race or language. Only in such a way will we win the vital space we need. Who still talks nowadays of the extermination of the Armenians?
>
> (*The New York Times*, "Partial text of talks on Poland," November 24, 1945, p. 7)

Questions

1. What order did Adolph Hitler give to German generals attacking Poland?
2. Why did Hitler believe the attack on Poland was justified?
3. In your opinion, why did Hitler refer to the extermination of Armenians by Turks during World War I?

New York Times headlines (1915)

(A) TELL OF HORRORS DONE IN ARMENIA (October 4, 1915)
The Committee on Armenian Atrocities, a body of eminent Americans who have been investigating the situation in Turkish Armenia, issued a detailed report asserting that in cruelty and in horror nothing in the past 1,000 years has equaled the present persecutions of the Armenian people by the Turks.

(B) GOVERNMENT SENDS PLEA FOR ARMENIA (October 5, 1915)
It is probably well within the truth to say that of the 2,000,000 Armenians in Turkey a year ago, at least 1,000,000 have been killed or forced to flee the country, or have died upon the way to exile, or are now upon the road to the desert of Northern Arabia, or are already there.

(C) MILLION ARMENIANS KILLED OR IN EXILE (December 15, 1915)
In a statement issued yesterday from the offices of the American Committee for Armenian and Syrian Relief at 70 Fifth Avenue further atrocities committed by Turks against Armenian Christians were detailed and additional evidence was given to support Lord Bryce's assertion that the massacres are the result of a deliberate plan of the Turkish government to "get rid of the Armenian question," as Abdul Hamid once said, by getting "rid of the Armenians."

Armenian Golgotha: A survivor's memoir (Armenian Golgotha, New York: Vintage, 2009)

"Golgotha" is the biblical name for the hill in Jerusalem where Jesus of Nazareth is supposed to have been crucified. The name has come to mean a place or occasion of great suffering. In the 20th century it was used to describe events that would later be called genocide.

Between 1915 and 1918 over one million ethnic Armenians living in modern-day Turkey were murdered or marched into the desert to die of exposure, thirst, or starvation by the Turkish military, police, and militias. The government of Turkey continues to deny that genocide occurred. It argues that the deaths of the Armenians happened because of World War I and that the number of deaths is inflated.

In March 2010 a committee of the United States House of Representatives approved a resolution that the Armenian Golgotha was genocide. However, the Turkish government, a military ally of the United States, continues to lobby against the resolution. It does not want it approved by the House and Senate and signed by the U.S. President.

In 1922, an Armenian priest named Father Grigoris Balakian published an account of his deportation from the city of Constantinople, now known as Istanbul, with 250 other Armenian intellectual and political leaders. Father Balakian was able to use his fluency in German to help him escape from the doomed caravan. In the edited excerpts included here, Father Balakian reports on conversations with a police captain named Shukri in charge of escorting the prisoners. He titled the chapter "The Confessions of a Slayer Captain" (139–150).

(A) Now it's not secret anymore; about 86,000 Armenians were massacred. We too were surprised, because government didn't know that there was such a great Armenian population in the province of Ankara. However this includes a few thousand other Armenians from surrounding provinces who were deported on these roads. They were put on this road so that we could cleanse them.

(B) After we had massacred all the males of the city of Yozgat – about eight thousand to nine thousand of them in the valleys near these sites, it was the women's turn . . . Every woman, girl, and boy was searched down to their underwear. We collected all the gold, silver, diamond jewelry, and other valuables, as well as the gold pieces sewn into the hems of their clothes.

(C) After stripping them all of their possessions and leaving them only what they were wearing, we made them all turn back on foot to the broad promontory [overlook] located near the city of Yozgat . . . Ten or twelve thousand Muslims were waiting there . . . The government order was clear: all were to be massacred, and nobody was to be spared.

(D) I had the police soldiers announce to the people that whoever wished to select a virgin girl or young bride could do so immediately . . . Thus about two hundred-fifty girls and young brides were selected by the people and the police soldiers.

(E) It's wartime, and bullets are expensive. So people grabbed whatever they could from their villages – axes, hatchets, scythes, sickles, clubs, hoes, pickaxes, shovels – and they did the killing accordingly . . . The Sheikh had issued a *fatwa* [order] to annihilate the Armenians as traitors to our state . . . I, as a military officer, carried out the order of my king.
(Grigoris Balakian, *Armenian Golgotha: A memoir of the Armenian genocide, 1915–1918*)

Questions

1. Who was the author of this memoir?
2. According to the Turkish officer, how many Armenians were killed in this district?
3. How were the people murdered?
4. In your opinion, based on this evidence should the treatment of Armenians in Turkey be considered genocide? Explain.

REFERENCES

Chapter 1 What is a Social Studies Approach to Global History?

Armstrong, K. 1993. *A history of God: The 4,000-year quest of Judaism, Christianity and Islam*. New York: Random House.

Bernal, M. 1987. *Black Athena: The Afroasiatic roots of classical civilization. Volume 1*. New Brunswick, NJ: Rutgers University Press.

Bigelow, B. 1997. "The human lives behind the labels: The global sweatshop, Nike, and the race to the bottom," *Phi Delta Kappan, 79* (2), 112–119.

Bigelow, B. and Peterson, B. 2007. "Students as textbook detectives: An exercise in uncovering bias" in W. Au, B. Bigelow, and S. Karp, eds, *Rethinking our classrooms: Teaching for equity and justice, Volume 1*. Milwaukee, WI: Rethinking Schools, 116–117.

Blackburn, R. 1988. *The overthrow of colonial slavery 1776–1848*. New York: Verso.

Blackburn, R. 1997. *The making of new world slavery: From the Baroque to the modern 1492–1800*. New York: Verso.

Bloch, M. 1953. *The historian's craft*. New York: Knopf.

Braudel, F. 1973. *Capitalism and material life, 1400–1800*. New York: HarperCollins.

Carr, E. 1961. *What is history?* New York: Vintage.

Childe, V. G. 1942. *What happened in history*. New York: Penguin.

Childe, V. G. 1951. *Man makes himself*. New York: New American Library.

Cohn, N. 1970. *The Pursuit of the millennium: Revolutionary millenarians and mystical anarchists of the middle ages*. New York: Oxford University Press.

Cook, M. 2003. *A brief history of the human race*. New York: Norton.

Davidson, B. 1995. *Africa in history*. New York: Touchstone.

Diamond, J. 1997. *Guns, germs, and steel: The fates of human societies*. New York: Norton.

Diamond, J. 2005. *Collapse: How societies choose to fail or succeed*. New York: Viking.

Finley, M. I. 1963. *The ancients Greeks: An introduction to their life and thought*. New York: Viking.

Harris, M. 1974. *Cows, pigs, wars and witches: The riddles of culture*. New York: Random House.

Harris, M. 1989. *Our kind: Who we are, where we came from, and where we are going*. New York: HarperCollins.

Hobsbawm, E. (1994). *The age of extremes: A history of the world, 1914–1991*. New York: Pantheon.

Linden, E. 2006. *The winds of change: Climate, weather, and the destruction of civilizations*. New York: Simon & Schuster.

Ó Gráda, C. 2009. *Famine: A short history*. Princeton, NJ: Princeton University Press.

Patterson, O. 1991. *Freedom*. New York: Basic Books.

Perry, M., Scholl, A., Davis, D., Harris, J., and Von Laue, T. 1990. *History of the world*. Boston, MA: Houghton Mifflin.

Schlesinger, A. Jr. 1992. *The disuniting of America: Reflections on a multicultural society*. New York: Norton.

Seldes, G. 1966. *The great quotations*. New York: Lyle Stuart.

Wilentz, S. 1997. "The past is not a 'process'," *The New York Times*, April 20, E15.

Williams, E. 1970. *From Columbus to Castro: The history of the Caribbean 1492–1969*. London: Andre Deutsch.

Chapter 2 Debating Curriculum: What is Important to Know and Why?

Cook, M. 2003. *A brief history of the human race*. New York: Norton.

Pezone, M. 2008. "Teaching about the scientific revolution and the trial of Galileo," *Social Science Docket*, 8 (2), 47.

Ravitch D. and Thernstrom, A., eds. 1992. *The democracy reader: Classic and modern speeches, essays, poems, declarations, and documents on freedom and human rights worldwide*. New York: HarperCollins.

Singer, A. 2008. *Social studies for secondary schools: Teaching to learn, learning to teach, 3rd edition*. New York: Routledge.

Chapter 3 How Should Global History Teachers Address Controversial or Sensitive Issues?

Beard, M. 2008. *Pompeii: The life of a Roman town*. London: Profile Books.

Beck, R., Black, L., and Krieger, L. 2005. *World history: Patterns of interaction*. Evanston, IL: McDougal Littell.

Cassirer, E. 1946. *Language and myth*. trans. Langer, S. New York: Dover.

Cowan, A. 2009. "An intrepid cartoon reporter, bound for the big screen but shut in a library vault," *The New York Times*, August 20, A23.

Hamilton, V. 1988. *In the beginning: Creation stories from around the world*. San Diego: Harcourt.

Hergé. 1991. *Tintin au Congo*, trans. Lonsdale-Cooper, L. and Turner, M. London: Sundancer.

McNamara, D. 2002. "High school-level activity: Editorial board meeting for a textbook publisher," *Social Science Docket, 2* (1).

Morris, B. 1997. *Israel's border wars, 1949–1956*. New York: Oxford University Press.

Chapter 4 Why is Global History Usually European Chronology with Tangents?

Cheney, L. 1994. "The end of history," *Wall Street Journal*, October 20, A22 (http://www.hartford-hwp.com/archives/10/006.html, accessed June 29, 2010).

Diamond, J. 1997. *Guns, germs, and steel: The fates of human societies*. New York: Norton.

Fishman, T. 2004. "The Chinese century," *The New York Times Magazine*, July 4.

Lewin, T. 2010. "World focus is gaining favor in high schools," *The New York Times*, July 3.

Marx, K. and Engels, F. 1964. *The communist manifesto*. New York: Monthly Review Press.

Chapter 5 What Does a Theme-Based Global History Curriculum Look Like? Part 1 – BC: Before Columbus

Cook, M. 2003. *A brief history of the human race*. New York: Norton.

Diamond, J. 1997. *Guns, germs, and steel: The fates of human societies*. New York: Norton.

Harris, M. 1989. *Our kind: Who we are, where we came from, and where we are going*. New York: HarperCollins.

Hobsbawm, E. 1962. *The age of revolution, 1789–1848*. New York: New American Library.

Hobsbawm, E. 1975. *The age of capital, 1848–1875*. New York: Scribner.

Hobsbawm, E. 1987. *The age of empire, 1875–1914*. New York: Pantheon.

Hobsbawm, E. 1994. *The age of extremes: A history of the world, 1914–1991*. New York: Pantheon.

Marx, K. and Engels, F. 1964. *The communist manifesto*. New York: Monthly Review Press.

Chapter 6 What Does a Theme-Based Global History Curriculum Look Like? Part 2 – AD: After the Deluge

Bigelow, B. and Peterson, B., eds. 1998. *Rethinking Columbus, 2nd edition*. Milwaukee, WI: Rethinking Schools.

Davis, J. and Hawke, S. 1992. *Seeds of change: The story of cultural exchange after 1492*. Reading, MA: Addison Wesley.

Faithfull, B. 2009. "Lesson plan on Afghanistan," *Social Education, 73* (7), 350.

Friedman, T. 1999. *The Lexus and the olive tree*. New York: Farrar, Straus & Giroux.

Hobsbawm, E. 1994. *The age of extremes: A history of the world, 1914–1991*. New York: Pantheon.

James, C. 1963. *The Black Jacobins: Toussaint L'Ouverture and the San Domingo revolution*. New York: Vintage.

Pezone, M. 2002. "Teaching about the French Revolution – A play," *Social Science Docket, 2* (1), 24–26.

Prentice Hall. 2007. *World history*. Upper Saddle River, NJ: Pearson–Prentice Hall.

Chapter 7 The Grand Narrative of Western Civilization

Beck, R., Black, L., and Krieger, L. 2005. *World history: Patterns of interaction*. Evanston, IL: McDougal Littell.

Bergh, A., ed. 1907. *The writings of Thomas Jefferson, vols 9–10*. Washington, DC: Thomas Jefferson Memorial Association.

Bernal, M. 1987. *Black Athena: The Afroasiatic roots of classical civilization, vol. 1: The fabrication of ancient Greece, 1785–1985*. New Brunswick, NJ: Rutgers University Press.

Bernal, M. 1991. *Black Athena: The Afroasiatic roots of classical civilization, vol. 2: The archeological and documentary evidence*. New Brunswick, NJ: Rutgers University Press.

Bernal, M. 2006. *Black Athena: The Afroasiatic roots of classical civilization, vol. 3: The linguistic evidence*. New Brunswick, NJ: Rutgers University Press.

Bernal, M. and Moore, D. 2001. *Black Athena writes back: Martin Bernal responds to his critics*. Durham, NC: Duke University Press.

Braudel, F. 1966. *The Mediterranean, vol. 1*. New York: Harper & Row.

Braudel, F. 1992. *The wheels of commerce*. Berkeley: University of California Press.

Broad, W. 2001. "In an ancient wreck, clues to seafaring lives," *The New York Times*, March 27.

Burke, P. 1998. *The European Renaissance, centres and peripheries*. Oxford: Blackwell.

Cohler, A., Miller, B., and Stone, H., eds. 1989. *Montesquieu: The spirit of the laws*. Cambridge: Cambridge University Press.

Coleman, J. 1996. "Did Egypt shape the glory that was Greece?" in M. Lefkowitz and G. MacLean Rogers, eds, *Black Athena revisited*. Chapel Hill, NC: University of North Carolina Press.

Diamond, J. 1997. *Guns, germs, and steel: The fates of human societies*. New York: Norton.

Finley, M. I. 1963. *The ancient Greeks: An introduction to their life and thought*. New York: Viking.

Goldthwaite, R. 1982. *The building of Renaissance Florence*. Baltimore, MD: Johns Hopkins University Press.

King, R. 2001. *Brunellechi's Dome*. New York: Penguin.

Jardine, L. 1996. *Worldly goods: A new history of the Renaissance*. New York: Doubleday.

Johnson, P. 1987. *A history of the Jews*. New York: Harper & Row.

Lefkowitz, M. 1992. "The use and abuse of Black Athena," *American Historical Review, 97* (2).

Lefkowitz, M. and Rogers, G. 1996. *Black Athena revisited*. Chapel Hill, NC: University of North Carolina Press.

Linder, B. 1979. *A world history*. Chicago, IL: Science Research Associates.

McKay, J., Hill, B., Buckler, J., Ebrey, P., Beck, R., Crowston, C., and Wiesner-Hanks, M. 2009. *A history of world societies, 8th edition*. Boston, MA: Bedford/St. Martin's.

O'Shea, S. 2000. *The perfect heresy*. New York: Walker.

Patterson, O. 1991. *Freedom*. New York: Basic Books.

Perry, M., Scholl, A., Davis, D., Harris, J., and Von Laue, T. 1990. *History of the world*. Boston, MA: Houghton Mifflin.

Pirenne, H. 1937. *Economic and social history of medieval Europe*. New York: Harcourt, Brace.

Pounder, R. 1992. "Black Athena 2: History without rules," *American Historical Review, 97* (2).

Ravitch, D. and Thernstrom, A., eds. 1992. *The democracy reader*. New York: HarperCollins.

Singer, A. 1999. "Teaching multicultural social studies in an era of political eclipse," *Social Education, 63* (1).

Sobel, D. 1999. *Galileo's daughter*. New York: Walker.

Stone, I. F. 1988. *The trial of Socrates*. New York: Doubleday.

Thompson, B. 1996. *Humanists and reformers: A history of the Renaissance and Reformation*. Grand Rapids, MI: Eerdmans.

Wiggins, G. and McTighe, J. 1998. *Understanding by design*. Alexandria, VA: ASCD.

Chapter 9 Who and What Gets Included in History?

Beck, R., Black, L., and Krieger, L. 2005. *World history: Patterns of interaction*. Evanston, IL: McDougal Littell.

Childe, V. G. 1951. *Man makes himself*. New York: New American Library.

Clavin, M. 2010. *Toussaint Louverture and the American Civil War*. Philadelphia: University of Pennsylvania Press.

Diamond, J. 1997. *Guns, germs, and steel: The fates of human societies*. New York: Norton.

DuBois, W. 1969. *The suppression of the African slave trade to the United States, 1638–1870*. Baton Rouge, LA: Louisiana State University Press.

Genovese, E. 1979. *From rebellion to revolution. Afro-American slave revolts in the making of the modern world*. Baton Rouge, LA: Louisiana State University Press.

Katz, W. 2007. "Toussaint L'Ouverture and the Haitian Revolution," *Social Science Docket, 7* (1).

Linebaugh, P. and Rediker, M. 2000. *The many-headed hydra: Sailors, slaves, commoners, and the hidden history of the revolutionary Atlantic*. Boston, MA: Beacon.

Lopez, R. 1971. *The commercial revolution of the middle ages, 950–1350*. Englewood Cliffs, NJ: Prentice Hall.

McKay, J., Hill, B., Buckler, J., Ebrey, P., Beck, R., Crowston, C., and Wiesner-Hanks, M. 2009. *A history of world societies, 8th edition*. Boston, MA: Bedford/St. Martin's.

Noddings, N. 1992. "Social studies and feminism," *Theory and Research in Social Education, 20* (3).

Patterson, O. 1969. "The general causes of Jamaican save revolts," reprinted in L. Foner and E. Geonvese, eds, *Slavery in the new world*. Englewood Cliffs, NJ: Prentice Hall.

Thompson, E. 1963. *The making of the English working class*. New York: Vintage.

Chapter 10 Religion in Human History

Armstrong, K. 1993. *History of God: The 4,000-year quest of Judaism, Christianity and Islam*. New York: Ballantine.

Beck, R., Black, L., and Krieger, L. 2005. *World history: Patterns of interaction*. Evanston, IL: McDougal Littell.

Cohn, N. 1970. *The pursuit of the millennium: Revolutionary millenarians and mystical anarchists of the Middle Ages*. Oxford: Oxford University Press.

Harris, M. 1974. *Cows, pigs, wars and witches*. New York: Random House.

Harris, M. 1989. *Our kind: The evolution of human life and culture*. New York: Harper & Row.

Hobsbawm, E. 1959. *Primitive rebels*. New York: Norton.

Hobsbawm, E. 1994. *The age of extremes: A history of the world, 1914–1991*. New York: Pantheon.

Chapter 11 Revolutionary Movements in the 20th Century

Alvarez, J. 1994. *In the time of the butterflies*. New York: Plume.

Bell. M. 1995. *All souls' rising*. New York: HarperCollins.

Bell, M. 2000. *Master of the crossroads*. New York: Pantheon.

Bell, M. 2004. *The stone that the builder refused*. New York: Pantheon.

Dickens, C. 1967. *A tale of two cities*. New York: Oxford University Press.

Fanon, F. 1965. *The wretched of the earth*. New York: Grove.

Flanagan, T. 1979. *The year of the French*. New York: Holt, Rinehart, & Winston.

Hugo, V. 1980. *Les misérables*. New York: Penguin Books.

Malraux, A. 1934. *Man's fate*. New York: Smith & Haas.

Malraux, A. 1938. *Man's hope*. New York: Random House.

Pasternak, B. 1958. *Doctor Zhivago*. New York: Pantheon.
Sholokhov, M. 1946. *And quiet flows the Don*. New York: Alfred A. Knopf.
Thiong'o, N. 1989. *Matagari*. Portsmouth, NH: Heinemann.

Chapter 12 Teaching about the European Holocaust and Genocide

Achebe, C. 1994. *Things fall apart*. Garden City, NY: Doubleday.
Arendt, H. 1951. *The origins of totalitarianism*. Cleveland, OH: World Publishing.
Beers, B. 1991. *World history: Patterns of civilization*. Englewood Cliffs, NJ: Prentice Hall.
Browning, C. 1994. *Ordinary men: Reserve police battalion 101 and the final solution in Poland*. New York: Harper Perennial.
Camus, A. 1967. *The rebel*. New York: Knopf.
Cornbeth, C. and Waugh, D. 1995. *The great speckled bird*. New York: St. Martin's.
Churchill, W. 1929. *The world crisis: Aftermath, vol. 5*, cited in Charny, I. 1999. *Encyclopedia of genocide: I–Y, vol. 2*. Jerusalem: Institute on the Holocaust and Genocide, 42.
Dawidowicz, L. 1986. *The war against the Jews, 1933–1945*. New York: Bantam.
Facing History and Ourselves 1994. *Holocaust and human behavior: Resource book*. Brookline, MA: Author.
Frank, O. and Pressler, M. 1995. *Anne Frank: The diary of a young girl*. Garden City, NY: Doubleday.
Garrard, J. and Garrard, C. 1996. *The bones of Berdichev*. New York: Simon & Schuster.
Genghis Cohn. 1995. British Broadcasting Corporation.
Gerard, J. 1933. "Adolph Hitler's *Mein kampf*," *The New York Times*, October 15, V1.
Graf, G. 2005. *We wept without tears: Testimonies of the Jewish sonderkommando from Auschwitz*. New Haven, CT: Yale University Press.
Hébras, R. 1994. *Oradour-Sur-Glane, The tragedy hour by hour*, trans. D. Denton. Montreuil-Bellay, France: Editions C.M.D.
Hitler, A. 1942. *Mein kampf*. New York: Hurst & Blackett.
Hobsbawm, E. 1994. *The age of extremes: A history of the world, 1914–1991*. New York: Pantheon.
Johnson, P. 1987. *A history of the Jews*. New York: Harper & Row.
Kellner, D. 1984. *Herbert Marcuse and the crisis of Marxism*. Berkeley: University of California Press.
Lemkin, R. 1944. *Axis rule in occupied Europe*. Washington, DC: Carnegie Endowment for International Peace.
Levi, P. 1996. *Survival in Auschwitz*. New York: Simon & Schuster.
Martin, D. 2002. "Gerhard Wessel, 88, German Espionage Chief," *The New York Times*, August 3, A13.
Milgram, S. 1963. "Behavioral study of obedience," *Journal of Abnormal and Social Psychology, 67*, 371–378.
Murphy, M. and Singer, A. 2001. "Asking the big questions: Teaching about the great Irish famine and world history," *Social Education, 65* (5), 286–291.
Némirovsky, I. 2006. *Suite Française*. New York: Knopf.
New York Times. 1944. "Germans raze villages and slay populations in Greece and France," July 9, p. 1.
President Commission on the Holocaust. 1979. *Report to the President*. Washington, DC: Government Printing.
Schlesinger, A. Jr. 1962. *The vital center*. Boston, MA: Houghton Mifflin.
Simpson, M. 1995. "Teaching about the holocaust," *Social Education,* 59 (6).
Snyder, L. 1961. *Hitler and Nazism*. New York: Franklin Watts.
Totten S. and Feinberg, S. 1995. "Teaching about the holocaust," *Social Education,* 59 (6).
United States Holocaust Memorial Museum. 2001. *Teaching about the holocaust, a resource book for educators*. Washington, DC: Author.
Uris, L. 1960. *Exodus*. New York: Bantam.
Uris, L. 1961. *Mila 18*. Garden City, NY: Doubleday.
Wyman, D. 1984. *The abandonment of the Jews*. New York: Pantheon.

Chapter 13 Three Waves of Global Integration

Friedman, T. 2005. *The world is flat: A brief history of the twenty-first century*. Farrar, Straus & Giroux.

Chapter 14 The Columbian Exchange and the Age of Colonialism (1420–1763)

Diamond, J. 1997. *Guns, germs, and steel: The fates of human societies*. New York: Norton.

Díaz del Castillo, B. 1973. *The conquest of New Spain*. New York: Penguin.

Gates, H., ed. 1987. *The classic slave narratives*. New York: New American Library.

Thomas, H. 1997. *The slave trade*. New York: Simon & Schuster.

Chapter 15 Imperialism: The Eagle's Talons

Bush, G. 2001. "Text of Bush speech," *The New York Times,* October 8, B6.

Churchill, W. 1898. *The story of the Malakand field force: An episode of frontier war*. Chapter 1 is at http://www.pbs.org/wgbh/pages/frontline/taliban/tribal/churchill.html, accessed August 16, 2010.

Grandin, G. 2010. "Empire of savagery," *The New York Times*, February 14, BR11.

Hari, J. 2010. "The two Churchills," *The New York Times Book Review*, August 15, p. 11.

Lenin, N. 1929. *Collected works of V. I. Lenin, vol. XX*. New York: International Press, p. 340.

Mill, J. 1848. *Principles of political economy, vol. III*, cited in E. Said 1994. *Culture and imperialism*. New York: Vintage.

Morel, E. 1920. *The black man's burden*. Manchester: National Labour Press.

Seldes, G. 1966. *The great quotations*. New York: Lyle Stuart.

Sheean, V. 1960. *Nehru: The years of power*. New York: Random House.

Simons, G. 1994. *Iraq: From Sumer to Sudan*. London: St. Martin's.

Toye, R. 2010. *Churchill's empire: The world that made him and the world he made*. New York: Henry Holt.

Twain, M. 1900. "Returning home," *New York World*, October 6.

Twain, M. 1905. *King Leopold's soliloquy*. Boston, MA: Warren.

Chapter 16 Globalization: The Fifth Horseman of the Apocalypse

Amin, S. 1990. *Maldevelopment: Anatomy of a global failure*. Tokyo: The United Nations University/Third World Forum.

Bowden, M. 1999. *Black Hawk down: A story of modern war*. New York: Atlantic Monthly Press.

Friedman, T. 2005. *The world is flat: A brief history of the twenty-first century*. New York: Farrar, Straus & Giroux.

Gettleman, J. 2009. "For Somali pirates, worst enemy may be on shore," *The New York Times*, May 9, p. 1.

Hobsbawm, E. 1959. *Primitive rebels*. New York: Norton.

Hobsbawm, E. 2008. *On empire: America, war, and global supremacy*. New York: New Press.

Keynes, J. M. 1923. *A tract on monetary reform*. London: Macmillan.

Klein, N. 2008. *The shock doctrine: The rise of disaster capitalism*. New York: Metropolitan Books.

Linebaugh, P. and Rediker, M. 2000. *The many-headed hydra: Sailors, slaves, commoners, and the hidden history of the revolutionary Atlantic*. Boston, MA: Beacon.

Rudé, G. 1964. *The crowd in history, 1730–1848*. New York: Wiley.

Singer, A., ed. 2004. *New York and slavery: Complicity and resistance curriculum guide*. New York: Gateway to the City Teaching American History Grant. Available online at http://www.nyscss.org, accessed July 7, 2010.

Singer, A. 2008. *Social studies for secondary schools, 3rd edition*. New York: Routledge.

Stiglitz, J. 2010. *Freefall: America, free markets, and the sinking of the world economy*. New York: Norton.

Thompson, E. 1971. "The moral economy of the English crowd in the eighteenth century," *Past and Present, 50*.

INDEX